Women in America

FROM COLONIAL TIMES TO THE 20TH CENTURY

Women in America

FROM COLONIAL TIMES TO THE 20TH CENTURY

Advisory Editors

LEON STEIN

ANNETTE K. BAXTER

A Note About This Volume

The drift to the big cities that began in the decade before the First World War moved only the more daring and adventurous. Millions remained stranded on farms, in towns and small villages in the impoverished cultural atmosphere depicted by Sherwood Anderson, Edgar Lee Masters and others. Based on a survey by the Economics Department of Cornell University, this book reflects the lives of seven million young women isolated on farms, and full of dreams and longings. It is written sensitively by Martha Foote Crow (1854-1924), who was a poet, a biographer of Browning, Stowe and Lafayette, and between 1896 and 1898 published four volumes of Elizabethan sonnet cycles which she edited.

THE AMERICAN COUNTRY GIRL

MARTHA FOOTE CROW

ARNO PRESS
A New York Times Company
NEW YORK – 1974

Reprint Edition 1974 by Arno Press Inc.

Reprinted from a copy in
  The University of Illinois Library

WOMEN IN AMERICA
From Colonial Times to the 20th Century
ISBN for complete set: 0-405-06070-X
See last pages of this volume for titles.

Manufactured in the United States of America

------◆------

Library of Congress Cataloging in Publication Data

Crow, Martha Foote, 1854-1924.
    The American country girl.

    (American women from colonial times to the 20th
century)
    Reprint of the ed. published by F. A. Stokes Co.,
New York.
    Bibliography: p.
    1. Farm life--United States. 2. Girls. I. Title.
II. Series.
S521.5.A2C76 1974   917.3'03'913   74-3936
ISBN 0-405-06083-1

THE AMERICAN COUNTRY GIRL

The American Country Girl. An abundance of sunshine, fresh air, good water, and healthful exercise in the open permit wonderful young life to reach its highest development.

THE AMERICAN COUNTRY GIRL

BY

MARTHA FOOTE CROW

AUTHOR OF

"ELIZABETH BARRETT BROWNING," "HARRIET
BEECHER STOWE," ETC.

*WITH FIFTEEN ILLUSTRATIONS FROM
PHOTOGRAPHS*

NEW YORK
FREDERICK A. STOKES COMPANY
PUBLISHERS

 *September, 1915*

TO THE

SEVEN MILLION COUNTRY LIFE GIRLS
OF AMERICA

WITH THE HOPE THAT THEY
MAY SEE THEIR GREAT PRIVILEGE
AND DO THEIR HONORABLE
PART IN THE NEW

COUNTRY LIFE ERA

CONTENTS

CONTENTS

ILLUSTRATIONS

ILLUSTRATIONS

NOTE

The author acknowledges with gratitude the kindness of her friends among the members of her fraternity, and among the graduates of Wellesley College, of Northwestern, Syracuse, and Chicago Universities, and of Grinnell College, who carefully found Country.Girl correspondents for her in all parts of the country; and especially of Professor Martha Van Rensselaer of Cornell University who generously shared with her some of the results of a questionnaire on *The Young Woman on the Farm,* which was sent out by the Home Economics Department of that University.

It would be impossible to name here all the helpers that this book has the honor to claim; the many specialists who have been good enough to advise the author; the enthusiasts whose fire has sustained her courage; and above all the many friends who have entertained her in their country homes and talked over with her their problems. The author would, however, acknowledge her special indebtedness to the Honorable John T. Roberts, the well known lover and sympathetic critic of country life, who gave valuable time to reading her manuscript and made some vital suggestions; and to Miss Mary L. Read, head of the School of Mothercraft, who gave some of the chapters a studious criticism.

While acknowledging many sources of inspiration the author alone is responsible for the opinions expressed in the book, opinions sometimes maintained against valued authority. All quotations from Country Girl experiences are made with direct personal permission of the writers; the kindness of the girls, who for the sake of other girls have given these permissions, is here mentioned with special appreciation.

NOTE

For illustrations the author is indebted to the Home Economics and other Departments of the Agricultural College at Cornell University and to the Home Economics Department of the School of Agriculture at Alfred, N. Y.; also to Mr. S. H. Dadisman of the Agricultural College at Ames, Iowa; to Mr. O. H. Benson of the United States Department of Agriculture; to Mr. A. A. Allen of the Cayuga Bird Club, and to Mr. James M. Pierce of the *Iowa Homestead* of Des Moines, Iowa. The list should also include Mr. R. M. Rosbrugh of Syracuse, N. Y., and Mrs. Mabel Stuart Lewis, efficient homesteader, of Fladmoe, South Dakota. Other names are mentioned in the text and need not be repeated here. To these and other helpers, great thanks are due.

This book has been written about the Country Girl and for the Country Girl; for her mother and father, and for everybody else as well; but especially for the Country Girl herself. It will reach its aim if some father says, " Why, here now, somebody has written a book about my little gal there. I should not have thought it was worth while to make a book about her. Well, now, perhaps she is of some account. Guess I'll give her a little more schooling; guess I'll let her go to that institute she was asking to go to; guess I'll let her have some music lessons, or buy her a piano, or send her to college." Or if some mother says wistfully, " My daughter is going to have a better chance than I had! " Or if the Country Girl herself should say, " I see my opportunity and I will arise and fulfil my mission."

The book will reach its aim, too, if another thing should happen. This is the first book about the Country Girl. There have been tons of paper devoted to the farmer; reams filled on the farm woman; not a line for the girl. May this first book be followed by many, correcting its misconceptions, rectifying its mistakes, directing its enthusiasms into the

NOTE

best channels for the welfare of the six and three-quarters
millions of Country Girls of this land! By that time there
will be seven millions — unless in fact these six millions shall
have run away to build their homes and rear their children
in the hot, stuffy, unsocialized atmosphere of the town, leaving the happy gardens without the joyous voices of children, the fields without sturdy boys to work them, the farm
homes without capable young women to — shall I say, to
man them? No, let us say to *woman* them, to *lady* them, to
mother them, and so to make them centers of wholesome
interesting life that, if the girls do their part, shall be the
very heart and fiber of the nation.

The author is sorry that she cannot write to all the Country Girls who have written her either through the questionnaire or through other means of communication in the
groups with which she has been so happily associated; but she
wishes that every Country Girl who reads this book would
write to her (using the address below) and tell her where she
thinks the book has spoken truly and where mistakenly.
She trusts the judgment of the Country Girls of America
absolutely, if they can but be induced to speak in unison
and after careful thought.

MARTHA FOOTE CROW.

Tuckahoe, New York City
August, 1915.

CHAPTER I

THE COUNTRY GIRL — WHERE IS SHE?

Woman will bless and brighten every place she enters, and she will enter every place on this round earth.

Frances E. Willard.

O Woman, what is the thing you do, and what is the thing you cry?
Is your house not warm and enclosed from harm, that you thrust
    the curtain by?
And have we not toiled to build for you a peace from the winds
    outside,
That you seek to know how the battles go and ride where the
    fighters ride?

You have taken my spindle away from me, you have taken away
    my loom;
You bid me sit in the dust of it, at peace without cloth or broom;
You have shut me still with a sleepy will, with nor evil nor good
    to do,
While our house the World that we keep for God should be gar-
    nished and swept anew.

The evil things that have waxed and grown while I sat with my
    white hands still,
They have meshed our world till they twined and curled through
    my very window sill;
Shall I sit and smile at my ease the while that my house is wrongly
    kept?
It is mine to see that the house of me is straightened and cleansed
    and swept!

Margaret Widdemer.

THE AMERICAN COUNTRY GIRL

CHAPTER I

THE COUNTRY GIRL — WHERE IS SHE?

THE clarion of the country life movement has by this
time been blown with such loudness and insistence
that no hearing ear in our land can have escaped its an-
nouncement.   The distant echoes of brutal warfare have not
drowned it: above all possible rude and cruel sounds this
peaceful piping still makes itself heard.

It has reached the ears of the farmer and has stirred his
mind and heart to look his problems in the face, to realize
their gigantic implications, and to shoulder the responsibility
of their solution.   It has penetrated to the thoughts of
teachers and educators everywhere and awakened them to
the necessities of the minute, so that they have declared that
the countryside must have educational schemes adapted to
the needs of the countryside people, and that they must have
teachers whose heads are not in the clouds.   It has aroused
easy-going preachers in the midst of their comfortable
dreams and has caused here and there one among them to
bestir himself and to make hitherto unheard-of claims as
to what the church might do — if it would — for the betterment of country life.

And all of these have given hints to philanthropists and
reformers, and these to organizations and societies; these
again have suggested theories and projects to legislators,
senators, and presidents; the snowball has been rolled larger
and larger; commissions have sat, investigations have been

3

made, documents have been attested, reports handed in, bills drafted and, what is better, passed by courageous legislation; so that now great schemes are being not only dreamed of but put into actual fulfilment. Moreover, lecturers have talked and writers have issued bulletins and books, until there has accumulated a library of vast proportions on the many phases of duty, activity, and outlook that may be included under the title, "A Country Life Movement."

In all this stirring field of new interest, the farmer and his business hold the center of attention. Beside him, however, stands a dim little figure hitherto kept much in the background, the farmer's wife, who at last seems to be on the point of finding a voice also; for a chapter is now assigned to her in every book on rural conditions and a little corner under a scroll work design is given to her tatting and her chickens in the weekly farm paper. Cuddled about her are the children, and they, the little farm boys and girls, have now a book that has been written just about them alone — their psychology and their needs. Also, the tall strong youth, her grown-up son, has his own paper as an acknowledged citizen of the rural commonwealth. But where is the tall young daughter, and where are the papers for her and the books about her needs? It seems that she has not as yet found a voice. She has failed to impress the makers of books as a subject for description and investigation. In the nation-wide effort to find a solution to the great rural problems, the farmer is working heroically; the son is putting his shoulder to the wheel; the wife and mother is in sympathy with their efforts. Is the daughter not doing her share? Where is the Country Girl and what is happening in her department?

It is easier on the whole to discover the rural young man than to find the typical Country Girl. Since the days of Mother Eve the woman young and old has been adapting herself and readapting herself, until, after all these centuries of constant practise, she has become a past master in the art of adaptation. Like the cat in the story of Alice, she disappears in the intricacy of the wilderness about her and nothing remains of her but a smile.

There are some perfectly sound reasons why American country girls as a class cannot be distinguished from other girls. Chief among these is the fact that no group of people in this country is to be distinguished as a class from any other group. It is one of the charms of life in this country that you never can place anybody. No one can distinguish between a shop girl and a lady of fashion; nor is any school teacher known by her poise, primness, or imperative gesture. The fashion paper, penetrating to the remotest dug-out, and the railway engine indulging us in our national passion for travel see to these things. Moreover, the pioneering period is still with us and the western nephews must visit the cousins in the old home in New Hampshire, while the aunts and uncles left behind must go out to see the new Nebraska or Wyoming lands on which the young folks have settled. We do not stay still long enough anywhere in the republic for a class of any sort to harden into recognizable form.

New inhabitants may come here already hardened into the mold of some class; but they or their children usually soften soon into the quicksilver-like consistency of their surroundings.

There is also no subdividing of notions on the basis of residence, whether as townsman or as rural citizen. The wind bloweth where it listeth in this land. It whispers its free secrets into the ears of the city dweller in the flat and of the rural worker of the cornfield or the vine-screened kitchen. The rain also falls on the just and the unjust whether suburbanated or countrified. There is no rural mind in America. There has indeed been a great deal of pother of late over the virtue and temper of " rural-minded people." This debate has been conscientiously made in the effort to discern reasons why commissions should sit on a rural problem. Reasons enough are discernible why commissions should sit, but they lie rather in the unrural mind of the rural people, as the words are generally understood, than in some supposed qualities imposed or produced in the life of sun and rain, in that vocation that is nearest to the creative activities of the Divine.

And if there is no rural mind, there is no distinctive rural personality. If the man that ought to exemplify it is found walking up Fifth Avenue or on Halstead Street or along El Camino Real, he cannot be discovered as a farmer. He may be discovered as an ignorant person, or he may be found to be a college-bred man; but in neither case would the fact be logically inclusive or uninclusive of his function as farmer.

The same is almost as exactly true for his wife and his daughter. If one should ask in any group of average people whether the farmer's daughter as they have known her is a poor little undeveloped child, silent and shy, or a hearty buxom lass, healthy and strong and up to date, some in the group would say the latter and some the former. Both varieties exist and can by searching be found along the countryside. But it is nothing essentially rural that has developed either the one set of characteristics or the other. To be convinced of this, one who knows this country well has but to read a book like " Folk of the Furrow," by Christopher Holdenby, a picture of rural life in England. In such a book as that one realizes the full meaning of the phrase, " the rural mind," and one sees how far the men and women that live on the farms in the United States have yet to go, how much they will have to coagulate, how many centuries they will have to sit still in their places with wax in their ears and weights on their eyelids, before they will have acquired psychological features such as Mr. Holdenby gives to the folk of the English furrow.

A traveler in the Old World frequently sees illustrations of this. For instance, in passing through some European picture gallery, he may meet a woman of extraordinary strength and beauty, dressed in a style representing the rural life in that vicinity. She will wear the peasant skirt and bodice, and will be without gloves or hat. A second look will reveal that the skirt is made of satin so stiff that it could stand alone; the velvet bodice will be covered with rich embroidery; and heavy chains of silver of quaint workmanship will be suspended around the neck.

On inquiry one may learn that this stately woman was of what would be called in this country a farmer family, that had now become very wealthy; that she did not consider herself above her "class"—so they would describe it—no, that she gloried in it instead. It was from preference only that she dressed in the fashion of that "class."

Now, whether desirable or not, such a thing as this would never be seen in America. No woman (unless it were a deaconess or a Salvation Army lassie or a nun) would pass through the general crowd showing her rank or profession in life by her style of dress. And that is how it happens that neither by hat nor by hatlessness would the country woman here make known her pride in the possession of acres or in her relation to that profession that forms the real basis of national prosperity. Hence no country girl counts such a pride among her inheritances. Therefore if it is not easy to find and understand the country girl as a type, it is not because she is consciously or unconsciously hiding herself away from us; she is not even sufficiently conscious of herself as a member of a social group to pose in the attitude of an interesting mystery. She is just a human being happening to live in the country (not always finding it the best place for her proper welfare), just a single one in the great shifting mass.

Although it may be difficult to find what we may think are typical examples of the Country Girl as a social group, yet certain it is that she exists. Of young women between the ages of fifteen and twenty-nine, there are in the United States six and a half million (6,694,184, to be exact) who reside in the open country or in small villages.   This we are assured is so by the latest Census Report.

By starting a little further down in the scale of girlhood and advancing a trifle further into maturity this number could be doubled.   It would be quite justifiable to do this, because some farmers' daughters become responsible for a considerable amount of labor value well before the age of fifteen; and on the other hand the energy of these young rural women is abundantly extended beyond the gateway of womanhood, far indeed into the period that used to be called old-maidism, but which is to be so designated no more; the breezy, executive, free-handed period when the country girl is of greatest use as a labor unit and gives herself without stint (and often without pay) to the welfare of the whole farmstead.   The American Country Girl is not by any means behind her city sister in her ability to make the bounds of her youth elastic, though the girl on the farm may go at it in a somewhat different way.   Then, perhaps, too, the word " youth " may, alas! have another connotation in the mind of one from what it has in the dreams of the other.

If we should, however, thus enlarge the scope of our inquiry, we should increase but not clarify our problems. Moreover it is the Country Girl that interests us, the promise and hope of her dawn, the delicate swiftly changing years of her growth, the miracle of her blossoming.   There is something about the kaleidoscope of her moods and the inconsistencies of her biography that fascinates us.   The moment when she awakes, when the sparkle begins to show in her eyes, when we know that a conception of her mission and of her supreme value to life is beginning to glow before her imagination — that is the crisis to work for and to be happy over when it comes.   As for us, we ask no greater happiness than once or twice to catch a glimpse of that.

That great host of six million country girls is scattered far and wide; they are everywhere present.   A certain number of millions of them are working industriously in myriads of unabandoned farms all over the Appalachain plateau, and on the wide prairies to the Rockies, and beyond. In thousands of farmsteads they are helping their mothers wash dishes three times a day three hundred and sixty-five days in the year, not counting the steps as they go back and forth between dining-room and kitchen. They are carrying heavy pails of spring water into the house and throwing out big dishpanfuls of waste water, regardless of the strain in the small of the back. They are picking berries and canning them for the home table in the winter; they are raising tomatoes and canning them for the market; they are managing the younger children; they are baking and sewing and reading and singing; they are caring for chickens and for bees and for orphan lambs; they ride the rake and the disc-plow and sometimes join the round-up on the range. Moreover they go to church and they go to town and they look forward to an ideal future just as other girls do. The Country Girl is a human being also.

It has been intimated that young women living on remote secluded farms have not, with all their singing, been always able to dispel the monotony of a thousand inevitable dish-washings a year; they are said now-a-days to have opened their ear to the lure of the town and to have started out, keeping step with their brothers, to join what some one has called, " the funeral procession of the nation " cityward. If we could, in fact, get them to confide in us, we should find that they have longings and aspirations, many of which are unsatisfied; and that is the reason why it seems to be high time for their voice to be heard.

Some of the younger farm women are showing themselves equal to the larger burdens in the business of agriculture. They are running their own farms in Michigan and their own automobiles in Kansas. They are taking up claims. They are developing them and proving up in the Dakotas and through Montana and Wyoming. From four to six in the morning they till an acre; then they ride twenty miles to the school and teach from nine to four; after that they ride back and work in their cornfields till the stars twinkle out. They stay alone in their shack and are happy and fearless and safe.

Moreover some thousands of the girls are laboriously teaching schools in thousands of one-room schoolhouses, where they provide almost one hundred per cent. of the common instruction for fifty per cent. of the population.

Besides this, there is no one of all the gainful occupations in which young women of this country engage which has not drawn upon the reservoir of country strength for supplies. Among those women blacksmiths and engineers, those clerks, secretaries, librarians and administrators, those lawyers, doctors, professors, writers, those nurses, settlement workers, investigators and other servants of the people in widely diverse fields, there are many whose clearness of eye and reserve of force have been developed in the wholesome conditions of the open country. The Country Girl has no reason to be ashamed of the part she has borne in the non-rural world. It has been said that about eighty per cent. of the names found in " Who's Who in America " represent an upbringing in the rural atmosphere. The proportion of women in this number or the special proportion of grown-up farm girls to be found among those women cannot be stated; but the number must be large enough to justify a belief that to spend a childhood in the open country or in the rural village will not, in the case of women any more than in the case of men, form an impassable barrier to eminence.

From this great rural reserve of initiating force, sane judgment, and spiritual drive have come, in fact, some of the most valued names in philanthropy and literature. Among them we find the leader of a great reform, Frances Willard; the inaugurator of a world-wide work of mercy, Clara Barton; the president of a great college, Alice E. Freeman; the wise helper of all who suffer under unjust conditions in city

life, Jane Addams; and the writer of a book that has had a
national and world-wide influence, Harriet Beecher Stowe.

It heartens us up a bit to name over examples like these.
They give us a vista and a hope.   But now and then there
is a Country Girl who would rather have, say, a better pair
of stilts over the morass or a stronger rope thrown to her
across the quicksand, than a volume of " Who's Who "
tossed carelessly to her in her difficulties.   For all the Country Girls on their farms do not sing at their work.   They are
not idle, heaven knows ! — but their work does not invariably
inspire the appreciation it deserves.

CHAPTER II

THE HEART OF THE PROBLEM

New times demand new measures and new men;
The world advances and in time outgrows
The laws that in our fathers' day were best;
And, doubtless, after us some purer scheme
Will be shaped out by wiser men than we,
Made wiser by the steady growth of truth.

Lowell.

CHAPTER II

THE HEART OF THE PROBLEM

THE reason why the American people care so much for the ideals that are presented to us in the Country Life Movement is that there is something very deep-seated and permanent within us to which these motives can appeal. We are a country-life people. The bogy of the overshadowing city, threatening to spread and spread until, like a great octopus, it should suck all the sweet fields into its tentacles and cover the green areas with a compact blackness, has given us a definite fright. The result of our terror is the " Country Life Movement." It is not that we were actually approaching an imagined danger-point; it was only that a vision of life constantly fed and inspired by the pure unadulterated influences of the country was before the eyes of a country-bred people, and was of so great preciousness that we must guard it at the first hint of peril. There are indeed grave dangers threatening some fundamental interests in the agricultural realm; to these the nation is now well awake. The republic has many problems but on the whole it is prospering, and perhaps one reason why this is so lies in the fact that the profession of agriculture is still the backbone of our national life.

The so-called Country Life Movement, then, is not a sudden onslaught upon our consciousness by an alien influence, as if we were fish suddenly commanded to go and live on the land. It is more as if a band of mountaineers with lungs adjusted to a height of several thousand feet, had been trying to breathe the air in a close and stuffy valley far below their proper levels, but who had now returned to their native height and were feeling the glow and triumph of their original energy; or who perhaps, being frightened lest they should be imprisoned in that low valley, were making frantic efforts to escape this doom and to reach their mountain homes where they could breathe freely and grow normally again. The Country Life Movement is not the despairing gasp of expiring effeteness; it is an exclamation of robust joy in the possession of a life healthily adapted to our needs.

At present there are well-nigh six million farmsteads in this country. They form what we may untechnically call the agricultural group, and represent roughly, but of course vitally, the great business of farming. In our consideration we have to include also the small rural villages, because the United States Census Reports include under the word " rural " both people living in the open country and those living in villages up to twenty-five hundred inhabitants in size.

In the agricultural group the unit is the farmstead. By that term is meant the whole complex organization of the farm, including the land and its products, the stock, the barns and the sheds, the whole family together with whatever houses it, the corps of workers, farmer, farmer's wife, sons, daughters, maiden aunts, working people unhired and hired — in fact, everything " animal, vegetable or mineral," as the children say when they play " Forty Questions," that ministers in any way to the success of the farm as a business and to its ultimate object, the happiness of the family living thereon. So when we say " farmstead " we mean not only fodder for beasts but also food for the human beings; but inasmuch as the human being is soul-endowed and has imperative appetites in the æsthetic and spiritual realm as well as in the physical, the farmstead covers the matter of the piano as well as of the hoe. A wealthy farmstead is indeed one that has cattle upon many hills, or that sends many carloads of milk to the city; but it can scarcely be called a wholly prosperous farmstead unless it has an unrestricted view of the scenery from its living-room windows, a public reading room within reach of its buggy's wheels — that means, say, within twelve or fifteen miles at most — or of its automobile — which may mean within forty or one hundred miles according to the roads and the car; and, we may add, unless it takes advantage of this and other cultural privileges.

It may be said that the ultimate end of the whole farm business is the happiness of the family; yet the minds of many do not travel to the ultimate — they pause at some one of the possible stopping places along the way and fashion that subsidiary idea into the fiction of an ultimate end. For instance, one may make the fattening of stock or the purchase of a certain additional strip of land into an ultimate end, and work for that, sacrificing much that is of immediate happiness value, or perhaps even of supreme happiness value, to gain that minor object. Meantime the real end, the one that if we should penetrate to the heart of our ideals, we should find seated in the most sacred place: namely, the welfare and happiness of the family group for which we live and labor, has been neglected, and nearer, more direct means to attain it have been overlooked.

This, then, is the heart of the matter. The farmstead is an intricate organism with many parts working wonderfully together. The object, the reason for the existence of every item and strain of it and for the thing as a whole, is that there should be at the center of it a radiant core of joy in which every human member of the little cosmos may have a share and so reflect back to the others a still greater brightness. In this farmstead world, each individual member must therefore be made happy. A tricky word — that word "happiness!" Perhaps it cannot be defined, but Americans are entitled to pursue it, whatever it may mean!

The wise ones, however, say that the one condition that can and will set alight a vigorous flame of happiness at the heart of any human farmstead is that there should be found there the opportunity for growth for every individual in the circle, for the development of his or her latent powers, so that each life may find that whatever it was intended to be, it has been fully able to become; that none of its God-given abilities have gone to waste for want of notice, furtherance, food, or inspiration. It would be a pity to find that there was one social structure among the devices of our high civilization that was stubbornly inhospitable to the entrance of that messenger, " Growth," who precedes and announces the heavenly visitant, " Happiness." The farmstead must not be accused of being such a structure as that unless it is absolutely necessary.

To what extent, then, does the farmstead offer opportunity for such growth? Is it too much to ask that the ultimate joy of living, the joy of growth, should be brought very near to the eyes of the people living on the farmsteads, that their imaginations should be touched even more keenly than they now are to a consciousness of the real possibilities in their environment? What can we do to create an atmosphere that will give its own enthusiasm to the people, that will bind each member of the farmstead indissolubly to the place; one in which there shall be so swift a certainty that it will seem like magic; that must so charm the mind and the heart of each one that the tie will hold against any kind of onslaught?

But the claim is being made in some quarters that the countryside home does not live up to its possibilities in this respect, and if not in this respect then the country life movement has a real pang behind it as well as an uprising of renewed life. If the father in the home, who is the farmer and head of the homestead, does not find happiness according to his needs, it may from all the signs be concluded that the government and the universities and the newspapers and the legislators are busying themselves to the greatest possible extent to relieve his disabilities; he may be left in their care for the present. Of the farmer's wife, who is the head of the home and the partner with her husband in the farm business, the government has lately in a group of letters addressed to fifty-five thousand farm-woman correspondents, asked the question, What do you wish to have done that your life may be more filled with content and that your disabilities may be relieved? It is safe to presume that the longings of their hearts will be by some means satisfied in longer or shorter meter. The sons are sharing the fortunes of the fathers, but if they are not, numbers of them may go out from the home valley and easily seek what they believe will be a better fortune along the outer avenues of a man's activities. And the daughter? While that ship comes slowly in that is to bring something comforting to her mother, while her father is giving the farm the benefit of his fast accumulating scientific information and lessening the daily labor by up-to-date machinery, what is happening to her? Is she having her share of content? Has she the chance to grow and fill full the possible round of her own personal development? Is the Country Girl happy on the farm? Or is she in her heart dissatisfied and glowering? Is she suppressed and sodden in mood? Is her face expressionless and too old for her years? Is she round-shouldered and heavy of step? Is she listless and suspicious and sensitive?

Or is she full of spirit and enthusiasm, a perfect dynamo of energy? Is she the life of the home, with a word and a joke for everybody and is she a perfect mischief among the other children? Is her face full of expression, with smiles and dimples all the time? Is she full of love and affection toward each member of the family, and endless in her devices for their comfort and entertainment? Is she a veritable steam engine to get the work done and equally a master hand at all kinds of games and plays, able to get up something in no time and carry out any kind of a scheme with nothing to do with? Does she sleep the very sleep of the dead the whole night long, and is she all day the

widest awake being that can be found for miles around?
Has she an appetite to startle one fully three times a day and
even more often, if something good to eat is being made?
In fine, is she receiving her share of possible growth?   Is
she having her chance to show all that she is able to become?   And thus is she being happy?   And also thus is she
making the rest of the circle in the home that is at the center of the farmstead, happier than it could ever have been
if she had not been there and had not been the fully developed girl that she is?

This is the question that seems most important at just
this time.   This is the problem on which light must be
thrown.

It seems to be an important question for several reasons.
It is said that the young men are showing their dissatisfac-
tion with farm life by going away in large numbers to find
occupation in the city; that the best and most energetic of
the young men, those who would have been leaders for betterment in the general countryside, are found among those
who desert the countryside, and that thus the farm community is depleted and deprived of good elements that it cannot well spare.   The wind of destiny for woman that has
swept through the country and the world during the last two
decades or so, has penetrated the valleys where in seclusion
the Country Girls have grown up, and has now whispered
inspiration and courage into their ears, so that if they are
dissatisfied with the conditions of their lives they will have
the daring to go forth also, following their brothers, and
to take up some industrial fortune in the city whither the
bright star of independence beckons them.   They are doing
this already; and the news of it should make thoughtful
people bestir themselves.   There seems to be a great problem here, and the Country Girl seems to be at the heart of it.
For if the rural question is the central question of the world,
and if the social problem is the heart of the rural problem,
and if the failure of the daughter's joy and usefulness

threatens the farmstead,— then once more in the history of
the world has the hour struck for woman; then does the
welfare of the world depend upon her as much as did the
life of the bleak New England shore depend on the health
and survival of the Pilgrim Mothers?

Of course no one would wish to claim that the young
woman in the farmstead is of more importance than other
members of the home; but as a chain will break if one link
fails, so the farmstead will be ruined if it lacks the cooperation of the daughter.   She has, at least, a function all her
own; and the happiness that comes through normal growth
must be hers in order that she may fulfil her mission.   The
farmstead girl must take her place in the farmstead or the
farmstead unit will lack one of its component parts and fall
to pieces.   It is her patriotic duty; it is her home and family duty; and it is her greatest happiness.   The young
woman on the farm must grow up with the idea that she is
essential to the progress of country life and therefore of
the national life, and that a career is before her just as much
as if she were aiming to be an artist or a writer or a missionary.   This purpose makes her life worth while.   She
must conserve her health for this; she must develop her
powers for this; she must train herself heroically for this.

We are, then, face to face with the question, so important to us at the present moment, whether the daughter in
the farmstead family is having her own full meed of happiness in her farm home or not.   Has she the opportunity that
is her right to grow and develop all her latent powers and to
become the person that by all the gifts of nature she is capable of becoming?

CHAPTER III

IS THE COUNTRY GIRL HAPPY
ON THE FARM?

Let the mighty and great
Roll in splendor and state!
I envy them not, I declare it.
I eat my own lamb,
My own chicken and ham,
I shear my own sheep and I wear it.

I have lawns, I have bowers,
I have fruits, I have flowers.
My lark is my morning's charmer;
So you jolly dogs now
Here's God bless the plow —
Long life and content to the farmer.
    Inscription on an old English pitcher.

CHAPTER III

IS THE COUNTRY GIRL HAPPY ON THE FARM?

THE young women who read this book will surely believe that no mere curiosity inspires the question at the head of this chapter, but a fully fixed idea that much depends on the answer. If it is not to be possible for the young women to be made happy in the rural environment, they surely are going to turn in great numbers and follow the beckoning finger of industries and engagements townward. And if multitudes of them do this, it will be increasingly difficult to keep that composite thing, the farmstead, in perfect balance; and in that balance the daughters have every year a more important part. Their share, in fact, is constantly growing more vital, more indispensable to the welfare of the whole.

There is also an even more important consideration. It is this. The daughters in the homes of to-day are the home-makers of to-morrow; if they are estranged irrecoverably from the countryside, what is to become of the countryside in the days that are to come? Can we entertain the hope that the city cousins will come to the rescue? Can we reply upon the inrush of new families from across the seas to enter our widespread fields and valleys and support for us the burden of scientific housekeeping, and high-minded home making, and modern education in the spirit of American institutions?

These are some of the thoughts and some of the fears that students of the situation entertain. The result is that a strong interest is felt to know if possible exactly how the country girl herself does feel about her life on the farm, whether she is dissatisfied with the conditions that surround her, whether she suffers from a deep-seated sense of neglect and suppression, and whether she is attentive to some distant call of the metropolitan.lure.

Many conversations and a wide and representative correspondence leave the impression upon the author that the Country Girls of America, however far apart in geography and condition, are alike in one characteristic — the sincerity and soberness of their testimony. The young woman on the American farm is thoughtful, well balanced, dignified. She takes herself seriously, and she is developing powers that promise well for the future of American life.

The first unthinking impulse of many country girls is their love for their country homes. Some are optimistic enough to claim that the farmer's family can enjoy all the advantages of village or city life without any of the disadvantages, and with the added enjoyment of the country itself. Now that books, pictures, and music are so easily accessible to the farm, now that the telephone puts one into communication with friends in city or country, and modern traveling conveniences make it possible to secure such urban benefits as lectures, church, lodge, post office, etc., they feel that they have all grievances done away with. Girls in thickly-populated New York and in wide-awake, modern Idaho give the same testimony. There is a large group who will even exclaim as one Missouri girl did that she never had had a single reason for wishing to leave the farm; that she knew of no other place which offered so much help in physical, mental, and spiritual growth and development.

A young woman with an ear to economic values suggests that on the farm a great part of the food can be produced at home and can thus be kept free from adulteration. This is not by any means a minor consideration. Another who perhaps has at some time known stringency in the city and can look at the problem from another angle, thinks that in the country it is rather a relief not to have to count the cost of each separate meal.

The Country Girl is the life of the home. She is a companion for the parents and a playmate for the little brothers and sisters.

The Country Girl and Her Pets. "The quietness of the country permits a greater spiritual and mental growth, with its abundance of life, plant and animal, which challenges the mind to discover its secrets."

The opportunities on the farm sometimes appeal to the fun loving propensities of the young girl. One has, or nearly always can have, they say, space for games, such as tennis, basket ball, etc. Many think that there is more real fun in the distinctive exercises of the farm than in those of the town; for there they have nutting, riding down hill, going berrying, riding on loads of hay; — all these are thoroughly appreciated.

In the varied business of the farmstead the daughter may see her love of animals gratified. On the big Iowa farm where one Country Girl lives the farm stock is to her the chief attraction. They make pets of nearly all their creatures, and she herself assigns the fanciful and literary pet names.

Some times the more mature country girl has reached the height where she finds the good of country life to consist in its liberty, its leisure, its varied interests, its fresh air and nearness to nature, and its distance from the pettiness of the towns people and their limited outlook. On the farm time may be devoted to the really big things of life without petty distractions. One gains there a wholesome, sane view of life. There may be plenty to do on the farm but what you do is of consequence.

Some of the more spiritual aspects are gathered together in this transcript of a Country Girl's thoughts and dreams. In trying to describe the charm that the country has for her, she mentions " the quietness and peace which permit of one's greater spiritual and mental growth, the abundance of life, plant and animal, which challenges the mind to discover its secrets; the rocks and streams which call out to one for study and discovery, the beauties of the sunrise, the clouds, the sunset, the moonlight, and the far off stars, — these call to our spirits to penetrate their mystery and lift up our souls to those levels above the commonplace where we commune with the Maker; the hills and the wide expanses make us reverent and teach us to walk humbly and patiently; the clean sweet air gives us health and strength of body and soul; and the freedom from restraint by formalities and conventionalities permits the development of the person in a sane and natural way."

Another thoughtful mind writes this: " Farming is creative; being experimental, it is interesting. On the farm both body and mind are exercised, therefore both are kept nearer a normal level. We have fresher, purer food and air; freedom from foolish forms and ceremony. We are nearer to God."

An aspect that many country girls have keenly felt is shown in this passage from the letter of a loyal girl of the countryside: " I fail to find the hardships of farm life, and it always makes me indignant to hear about them. Save as all life has its hardships, these special hardships are a bugaboo that does not exist. A few weeks ago I was hostess to fourteen of the girls from a large drygoods store in the city. I was grieved to see what undersized, ill-nourished little people they were. They ranged in age from sixteen to twenty, and every one was prepared to despise the country and to look upon it with contempt and the people with pity because they do not live in the city. Their prevailing idea seemed to be that they had come to another race of people whom they regarded with a tolerant pity and contempt. I heard them telling my cousins, honest manly fellows, how very different they were from boys in the city. Ah me! the simplest things about nature which they did not know would fill many a book."

This delightfully peppery communication may be followed by one that gives that feeling of joyousness that we believe should always be found in real country life, and at the end strikes clearly the most important note of all: "The attractiveness of farm life lies in as many, diverse, and wonderful things as the breadth of the individual girl's mind can comprehend and enjoy. To some the sense of freedom in country life is a large means of happiness. The feeling of exultation in the far sweep of vision, the glorious sunsets, and the movements of the clouds in the wind and the coming storm. Then there is the pleasure in seeing and helping things grow, in the frolic of the lambs in the spring, of the colts at play, and in the young plants sprouting and growing in the summer showers and sunshine; especially if you have pulled the weeds and hoed about them yourself. Frequent outings to the lake or river for an afternoon or evening holiday with bathing and canoeing in the afternoon and a bon-fire in the evening with a group of friends to toast marshmallows or roast corn, and later with stories and songs, add much to the pleasure of farm life. Then there is the quiet and peace of the country where one may be alone at times and think. In the country there is a more compact home life than anywhere else, for each member of the family is working together for the home." This most important point might receive further emphasis.

The young women in our farm homes, are, with true American spirit, appreciating the possible play in rural life of freedom and independence. Young women of the rural communities seem to be at one with the time spirit of the whole country. Nothing has set them askew, not even a world-wide women's movement! It delights them that country life fosters individuality; but they absolutely identify themselves with the welfare of the farmstead as a whole. The idea that their good could be separated from the good of the family and business group in which their life is embedded, does not seem to influence the minds of our country girls, north, south, east, or west. And they have their far thoughts; they look ahead and see that life on the farm furthers the unity of the family; that it is the best place to rear children; that family life and affection are more successfully fostered in a country town than in a city flat, hotel or mansion. They find that simplicity of living is easier to attain in the farm home and they believe that this is favorable to the welfare of the family.

Moreover, the coordinating spirit of the age has touched the minds of some. They see now that the farmstead is closely knit up with the larger unit of the farm community. They find along the countryside greater friendliness among neighbors than is found in the crowded city; they realize that the farmer's family can set its own standards without losing social recognition; and they prize the informality of social intercourse which is found in the rural world.

These are some of the things that the young woman in the rural realm will set down in her brief for country life. Her voice is an even-tempered voice; there is self-control in it and there is a dynamic element behind it that will compel a hearing. Talking with many Country Girls and reading long letters from them, one gains an impression that, like the composite photograph, reveals a country girl personality whose sanity and thoughtfulness win our respect, and whose serious facing of the facts bodes ill for such country life leaders as may in the future neglect the resources to be found in the sagacity, alertness, and powers of execution stored up in the young womanhood of our rural life.

CHAPTER IV

A CALENDAR OF DAYS

A country life is sweet!
In moderate cold and heat,
  To walk in the air how pleasant and fair!
In every field of wheat,
  The fairest of flowers adorning the bowers
And every meadow's brow;
  So that I say, no courtier may
  Compare with them who clothe in gray,
And follow the useful plow.

They rise with the morning lark,
And labor till almost dark;
  Then, folding their sheep, they hasten to sleep,
While every pleasant park
  Next morning is ringing with birds that are singing
On each green, tender bough.
  With what content and merriment
  Their days are spent, whose minds are bent
To follow the useful plow.

                                        Anon.

CHAPTER IV

A CALENDAR OF DAYS

THE wisest find life a difficult thing to classify; therefore young girls must not be blamed if they do not critically analyze the causes and the effects that appear in their personal environment. When asked, however, to give pictures of their daily experiences they do not fail us. Such glimpses of the real life of some Country Girls in their farm homes will be afforded by the partial recitals given in this chapter. To other Country Girls or to those to whom the welfare of the country girl is dear, or even to those urbanized city residents who consider the dwellers in the open country as a sort of alien race whose ways must be made a matter of study before they can be comprehended — these and perhaps others will surely be interested in these fresh and vivid accounts of the everyday doings in the farm homes of our country.

A fortunate country girl when asked to write a description of a representative working day of her life, sends the following joyous account. She is fifteen years old. Her life is under the protection of highly educated parents and the safeguards of right home training, taste and refinement. They come from magnificent stock and work a farm of medium size in the Northwest. She said:

"I get up at about half-past six in the morning, and have breakfast at seven. Then I help Mother what I can before I start for school. Mamma puts up my luncheon while I get ready. About a quarter past eight I start on my two mile walk to school. For about three quarters of a mile I follow the road, then I turn off into woods. By following a half-beaten trail for a ways, I come to a bridge

33

made of wire. The sides and bottom are of wire; on the bottom are laid rows of planks with cross pieces to keep them where they belong. The bridge sways when you walk on it and sometimes it sags quite a little. Across the river I go through more woods. The schoolhouse is set on the top of a little hill. There are about twenty pupils in the school. At recess and noon we often play baseball. We have a fine teeter and swing. At noons all of the girls and sometimes the boys take their dinners and go out and find some pretty spot in the woods to eat. In the spring-time we often go flower hunting. I never get home in the afternoon until about half past four. After school I play, sew, or help in the garden till supper time. After supper I do the supper dishes, then we all have a nice time sewing, reading, or playing games around the fireplace."

A rest-breathing idyl like this shows that it is possible for bits of heaven to appear here upon earth now and then! The picture is made still more vivid by this little note:

" Several times we took lunch to an unworked mine near by and enjoyed the beautiful view and amused ourselves by picking gold out of the crevices in the rocks." The final touch of romantic beauty!

A roseate story like this should be followed, for contrast's sake, by one picturing the harder side. The following, written by a girl of sixteen, a description of a day in haying time, shows how a blithesome spirit can make work light and joyous:

" Haying time is a very busy season for all on the farm. At 5.30 o'clock Mother comes to our room, saying, ' It is going to be a good hay day, girlies. You must get up now; the men are nearly through milking.' She is forced to call several times, but finally we are up and dressed; we help finish getting breakfast, feed the chickens, and drive the cows to pasture. After breakfast my sister and I take the milk to the milkman who carries it to the milk station. Father hitches our horse and loads the milk for us, and then

hurries away to begin his mowing so that the hay will have
time to be well cured in the afternoon. We drive a half
mile to the milk stand where our milk is unloaded by the milkman; exchange good-mornings with him and perhaps with
a neighbor or two, and drive back home. We take care of
our horse and wagon and then help with the morning housework. About half-past eight my sister and I start out after
huckleberries in a near-by field. It is a beautiful morning
and we enjoy the walk. We pick enough berries for a pie
and for supper that evening and a few more. But we hurry
back in order to have a little rest before half-past ten, when
I must start raking. At half-past ten, then, I hitch my
horse to the rake and ride off to the lot to work. I rake
until dinner time and have perhaps a third of the raking
done. I unharness my horse, water him, and put him in
the barn. I go to dinner with an enormous appetite and a
feeling of anticipation, both of which are soon appeased.

" Soon after dinner I begin raking again and rake until
six o'clock. Father and the hired man draw in six large
loads of hay. The haying for the day is done and it is
pleasant to lie in the hammock and read a paper or book
while the men finish unloading their last load. But before
I enjoy this I must take care of my horse and carry him a
drink of water from the well. After supper my sister and
I help with the dishes and then run off to play in the swing
while the men finish milking. When the milking is done we
take the cows and the horse to pasture. Then we feed the
calf, Claire by name, who is a very dear little creature and
always greets us with great joy when she sees us coming.
We shut up the chickens also. Then there is about a half-
hour or more left for play, and we have a good time, forgetting that we ever worked.

" All our days are not so busy as this one; and when the
haying and summer sewing are done, we have a chance for
good times. Our haying was done this summer in eight
days or perhaps less. At quarter of nine we go to bed. I

read a chapter or two in some book I am reading, but by ten o'clock we are both asleep with the starlight and the moonlight shining in on us through the open screen."

If our sixteen-year-old girls can be completely satisfied to have but half an hour a day for recreation and to spend all the rest in unintermittent and heavy toil, and then can come out of it not only with unbroken courage but also with buoyancy and a poetic mood, then our respect for the country girl's character and nerve ought to be enhanced. This one ends her story thus:

" Indeed my sister and I love the farm very much and have no desire to leave it. We often declare that we would not live in the city for anything."

Perhaps the above letter will be recognized in some mysterious way as belonging to one of the Middle States; the following delightfully individual letter can come only from a big ranch in the Northwest. One feels the personality of the writer, like a dynamo, through all she writes. A Rocky Mountain breeze blows through her words; and her day, we know, is only one among many equally dramatic and interesting.

" This morning I was wakened by the sun as it first shone in at my window. As it was only a quarter of five I covered my eyes for one more nap. We have cool nights, but yesterday it was 104 in the shade. Soon I heard Papa get up, so I did likewise. I built a fire in the kitchen range and cooked my own breakfast. ' Cookie Sis' was not up and Papa does not eat breakfast.

" I thought the rest had slept long enough, so I turned on the water near the house and began to carry wash water. That got them up. While my water was heating, I gathered the clothes, swept four rooms, irrigated a little on the garden, and picked up chips. Then I washed — they call me the ' family laundry.' I must be somewhat Irish, too, for I must have everything in the house and on me washed clean.

"At noon I was still washing. While waiting for dinner, one of the hired men struck a bargain with me. He is to bring down his spring and summer collection of seventeen dirty shirts; I am to show him how to wash them and then I may iron them. I promised because I believe in helping my neighbor, because this fellow sometimes takes my sister riding in his new buggy, and because he and I have red hair.

"Dinner was good even though served on our decrepit ranch dishes. We are running three kitchens. We have good meals always. We eat well and work hard for what we get here in the West.

"In the afternoon I finished the washing, helped clean the house, and mended. After three o'clock I sat here in a cool room by an open window watching Papa mow alfalfa and the men stack grain. The children were in swimming. By and by one of my chums drove by on her way home from town. We visit thus mostly.

"Supper at six. I ironed before and after, as long as the irons were hot. Now at sunset my work is done. But Papa is irrigating — that takes twenty-four hours a day.

"This was a typical working day; but it would have been as natural for me to have described one of the six days last week when I spent ten hours a day hoeing corn. To-morrow we girls will put on overalls and shock hay. Don't let it shock you — we live in the West!

"The trouble with farming is that the days are not long enough for work or the nights long enough for sleep."

The writer of the following "typical day" has become early the possessor of husband and child; but we shall not omit her story on that account. She lives sixty miles from the railroad station and has wonderful mountains about her horizon. Her account of one of her marvelous days may be commended to all country people wherever they may be found. The joy of work and the joy of living, here reach a climax together:

"It is dusk. The children and I have just come in from

the corral, where I milked seven cows. I am so in love with life that I find a day very short to hold its allotted joys.

" First, I awoke a little earlier than usual this morning and lay thinking over the ' had-to-be-dones.' It was baking day ; but that is a glad-to-be as well as the other, because I love to experiment outside of the cookbooks. At half-past five I arose and by half-past six had breakfast on the table and my bread set. By eight o'clock we had breakfasted and I had the seven cows milked. How I love my gentle cows! What an inspiration their calm patience is! And I love to get out at that hour. At this altitude the mornings are always chilly but by eight it is pleasant. At half-past eight I had the three larger children dressed and at breakfast, while I ran the milk through the separator. While the children finished, I went again to the barnyard, where I fed my little chicks and turkeys and looked after the rest. I have two rows of flowers between the barnyard and the house, so I stopped a few minutes to smell the sweet-peas, to admire the gorgeous colors of the poppies, and to pull a few weeds. By ten I had baby Robert bathed and all his little wants attended to, the breakfast dishes and the milk things washed, my bread in the oven and my dinner started. So I sat down to churn and to read while I churned. I use an old-fashioned dash churn, therefore I have an excuse for sitting down. I am glad of it, for I can read then. By twelve I have my sweet golden butter printed, have heard Jerrine's lessons and have dinner ready. By half-past one we have had dinner and I have the kitchen in order and we all lie down for a rest. At two I begin making the beds, by three the whole house is straightened, so I have two hours for myself. I read a little story for the kiddies and then send them all to play while I read a little. I write a couple of letters and then go out to hoe and pull weeds a while. I cook most of my supper while I cook dinner so I can prepare supper in a few minutes. So I feed my biddies, and the children gather the eggs, until we hear the men coming in from the field.   By seven o'clock we have had supper, and Baby is put to bed.   Jerrine helps me put the kitchen to rights.   Then comes the goodest part of the day.   We go to milk.   Jerrine and Calvin sit in the wagon out of harm's way and I milk.   Jerrine lets the cows in for me and empties the milk.   We all enjoy the beauties of the sunset, the beautiful colors, the crisp little mountain breeze.   By nine the kiddies have had their bath and are in bed.   Daddy-man is playing the phonograph so they can go to sleep lulled by *Annie Laurie, Bonnie Doon* and *The Sword of Bunker Hill.* Now that I have that line written I see it is rather an odd thing to be lulled by a sword, but I reckon you can figure out the meaning.   At ten o'clock my day will be finished.   I shall finish this paper and read a little with Daddy-man and then it will be my bed-time.   As I finish I see I have left out many little joys.   I have kissed little hands to make hurts well perhaps a dozen times.   I matched some colors and cut some blocks for Jerrine's patch work; I made a finger-stall for the hired man.   I have answered the 'phone a few times and — Now if some university can help me to make my days more elastic so that they can encompass all my joys comfortably, I shall be glad.   There's so much I want to do but — Good-night.''

The writer of the following story goes beyond the one typical day and for the sake of a more accurate treatment of her program includes a whole week.   Thus is recorded the general plan of the American housework system as it is carried on to-day.   She says:

'' A representative week of my life at home in the summer is easier to describe than one day, for each day is individual to itself.   To begin with the most interesting occupation of the morning, I get up at about five-thirty in time to toast the bread for breakfast.   After breakfast I take care of the milk and then Mother and I wash the dishes. Sweeping, dusting and putting in order the kitchen, dining-room and living-room comes next. The hard-wood floor in the kitchen is mopped twice a week. Next the bedrooms are put in order. This regular morning work takes from an hour to an hour and a half. On Monday we always do the family washing, which generally takes me about three hours and a half when Mother hangs up the clothes. Mother bakes the bread, prepares the vegetables for dinner and plans the desserts. If she needs me I sometimes help with these. She lets me bake the cake and what extra bread is needed for variety, such as brown bread, graham, corn-bread, etc. Monday afternoon we generally iron for an hour and a half to start on Tuesday's work. After the ironing is finished I sweep and dust the bedrooms, unless something extra comes up, such as indoor painting, varnishing hard-wood floors, cleaning of cupboards, etc. Tuesday afternoon is open for sewing. On Wednesday and Thursday after the morning work is completed Mother and I sometimes go visiting, but generally I spend these days sewing. On Friday there is the weekly sweeping of the living-room, the lamp chimneys to be washed, the windows to be polished and the porch to be cleaned. Sometimes there is company expected Saturday or Sunday, so that I do part of this work Thursday. Saturday morning there is a cake to be iced and in the afternoon we often have callers or else we go somewhere.

" Sunday is a day looked forward to all the week. We sleep a little later Sunday morning and after the morning work is done all the family, consisting at present of Mother, Father, my two brothers and I, get ready for church. In the afternoon we sometimes either go away or have company, but the kind we like best is the good old fashioned kind that we enjoyed when we were children, just to read a favorite book or story for the two or three short but precious hours before chore time. In the afternoon after their naps Mother and Father always enjoy a walk back on the farm. The evening we either enjoy quietly at home or if it is fair weather we attend the evening meeting at the church.

" This is the frame-work of the program of the summer days on the farm. I have said little of the heat because our kitchen is cool, nothing of the work because nothing is worth while which isn't hard work, made emphatic with backache and punctuated with drops of sweat. Gathering the berries, early apples, etc., was omitted because they come in just any time and are fun. Driving on the horse fork, canning fruit, etc., all come in their time, making every day full of busy little tasks."

The following gives the experience of three sisters in an opulent home on the western slope of the Catskills. It seems likely that the writer depreciates her own share in the work and in the success of the systematic household. She says:

" It is difficult to select any one day for a representative farm day program. The work changes with each day in the week and also changes very much with the seasons. In the spring there is the gardening, house cleaning and the raising of chickens, besides the shipping of many crates of eggs to New York. All this is done in the house and, although it is done all the year, in the spring when there are more eggs the work is heavier.

" The chickens are hatched out by incubators in a small house built for that purpose and when hatched they are moved to the brooder house. Here they are cared for until strong enough to be put out doors in brooders. Later they are sorted and put into larger colony houses out in the field. The entire responsibility and work of this is taken by my sister Isabell, so it is needless to say that her program through the spring months would show days that were more than busy.

" In the creamery, from which butter in pound prints is shipped twice a week to private families, the work of wrapping, packing and marking is also done by Isabell.

There is more of this work to be done during the winter months than in the summer because so many of the people who take the butter go abroad for the summer months.

" The management of the house, the cooking, and to a large extent the management of the business fall to my oldest sister, Elizabeth. We have two dining-rooms, one for the men, of whom there are sometimes as many as eight — and the other where we eat. For the housework we have no outside help except a woman who comes in once a week to bake for us and who also does the washing for the men. Our own washing is done by Elizabeth, with the aid of a power machine and steam which is piped from the creamery to the laundry.

" During the summer Elizabeth cans berries, fruits, beans, corn and tomatoes in as large amounts as our garden may produce for winter use. Ham, bacon and sausage are also made on the place. Even soap is made in the big iron kettles in just the same way that our grandmothers used to make it. Many people marvel at the amount of work which.is done here without any apparent confusion, and the reason for this is to a large extent due to my sisters' management. We have electric lights and steam heat and the kitchen is arranged in every way to save unnecessary labor.

" As for social life, we are not able to have as many guests here or to go to as many things in town as when we had sufficient girls in the kitchen. Most of our friends live in town six miles distant. This is due probably to the fact that we all went to High School there. We have a driving horse and go to most of the social things in town which occur in the afternoon. We rarely go down at night unless there is some exceptional event. My sister belongs to several clubs in town and recently has organized a study and social club among the farm women of this immediate vicinity. I think if one asked my busy sister what kind of recreation she enjoyed most, she would answer horseback riding and shooting. Most of the time we are too busy and interested in things here to complain about being far away from things in town. Sometimes, however, when the roads are bad, it becomes monotonous to be shut away from the outside world, and I can easily see how this phase of farming is often the reason for great discontent.

"My part in the community is rather small. I just help, and when the other members of the family go away, I fill their places. The year Isabell was at Cornell I had charge of the chickens. Now the bees occupy a great deal of my time.

"I don't know as it is necessary after writing all this to add a program of a day, but I will simply put down the things I do in a day which isn't especially rushed.

"I get up at about 6:15 or am supposed to. My sisters get up earlier. After I have eaten my breakfast I prepare the potatoes for dinner. By that time all the men have had their breakfast and I wash the dishes and clean up things in general. Then there are beds to be made and perhaps rooms to be cleaned. After that some mornings I go to the creamery and wrap butter, but recently I have worked for an hour or so fixing bee equipment. About 10:30 on some mornings, I put on my bee togs and work with them until nearly dinner time, when I set the table and help get dinner. After dinner I wash the dishes and, unless there is garden picking or preparing of something for canning to do, as there often is, I am free until about four-thirty. If I go to town I leave directly after dinner and get back about six. We don't go down a great deal however. During the afternoon the mail comes bringing the daily paper and at the end of the month the magazines. The entire family take turns reading the paper, and the magazines are read at the first opportunity. We sew, do little odd things, and are never at loss as to how to spend the time. Supper is at five, so the men can milk after it. I wash dishes or gather eggs after supper and unless something turns up to do am free.

We often pick garden things for the next day because it is cool then."

The itinerary of the American Country Girl might thus be followed from the energizing cool of the morning when the impact of the day's work is so buoyantly met to the quieting cool of the evening when rest is so joyously welcomed.   So far in our investigation there has always been some source of hope and enthusiasm to be discovered.   If the margin of unbearable drudgery seems to be reached, there is the solace of music at evening when the whole family join in an orchestra of violin, cornet and piano.   If the days seem to grow unendurably monotonous, a pageant looms on the horizon to capture the interest and to make life fascinating at once. A fourteen-hour day of hard labor is broken by a recess in the midst to write a letter and send it out to some girl friend in the great big world that shall keep the secluded spirit in some touch with the outside currents of life.   At the stroke of eleven the daily paper comes; at the twentieth of the month the magazine.   A French or an organ lesson is possible; and life, though burdened is kept enlivened on every side.   In such homes, work is not drudgery and the word " monotonous " has no fatal meaning.

Perhaps it may be said that there is always something that can be found, if it is looked for searchingly enough, to make a life of hard work bearable.   Work is good; all of us write that down on paper and believe that we believe it.   But when the principle is illustrated in a practical form many things are required to sustain our conviction.   There must be a meaning, a hope, a definition, a goal.   Each life is a system set in with other systems.   To make one of them a success, all must move on right lines toward the chosen end. Other letters from these sensible young women in the rural realm will perhaps make us feel this more keenly than the foregoing.

CHAPTER V

WHAT ONE COUNTRY GIRL DID

THORN APPLES AND SWEET ACORNS

I love the taste of thorn apples and sweet acorns and sumac and choke-cherries and all the wild things we used to find on the road to school.
And I love the feel of pussy willows and the inside of chestnut burrs.
I love to walk on a country road where only a few double teams have left a strip of turf in the middle of the track.

And I love the creaking of the sleigh runners and the snapping of nail-heads in the clapboards on a bitter cold January night.
In the first cool nights I love the sound of the first hard rainfall on the roof of the gable room.

And I love the smell of the dead leaves in the woods in the fall.
I love the odor of those red apples that grew on the trees that died before I went back to grandpa's again.
I love the fragrance of the first pink and blue hepaticas which have hardly any scent at all.
I love the smell of the big summer raindrops on the dusty dry steps of the school house.
I love the breath of the great corn fields when you ride past them on an August evening in the dark.

And I love to see the wind blowing over tall grass.
I love the yellow afternoon light that turns all the trees and shrubs to gold.
I love to see the shadow of a cloud moving over the valley, especially where the different fields have different colors like a great checkerboard.
I love the little ford over Turtle Creek where they didn't build the bridge after the freshet.
I love the sunset on the hill in Winnebago County, where I used to sit and pray about my mental arithmetic lesson the spring I taught school!

Elizabeth Wilson.

CHAPTER V

WHAT ONE COUNTRY GIRL DID

IT may be interesting to some of the Country Girls who read this book to see not only some pictures here and there from the life history of girls but also to look over several more detailed accounts, so that they may realize more fully what the new era in country life means to a young woman on the farm who takes hold of her problem with vigor and enthusiasm. To gratify this desire there will be given in this and the following chapters, with the kind permission of the writers, a number of sketches in some detail of the experiences of several girls, who though they represent widely separated regions of the country, still seem to be moved by a like impulse toward an advance in efficiency and power of service.

The first of these accounts expresses the great awakening of southern womanhood in the new activity of the " beloved southland." This story is especially interesting because it shows what one girl has done just with what she had, and how she found that she had a great deal more to work with than she had dreamed. The writer of the many letters from which the account is framed, is a little over twenty years old, and lives on a farm of two hundred acres, twenty-five of which are cleared. The nearest village, which consists of just a score of houses, is three miles from her farm. The land is not productive without fertilizer, but at the best produces a fair crop of corn and sweet potatoes.

This is the way the farm looked when she first saw it: " Around the house was an old-fashioned flower garden

47

planted years before.   The woods and creek were beautiful.
The day we arrived, after we had crossed the creek and
were inside the clearing, what we saw made us forget the
long drive through black stumps and fallen trees.   The oaks
were just coming into leaf.   The dogwoods formed a semi-
circle around the place and were white with bloom against
the green of the pines, while the wisteria hung in great clus-
ters and the bridal wreath was one heap of white flowers."

This was the first entrancing glimpse.   But any one who
knows about farm work, realizes that this view of a run-
down, neglected old place means a long struggle.   Nature
has reached out hands to pull the whole cultivation back
into the wilderness.   In that tangled fragrant clearing was
waiting a severe test for a trained farmer, not to say, for
a beginner.   But this girl was determined to live on the
farm, and she stood ready to face all difficulties in the attainment of her desire.   That neglected garden was typical.
She soon had it cleaned and the bulbs reset, and it was not
long before there were flowers for every month in the year.
All difficulties seem to have been met with a spirit of determination and of cheer.   " We were crazy," she declares,
" to live on a farm and determined not to fail; but as soon
as one problem was solved, another would bob up.   There
was never a day without some unexpected happening, and
adventures were plentiful."

She would have amply proved that she appreciated the attractiveness of farm life if she had not classified her
thoughts and set them down so neatly.   To her the charm
of life on the farm consists, first, in the fresh air and wholesome food, with plenty of fruit and vegetables, together with
the pleasure of helping to produce and prepare the food.   In
her opinion having to depend upon one's self to decide
courses of action as much as you do in farm life, gives one
back-bone and trains one to rely upon self and to be an effective leader.   She has, as most true country people have,
an ineradicable and fundamental passion for independence.

In town one may have the advice of the minister, the doctor and the lawyer; but in the country, she says, it is the Lord and I.   Again, it takes much less time and less expense to keep up appearances in dress in the country; one is freer from interruptions than in town, and ties of kinship are stronger among people of the country.   No, the farm is not monotonous; one acquires a liberal education just by being alive; nature study, the work in the flower garden, affords constant variety; and there are new interests and adventures every day.

This girl has also thought on the other side of the question, and she can see that there may be reasons why one may prefer to leave the farm.   One may feel the lack of companionship near one's own age and the lack of recreation. Too much importance may be placed on field work to the neglect of the garden; unkind criticism by neighbors may be the only recreation available; and not paying the women of the family for their aid in the household service, may be in her mind sufficient reasons for desertion.   These, in short, are some of the things she emphasized.

An average day of her life on the farm is a busy one. She says:

" The sun wakes me up in the morning, or maybe it is the mocking-birds singing.   I work in the garden gathering the vegetables, picking the flowers, or cultivating, until breakfast time.   After breakfast I make the beds and straighten the bed-rooms; then I work in the garden again until about 9:30 or 10:00 o'clock.   Then I come in and help with the dinner or sew or study or write, and if it is bread-baking day I always knead the bread and prepare it for the oven.   As we have breakfast about five-thirty o'clock we get so hungry we have dinner about 11:30.   After dinner we rest a half hour either by reading or by lying down.   In the afternoon after a bath I study or sew until it is cool enough to work in the garden.   For supper we only make coffee and warm over something left from dinner.   We have supper at five o'clock, but usually have a bowl of clabber or a glass of milk before going to bed. I work in the garden until dark; then we talk a while and go to bed about nine o'clock. In the winter we talk or read after supper until bed-time. However, in canning time the study, the sewing, and a good part of the reading are put aside."

It is evident that her share in the housework is not a small one. She does the sewing and much of the gardening, taking entire care of the flower-garden. She does marvels of canning; she keeps the accounts; she straightens out the rooms, and helps with the cooking. She runs the errands, waiting on the father, who is permanently disabled. To facilitate her work she has a sewing machine, an oil stove, a pump near the door, and a wheel-hoe. What she desires in the way of equipment in order to make her housekeeping easier are these only — her thoughts for herself have not flown very high! — a kitchen cabinet and a clothes wringer. Since they eat a great deal of cream cheese and lots of fruit and vegetables raw, she does not feel that they need a fireless cooker; but she does greatly need a canner. Since the canner is so frequently offered as a prize, this need will no doubt be soon supplied.

The recreations of this hard-working girl consist of reading, going visiting, walking, studying nature, making a flower garden, and writing letters. She also naïvely includes going to Sunday School among her recreations. She takes an excursion to the shore once in a great while; but only seldom has she the time for that. She can have the use of a conveyance at convenience, and on Saturday she and her mother drive to town and occasionally on Sunday to church. Has she no games? No, she is an only child and has never had any playmate in the home. Besides the flower garden and nature study form her recreation. But she thoughtfully encloses in one letter a list of games that she thinks girls may like to know about and gives a bibliography of articles on games for young folks in the woman's paper they are accustomed to take in her home. In her community there are perhaps twenty-five young people. They have a dance once or twice a month and a picnic twice a year; and there is a school social every two months. The social life of the village centers about the school as much as anywhere. Perhaps they could attract more interest to the church if the members of the church choir only had tact and facility enough. They have no resident minister and therefore the church lacks a centralizing element. But the village has a hall with a platform, a two-roomed school house, and a tennis court, as facilities for a social center. There is also a rest room at the ice cream parlor and back of the church there is another hall. One would say that there was no excuse for this town if it did not have a thriving social life and a good time for everybody on the highest lines. And ought they not to overcome all separating difficulties, if there be any such, and establish a regular pastor and begin to have a real community life? For how can a town with all those advantages hold up its head among the towns of America if it has a church building and no church therein? Certainly though one girl can do much, she cannot do all.

One may judge any girl by the books she sets down as her favorite reading matter: This farm girl mentions The Bible, Shakespeare, *Silas Marner, Days Off, The Calling of Dan Matthews, Alice in Wonderland, Little Women, John Halifax Gentleman, Lorna Doone, David Harum, The Little Minister, Distractions of Marietta, The Chimes, Treasure Island, Josephus, Lady of the Lake, Rose and Ring, Prince Otto, Red Badge of Courage, Poems of All Great Poets, Idylls of the King,* Department of Agriculture Bulletins, Botanies and School books. To this list she adds the name of the woman's paper she and her mother had taken, the file of which she has preserved for some years. Those she underscores as the ones she reads with most delight are these: *Little Women, Little Minister, Alice in Wonderland,* and all the stories in her woman's paper. The serial story appeals to her most, because she has to wonder how it is going to come out.

She does not let anything interfere with reading an hour or so every day. She and her mother read together a great deal. She reads to her mother articles in the woman's paper, and the poetry of Lewis in the Houston *Post*. They take several weekly papers, three monthly magazines, and a daily city paper. She herself took two of these, the woman's paper and one of the most vital of the national weekly journals. She likes these two best — one because it gives the home view and the other because it gives the world view. They supplement each other, she thinks, and help one to develop a well balanced mind and character.

Her other cultural interests, however, are centered in the household tasks and in helping in the Sunday School, and she finds these so interesting that the days are all too short. The Sunday School must mean a great deal to her for she mentions it as a cultural as well as a recreational resource. It was about four years ago that the Sunday School was started. They had good music for about two years, one family playing all the instruments. Through the librarian she loaned her books, bringing them as they were called for. The librarian saved her the trouble of asking for the return of the books and in five years only one was lost. They also had a plan for passing their magazines about. Every Sunday when she went to church she would take armloads of flowers to give away; and if any one wanted plants or bulbs she brought them on request. This seems so delightfully practical. Why should not the church door be a place for the exchange of free will offerings of all kinds?

There seems on first view very little opportunity for a girl in some secluded farm to learn much about the great fields of classic art. This girl is one to whom art subjects have a great appeal though she feels the lack of opportunity to develop this interest. She draws enough to have some appreciation of form and tone and she studies reproductions of famous paintings; she enjoys especially watching the sunrise and the sunset, and the stars on a clear night. Nothing in nature is alien to her. Trees, birds, ferns, wild flowers and garden flowers, all are beloved. She has the scientific spirit as well as the artistic. She has made collections of pressed wild flowers, and the expert consulting botanist of the United States Department of Agriculture Bureau of Plant Industry names them for her. She made two sets of specimens, numbering them, keeping one and sending the other to Washington.

With delightful frankness this efficient Country Girl recounts her financial endeavors. Her chief way of earning money is by raising vegetables for the table and by cutting down expenses by careful planning of the diet. During one year the family had only to pay out $71 for bought groceries, and the eggs helped to pay for that, so that the bought groceries were only $1.50 apiece per month for the four members of the household. Circumstances have thrown a load of responsibility upon this young girl, but unconsciously she was being trained for the work. She was already a unit in the complex structure of the farmstead before she was so acutely needed. In her earlier girlhood her father paid her a salary of ten dollars a month for her household assistance. In doing this he was enlisting her interest in an enterprise to the success of which she was led to feel that she was essential. She responded to this educational method by being ready when the need came to plan wisely and efficiently and to carry out these plans successfully. That first money she earned she was permitted to save. She let it accumulate for a time and when she had a good opportunity she bought a lot with it. After a while she moved a house upon the lot and fixed it up. The family lived there for about a year and then she sold it, making a good profit. During that time they owned a garden and a cow. The garden was held to be her own special property; but her enthusiasm for the whole farm project was no doubt to a good extent the result of the training in responsibility she had received at the hands of her wise parents.

When she found that she could obtain government publications on farming problems, she promptly availed herself of this means of help. Almost as soon as she moved to the farm, her Congressman at her request sent her the publications of the Department on Agricultural Education. There she read about the correspondence work at the Pennsylvania State College; and by the time she had been on the farm four months, she had begun correspondence courses in domestic science and agriculture under that patronage. She completed thirteen subjects: Principles of Cooking, Heating and Ventilation, Canning and Preserving, House Furnishing, Butter-making, Dairy, Breeds of Cattle, Vegetable Gardening, Dressing and Curing Meat, Stock Feeding, Principles of Breeding, Farm Manures, Commercial Fertilizers, and Farm Bookkeeping. For this work she received two certificates. The tuition was free and no books had to be specially purchased for these subjects.

For her home library and text-book facilities for these studies this energetic and persevering girl had at command, besides the bulletins of the United States Department of Agriculture, only the file of that household journal that she had taken since 1893. Added to this was the constant advice of her mother, who had had opportunity to observe the work in a large hotel where her husband had once occupied some position that gave her the entrée to the kitchen laboratory. This aid came in well on the household side of the problem.

As one would certainly expect, it is found that this correspondent takes part in all meetings and movements to promote better housekeeping that are at hand. She has the Girls' Canning Club and The United Farm Women. For information in regard to clubs and societies she sent to the colleges receiving federal aid as listed in Circular 971, Office of Experiment Stations. By this means she has begun a thriving intercommunication by letters with many other girls, with whom she exchanges items of information as to what they find out in their canning and gardening experiences. After a little the Bureau of Plant Industry asked her to report the blossoming and ripening of fruit for the region where she lives; in return for this they sent her a whole mail sack of bulletins. These bulletins and others from the Department, together with the household journal which she and her mother had taken for several years, she used in studying the lessons in her correspondence course, making a list of references for each lesson.

The Girls' Canning Club meets at her house, and she prepares the questions for them. She has copied over two hundred recipes on canning for the Department of Agriculture. She hopes to get the National Plant, Flower and Fruit Guild started in her vicinity so that she can send things to the Orphans' Home in the nearest city. For two years she has sent an exhibit of canned products to the Fair — twenty-one varieties in 1912. She read in the papers about the Girls' Tomato Club in an adjoining State and she wrote at once to the professor in charge of the Extension Department of a Polytechnic Institute in her own State, asking him to help start some clubs for girls. This professor soon journeyed to her county to look the situation over and to see what could be done. He became enthusiastic about it and won the interest of the County Superintendent; thus the clubs were soon started under the patronage of the school teachers. At present there are 165 girls in the Canning Clubs of that one county alone. In the Club in the one little village there are seventeen members, nine girls and eight women. They have four meetings and a Canning Party annually. At the last meeting the founder read a paper on *The Uses of Tomatoes;* she also asked forty questions on tomatoes, five on berries, five on beans and cabbage, and five

on jelly.   The club is now working on a Tomato History;
they will send their exhibits to the Fair where they stand a
good chance to win one of the five prizes offered.

The Canning Club also belongs to the United Farm
Women.   By this organization programs for suggested
meetings are sent and at the time for the meeting various
bulletins and booklets on the subjects chosen also come.   The
girls consider those in the *Better Babies* group a valuable
collection.   The Club asked the storekeeper in the village to
hand out the bulletins on the *Care of the Baby* to the country
customers wherever he hears of the arrival of new babies.
He says the people are very thankful for the bulletins.

Among other resources of various kinds that this girl
and her friends can call upon is the Daughters of the American Revolution, who through their Conservation Committee offer seven canners as prizes to the Canning Clubs of
that State.   The members of the Club also receive magazines from the Church Periodical Club, and they pursue
extension courses in agricultural subjects.   Certain colleges
that have correspondence courses on subjects connected with
the farm home have been called upon for aid by some of the
young women who belong in the realm of this girlhood
endeavor.   When the girls began to feel the need of beautifi-
cation about the Church surroundings, they asked the Landscape Gardener of the Bureau of Plant Industry for aid and
he drew a blue print plan for setting out the trees and
shrubs; now they are asking the same favor for the country
school houses in their vicinity.

Community spirit has reached such a height now that
effective meetings in the interest of Good Roads are being
held.   Many people think that this is the final stage in community success, for all things become possible if the roads
are good.   Says this young enthusiast: "When we have
as good roads as they have across the line in the next State,
we shall have to move to a pioneer country to find some
new problems."

This concludes the report of a wonderful young life — a life full of promise, one that seems to be developing through service, making economical gain and keeping economical balance as she goes along. Nothing greater could be asked, as far as ultimate good is concerned.

CHAPTER VI

STORIES OF OTHER COUNTRY GIRLS

Well then, I now do plainly see
This busy world and I shall ne'er agree;
The very honey of all earthly joy
Does, of all meats, the soonest cloy;
   And they, methinks, deserve my pity
Who for it can endure the stings,
The crowd, and buzz, and murmurings
   Of that great hive, the city!

Cowley.

CHAPTER VI

STORIES OF OTHER COUNTRY GIRLS

THE first of the three stories in this chapter represents the work of a young woman who spends more than half of her time with her mother and an aunt upon an ancestral home in a mountain region of New England. Again we discover what a girl can do who looks about her to see what the needs are and then stands ready to help in any way she can. The ways that are opening before her are many and her life seems likely to be marked by the most joyous of fulfilment in helpfulness and radiating energy.

The farm where she lives has about nine hundred acres and is situated in the edge of a village of some four hundred inhabitants. The place is full of historic interest, and has wonderful views over the mountains in every direction. Such a home as this naturally makes a great claim on the attachment of the open-eyed young woman who writes about it; but she possesses also a pure straightforward love for the simple country wherever found. Watching the growth of plant and animal life has a charm for her. The fresh air, the good water, the abundance of fresh vegetables, and the freedom from the noise and hurry of the city, make a strong appeal. Yet she sees that there might be reason in some complaints against the country system as it is. An absence of cash results for work done by members of the family in the home or in the field; a lack of interesting recreation; a longing for freedom; the narrowness and spirit of criticism in village life: any of these may justify a young woman in going away. As for herself she has no grievance.

Her share in the work on the farm and in the home consists of a good part of the cooking, cleaning, canning and gardening, but it is not too much for her.   They have many household conveniences: running water in a barrel, a blue flame oil stove, a bread-mixer, and a carpet-sweeper.   She would like a kitchen cabinet, electric lights, a furnace, a vacuum cleaner run by electricity, and a system of plumbing. But these, in that thickly populated region, will doubtless come in the near future.

In the summer her regular work is the care of the garden, and bringing in the vegetables.   When they have no hired girl, she washes all the dishes, fills the lamps and the wood-box, and does most of the sweeping and cleaning.   She does a great deal of sewing and is occupied with everything from upholstering chairs to making posters for lectures and plays. During the canning season she cans string beans, corn, swiss chard, spinach, beets, carrots, pears, plums, cherries, berries, etc., and makes astrachan jelly enough to supply the church suppers for the whole year.   She seldom has a chance to sit down unless it be to prepare the vegetables for dinner.   Her afternoons are taken up with club work, or with other outside activities, with time for an occasional walk with her mother, or an informal call.   Evenings there is either choir practise, Christian Endeavor meetings, Grange, church suppers, Club work, or plays, with business letters and sewing to fill up whatever time remains.

Yet room is made for a little music.   There is a piano in the home and they sometimes have hymns and old standard songs in the evening.   When sewing is to be done, some one always reads aloud.   The house is well supplied with books. There are most of the standard books though few novels and little light reading.   The newspapers and magazines are read aloud evenings.   The table is well supplied with periodicals: they take the *Outlook,* the *Independent,* the *Geographic Magazine,* the *Atlantic,* the New York *Times,* the *Hampshire Gazette.*   For herself alone she takes *Wohelo,* the Camp Fire magazine, and if she should add another it would be the *Survey*. That would help her most, as her reading at present is along the lines of sociology. To be sure, her reading is somewhat interfered with by housework, sewing, and occupation with outside interests. Besides she has too much physical vitality to sit still long. But if she does need more books than her own house supplies, there is a public library a quarter of a mile away. She is a trustee of this library and goes there twice a week. She helps the librarian catalog the new books, obtains loan agricultural library books, exchanges books with other towns, and obtains agricultural bulletins,— thus making herself an invaluable helper to the whole region. She sees to it that the library gives help to those that are interested in nature study. She herself has an interest in birds and wild flowers. In her home they have a stuffed collection of fifty or more species of birds. She modestly says that she "knows ferns somewhat." Thanks to her ministrations the town library has books on all those subjects. The chief sources of culture in the village, she says, are the library, the Grange, the stereopticon lectures, and a good pastor.

In order that she may do her full share in helping to promote the general welfare, she has become Guardian of a Camp Fire Club and in that group does all she can to encourage efficiency among the girls. She takes a vital interest in all the organizations for young people. There cannot be a girl in that region who does not know that if she wants any good thing this older girl stands ready to help her. She is herself a Unitarian but she has no sectarian prejudice against working in the Christian Endeavor Society and she shows this by taking part in the meetings every Sunday evening. She owns the only stereopticon in town and generously sees to getting the slides for the monthly lectures. She sings in the church choir. She keeps more or less in touch with the school superintendent who is very responsive to suggestions and she tries to help him and the five district school teachers in every way she can. She is medical temperance superintendent in the Women's Christian Temperance Union.   In this connection she puts up posters and prepares charts for the school children.   She is Guardian not only for the Camp Fire Girls but also for the Bluebirds, which is organized for the girls under twelve.

As to earning money, she is so happy as not to have to work for that at present.   However, " on the place," she says, " I think I could earn by making jelly, if I could find a market.   In the past, when we were living elsewhere, I was given seventy-five dollars a month to pay my share of the housekeeping accounts (which I ran) and to lay aside. Now on the farm, I do not have any set sum, but I own a share in the farm."

Asked if this sharing in the ownership made her more enthusiastic for the success of the farm, she answered that she thought it did.   She would like to know of more ways of earning money that she might recommend them to her Camp Fire Girls.   She has had no special education for farming as a business or for home-making; but she follows the suggestions of an agricultural teacher in a high school in the next town, and she reads up on various lines of home work in connection with the judging of the work of the girls in the Camp Fire, and she has taken two courses at a college in household chemistry.

A life of such incessant activity must have a great deal of joy in it.   There are, however, some special forms of recreation accessible to her.   There is a Fourth of July celebration with floats and a parade; there are athletic contests; there is baseball, and there is an entertainment consisting of a play, and other exercises.   There are occasional school picnics, and plays are given by the Grange or by the Camp Fire Girls.   Sunday evening stereopticon lectures are run by the Christian Endeavor Society.   She attends the baseball games, the W. C. T. U. parties; the Cradle Roll parties, the Camp Fire parties, and the Bluebird parties for the little club girls.

Social life centers about Church and Grange. There are enough girls to have societies of their own and though they live widely apart, it seems that this girl with the spirit of a leader is able to draw them together. Though she is very modest about her part of the attraction, she could doubtless say, if she would, " a great part of it I was!" There are about a dozen young people in about a dozen houses in her village and there is something going on once a week or oftener which is specially for the girls.

There is a great deal more that might be said about this faithful and enthusiastic worker. Her loyal following in the path that first opened before her has led her into a special field of moral education where her efficiency and fine spirit are making her useful not only to her own region but to a much wider circle. She has been trained for a service which it is a joy to render.

The second record in this group represents the great bounding life of the Northwest, and is as full of the new elixir of country life as the other accounts given.

The writer says: " I could tell you volumes about our Western rural life," and if there were room, those " volumes " should be included. She is twenty-one years old, and is one in a family of ten children. The farm she refers to is one owned by her grandfather and there she spends a great deal of her time and lavishes a great deal of work. There are eighty acres; forty of them are hilly, unirrigated lands, while five acres are still in sage-brush. The rest is irrigated by electric pumped water. The nearest town is six miles away and has twenty-two hundred people.

Many charming glimpses are given of the home this girl represents. She is an enthusiast for the possibilities of farm life. She prizes it because she finds that freedom of action is possible there in matters of dress and in the choice of companions. All desired urban benefits — such as lectures, church, organizations and social events, seem to have become accessible to her. She thinks, too, that the farm

realizes outdoor life at its best.   There is plenty to do —
this she rates as one of the great advantages — and she adds
this pregnant sentence, " what one does is of consequence."

She acknowledges that parents might desire to go away
from the farm in order to put children in a town school.
But she adds: " I'd rather take them to a good centralized
country school.   I have taught in town and country both,
and am now teaching a country school under town super-
vision with ten pupils and every advantage.   As I keep
house for my grandfather on a dry homestead two miles
from school, I have the fun of walking to and from the
schoolhouse."

Again she says that people may go to the town in order
to spend their money; town, she says, is a good place to go
for that purpose.   She adds this caustic note: " But my
father made money in town and spent it in the country —
as long as he kept tenants on his farm! "

Her share in the housework is ample and joyous.   She
says: " Myself and two grown sisters, both younger than
I, take turns about doing the entire housework.   The rest
work in the garden and the field, irrigating, hoeing, etc.   I
prefer outside work too, but I always wash and iron, even
when I am working outside."   Her home conveniences are
a washing-machine, a pump in the house, running water
at the door, a telephone, the daily weather reports, a type-
writer, a sewing-machine, screened windows and doors, and
home-made soap.   Who but a girl of the great untram-
melled Northwest would call the weather reports a home
convenience, or think of including home-made soap?   Of
course she is not satisfied: she would like electrically pumped
water, electric lights, ice, and a gasolene stove.   Some of
these she hopes to have next year, and the electric stove
will doubtless come too and other new and important things.

Opportunity for recreation is not wanting.   There are
fishing on the place, swimming in the large irrigation canal,
and buggy riding.   In winter there is dancing at farm

homes; visits are made over the 'phone. Sewing and sewing bees are recreation; so are reading and writing letters. Caring for small brothers and sisters seems to come under the same head; water-color painting, hunting jack-rabbits and grouse, taking kodak pictures, going to picnics and celebrations, camping in the mountains, lectures, lodge, and socials in town, horseback riding and day dreaming do not seem so difficult to include. She harnesses and drives, hitching up to the buggy, the democrat, or even the jockey cart; she rides the bicycle and expects to drive an auto — " some day." All the games they play in that large and varied family are " to work, and to tease one another." Evidently here is a place on the planet where work and play run into each other and become one and the same thing! She says: " There seems to be no necessity for games." She adds: " We older ones often amuse and watch the three children play."

As to the number of young people in the vicinity she says that there are about twenty " within this natural district." During the school year they have about six social gatherings; in summer there are informal picnics and Sunday visits with refreshments. Social life centers about the school and the doings in the adjacent town. Among some of the neighbors there is a German Club. As facilities for a social center, they have the schoolhouse (but with stationary seats), a playground, any number of natural groves and of fishing holes, and the big ditch for swimming. For the girls alone they have swimming parties and visiting parties; and they help one another during haying and threshing. This she puts down among the social gatherings for girls in her neighborhood!

In the house there is a library of about two hundred and fifty volumes. Lack of time is the only thing that prevents reading. There is a public library in the nearest town and she goes there every week in winter. In summer however she is too busy with farm work to go so often. In the family evenings either she or her mother reads aloud: also on Sunday afternoon.   The books that they have thus read together of late are *Lorna Doone* and one by Wason called *Friar Tuck* which she marks an underscored " Good."

They have a piano and the favorite songs are such old favorites as *Annie Laurie* and *Juanita*.   Also they sing church songs, and popular tunes, such as *The Trail of the Lonesome Pine*.   They adapt the music to the different tastes in the ten-children family.

Besides the daily evening paper and the local weekly paper, they take *Successful Farming, Better Fruit, Scientific American, American Magazine, Cosmopolitan, Epworth Herald,* some law papers, the government bulletins and reports, *Current Opinion,* etc.   For her own interests she is going to take *Epworth Herald, Primary Education, Youth's Companion, American Geographical Magazine, Current Opinion, Stock Reports, Successful Farming*.   Her other cultural interests are these: Music; school, especially high school entertainments, correspondence with normal school friends; teachers' institute, each fall, one week; water-coloring; making beautiful clothes and fancy work; Rebecca Lodge; Church in town; amateur photography; and reading, underscored again.   It is fascinating to see what a girl like this will include under the head of " cultural interest."

On the question of earning and using money, she says: " From the time we were very small we earned all our spending money by being paid for extra work.   I have been absolutely independent, even to buying my clothes, since I was seventeen years old.   I figure that my work more than pays my board."   First among the ways of earning money, she names hoeing corn; next she mentions teaching school.   " I teach school nine months of the year.   Before I began that and ever since, I have earned money.   I put myself through the Normal School.   I packed prunes (at four cents an hour), sold garden truck (twenty-five cents a day, average — did no peddling), and sewed for others at usual rates."

No special sum is set apart for her use but she has all she earns. In teaching she receives sixty dollars a month. She has taught for this salary for two years and with this she has paid two hundred dollars she had borrowed for her school expenses. She has four hundred dollars remaining. Most of this is now in interest-bearing notes on farm securities. She adds: "I buy my clothes, go one-half on board with grandfather on the homestead, and am beginning a 'hope-box.'" She is to have a share in the corn crop. "When I am married," she says, "I expect to invest some in cattle for beef." The vital question as to whether her sharing in this ownership makes her have more enthusiasm for the success of the farm, receives this answer: "Certainly; you should have seen me top the corn when it got frosted June 6. It's doing fine now; I think we saved it, for it was frozen to the ground." She has read all on the subject of farming that she could find. She took some work in the Normal School — enough, she says, to make her realize that she knew very little; she believes she could do much through correspondence. Her interest is now about equally divided between farming and home economics: but, she is good enough to confide, "I expect to make home-making predominate some day." Ah, then this is the true meaning of that "hope-box"! This efficient girl is to be a farmer's wife and she wishes to know how to do her part in helping run a grain-haystock ranch of a thousand acres successfully. So she has taken one year at the Normal School in Home Economics and some studies in agriculture also; she studied family sociology in a forty weeks' course; and she has given some study to the laws governing women's property. May her hope-box overflow! May she in time run her own car, and may all her schemes work out perfectly!

Is there room to put down just one more story? This one has been sent by a friend who for years has been teaching in the Idaho Industrial Institute, a school where they train boys and girls for farm life. The writer of the paper, a girl of nineteen, interested her especially and she asked her to write a brief record. The farm where this girl lives is in a hilly region and is productive; they have from it oats, wheat, clover, timothy, and potatoes. There are 160 acres, and they are six miles from town.

" Farm life to me is attractive," she says, " because on the farm one has the freedom that cannot be gained anywhere else in the world. One learns the habits of birds and animals and one comes in touch with nature and hence with the Creator himself. Children raised on the farm grow strong in body and spirit, and they store their minds with more venturous thoughts. By living on the farm one gets all the fresh vegetables, fruits, butter, milk, eggs and meat that one desires. But of course there may be reasons why one might desire to leave the farm. One may get the idea that one has to work harder for less pay than elsewhere. One may think that the pleasures are few and that farm life is not respectable enough, and that if one could only leave and go to the city, one would be contented. But any one leaving the farm will never be happy while away and will soon learn that there is no place in life like the farm."

This young woman shows the usual picture of work and of small opportunity for social enjoyments. These are her books: The Bible, *Stephen, Soldier of the Cross, Jesus of Nazareth, The Coming King, Tempest and Sunshine, The Broken Wedding Ring, Sweet Girl Graduate, Daddie's Girl, Wild Kitty, Girls of the Forest, Ruby or a Heart of Gold, Taking Her Father's Place, Now or Never.* She was very much delighted, she says, with all in this list. She has the long winter's evenings to read in but the additional work in summer interferes somewhat with her reading. They have no musical instrument in the home but they have many of the best hymn-books and country songs, and they sing hymns together. She is very much interested in ways of making better homes.   She herself takes the *Mother's Maga-zine* and *The Christian Endeavor World,* and is pursuing a course in Home Economics at the present time.

A single working day of her life is thus described:

" One bright morning in early July I was awakened by my mother who told me that it was half-past four.   I arose immediately for I had had a good night's rest and did not feel sleepy.   I dressed in my riding habit and went to the barn and waked my brother who was sleeping in the hay-loft and asked him to come and saddle my pony, ' Daisy.' He saddled her and I mounted and went to the timber for the cows.   The air was fresh and cool.   It filled me with joy and seemed to affect Daisy the same, for she threw her ears forward, listened a second for the cows, and hearing the tinkle of the bell she started out on a gallop.   After about a half hour's ride I found the cows and drove them home.   When I had taken the saddle from Daisy and given her her breakfast and a few loving caresses I left her and went to the house, arriving just in time for breakfast. After breakfast I told my two sisters I would do the house-work myself while they washed.   I had an early start, was in high spirits and ready for the day's work before me.   It did not take me long to plan my dinner, which I decided should consist of baked potatoes, creamed carrots, greens, and radishes, all fresh from the garden.   For dessert I made blanc mange with cocoa sauce.   I had plenty of fresh butter, cream, and light-bread at my disposal.   The first thing I did on entering my kitchen was to mix up my light-bread.   It did not take me long to clear off the breakfast table and put the dining-room in order.   When I came to the kitchen I did not find it so easy; but my greatest delight being to set a kitchen in order I did not mind the task be-fore me; but before starting it I did up the milk work which only took me half an hour, there being no churning that morning.   I had my kitchen in order and the bread molded by ten o'clock.   I then cleaned myself up and read a short

story in the Sunday School paper before starting my dinner which I did at ten-thirty.   My dinner was a success or
at least my father pronounced it so when he had finished
eating a not small portion of it.   After I had the dinner
work cleared away, everything in order and my bread baked,
I made my small brother a suit and had it done by the time
that my mother had supper ready.   After supper again I
saddled Daisy and went for the cows while my sisters
washed the supper dishes.   That evening as we gathered
around the kitchen table and my father read a chapter from
the Bible, I think I was one of the happiest girls in the world
even if I was tired.   As I went to bed that evening I thanked
the dear Father that I had a father, mother, brothers and
sisters to love and help care for.   This is only one day
out of many that I have spent in this way."

When one reads this account, one pictures the strong vivid
life of this sound generous-hearted girl.   It seems glorious
to be so able and so willing.   What, then, will be the surprise when on looking down the page a little farther one
sees in the handwriting of the friend who had asked her to
write an account of one of her working days, a paragraph
like this: "The writer of the above is a cripple, getting
about with the aid of a crutch.   She entered the Institute
this fall and pays half her expenses by working more efficiently than most pupils."   After reading this, what words
of praise would not sound futile!

CHAPTER VII

THE OTHER SIDE

I cannot bear to think what life would be
With high hope shrunk to endurance; stunted aims
Like broken lances ground to eating knives;
And low achievement doomed from day to day
To distaste of its consciousness.

George Eliot.

CHAPTER VII

THE OTHER SIDE

THE experiences related in the last chapters have been purposely laid before the reader with little comment. They make their own impression. They may help to dispel an apprehension lest the girls on the farms should be having too hard a time, or lest when the work in which they are asked to join is closing somewhat too strongly upon their young strength they should be weighed down with the sort of dullness that comes from continued pressure on one nerve. They seem to give an assurance that the country girl's day in many, perhaps the majority, of cases, affords some time for reading and for music; there is a concert in the evening or a spare afternoon hour for the village guest. They encourage us to believe that when the point of joylessness approaches there will be ready a new supply of energy for rejuvenation and refreshment. As long as this state of things exists the case is not so bad.

Into this serene atmosphere a bomb must be thrown; for both sides have a right to be heard. The testimony of the Country Girl when she is speaking in favor of country life has been accepted; the same courtesy must be given her when she tells us more or less frankly — frankly when she can be brought to speak at all — what objections some may have to a life which it seems to many ought to be good for any one, and which, if it is not, surely can very easily be made so.

It is no more than right that a system should be judged not only by the most fortunate example of its working, where factors that have little to do with its essential principles may have crept in to modify the outward appearance, but also by the less known cases, by flagrant examples of what is possible under the existing plan. What wrongs can be found? What sufferings to certain individuals? What must be rectified in order that the machinery may be wholly approved? Is the system, which was evidently designed to foster justice and happiness, accomplishing this end for a reasonable majority? These are very natural questions to those who listen to the testimony of the girl of the rural districts when she discloses her problems almost without knowing that she is doing so. What about exceptional cases? What about a vital minority?

The following description of a Country Girl's working day is taken from the life of a fourteen-year-old girl, who lives on a farm of medium size, so fortunately or so unfortunately placed as to be not very far away from a summer colony. There is no mother in this farmstead.

" Description of my average working day? Here it is. I rise shortly before five o'clock and dress hurriedly. Father is calling me to come and strain the milk and get his breakfast. Go down cellar and strain the milk into pans, set them on a large stone table, and skim the milk for cream for the campers along the lake. Measure out ten to twenty quarts of milk and put them into separate pails to be sent out to customers encamped on the lake. Take cream up stairs and put it in a warm place to ripen for churning. Get breakfast, call the children, and after the others have eaten and the boy has started on his morning delivery, I eat breakfast and clear away the dishes. While sister washes them, I mix bread and set it away to rise. Stir the cream, and then sweep three floors and make five beds. By this time it is nine o'clock. Then there are berries to pick, and vegetables to be got ready for market and I go out to help till about half-past ten, when I come in and make three or four pies and a cake or a pudding. While these are baking I clean the vegetables for dinner and put them on to cook, set the table and put the dinner on, meanwhile watching the baking pies, the rising bread, and the ripening cream. In the course of the morning ten or a dozen persons have come in for milk, eggs, butter, or something else, and I have to wait on them and keep their accounts up in my book. After dinner the bread is ready to make into loaves and is then set to rise again before baking. While the bread is rising I scald out the churn and rinse with cold water and then put in the cream and churn it by hand. After the butter has come and gathered, I remove it from the churn, rinse the buttermilk out and work the butter; salt and work again and set it in the cellar till the next day, when it must be worked again and put into pails or jars. Then I pour the buttermilk from the churn into a jar and set it away for future use, clean and scald the churn, setting it out in the sunshine to dry. By this time the bread is ready to bake and must be watched rather closely and the wood fire also. I begin to get things ready for supper, going out into the garden to pick berries, gather vegetables, dig potatoes, etc. Meantime I wait on more people. After straining milk and skimming other milk, I eat supper and then measure out milk for evening delivery, get vegetables and bread ready to be delivered also and start the boy on delivery. Wash dishes and meanwhile wait on milk customers who are transients. When boy returns from delivery, I wash milk cans and put them out in the air, write up books of accounts, plan out next day's work, make list of groceries, etc., that must be bought to replenish our slender stock. By this time it is ten o'clock; I am weary and my hair is a sight. After taking off a little of the dirt with a sponge in the wash basin I tumble wearily into bed until the next morning."

An account like this arouses a perfect hornets' nest of question-marks. It cannot be well for the nation, and especially for those that are to bear the burden of the day in decades to come that the girls of the present time should in any large numbers be required to endure such strain as this sixteen-hour-day of unremitting, heavy and exacting work imposed upon a young girl between the age of thirteen and seventeen, in one of the largest and most prosperous farming States of this country.   Fortunately she has had phenomenal strength and physical persistence, and the baneful conditions have not caused her absolute break-down.   But — she has run away!   Otherwise she probably would never have gained the development that gave her a voice to speak out for herself as she has spoken in this letter.

More laconic, and yet expressive of a more deadly blight, was the letter from a girl of fifteen in another State.   This girl lives on a prosperous seventy-five acre farm, three miles from a good-sized town.   There is a public library in that town but she never uses it: and there is no home library to give her any aid.   There are no contests, no prizes that are accessible to her to awaken her ambition; and there is no association or society of any kind for girls in her vicinity.   There is no music in her family, no games are played, and no magazines are taken; she has no share in any part of the farm business except to work tirelessly as directed; nothing on the farm can she call her own; and no sum of money is set apart for her use.   She has no enjoyments, no encouragement; she is hard at work all the time.   She neither knows why any one should find the farm attractive nor why one should desire to leave it.   Time and interest for her have ceased.

It is news from such a girl as this that most startles us. But such a Country Girl exists, hushed, unexpressive, unresponsive, undeveloped.   She is the blind gentian in the country garden.   Are there many of these?   Who can tell? If diligent search is made for them they are found upon the most remote farms where no newspapers ever penetrate, where the roads are bad and the neighbors are far away or are beyond forbidding hills, where the deadly round of dish-washing or the weight of work too heavy for the years of the girl are exhausting her strength, stifling her exuberance, and deadening all the power of expression she may have been capable of having. The least fortunate girl is the one that has her power to express developed to the least extent; she does not now know her own wants; but yet when told she too will begin to live and to do her lovely part in the rooms of life.

One of the group who has thus begun at last to live voices a part at least of the inwardness of the reason why the young women and young men of to-day will not be satisfied with the ways of their farming ancestors. She says: "There exist on many farms conditions which make life there almost unbearable, to young people particularly. One of them is lack of congenial companionship; which may be due to lack of material, or to the thoughtlessness of the parents, which makes it impossible for the young people to have their friends come to their homes. Then in many farm houses there is a woful lack of books, magazines and papers of the best sort; again due to the lack of education or of interest on the part of the parents. So also with pictures, music and recreation. But perhaps greater than any other, excepting perhaps the first named, is the dull weary succession of duties following each other day in and day out without rest or respite, and without any or with few of the modern conveniences to lighten the work. So many farmers, of the old school at least, understand little of the reasons for the why and wherefore of the things they do. They were taught of their fathers who were taught of their fathers and who did things in such a way because they proved expedient. By trial, or accident, one may have discovered something to be more expedient some other way, but the wonderful process and reason back of it, they understood little or not at all. This also is true of the farmer's wife. This blind way of doing things suits the young folks not, for the unrest, that spirit of the times which is forever questioning things, is within them, filling them with nameless longings even though they know it not. In their ignorance they believe they will find something better in the city, something more beautiful, more interesting, more thrilling. Were these young people taught the reason for things and the possibilities of experimentation to find a better way, were they given conveniences with which to work, so that there might be some leisure for books, music and friends, there would be, I believe, little discontent." Again we find our Country Girl closing with a hopeful note.

The gentle critical comments of those that in spite of their love for country life reject its claims as a mode of living favorable to human development and content, are based upon motives that are sometimes vocational and sometimes social in character. When they deny to the country their allegiance it is because they fail to find in rural life as they know it, those boasted possibilities and opportunities. Farming seems to them drudgery, which means labor without inspiration or acknowledgment. They have no interest for the work. They may have taste and fitness for some other occupation; but there is the fact — they do not take to farming. They feel intensely the monotony of farm life, the stagnation of the rural community. The sameness, the humdrum tediousness of the every-day life drives them to the city.

In the work of the farmstead, the Country Girl of this disheartened group plainly sees that the subsidiary, detail work, which has no intellectual and very little social stimulus will be assigned to her. She knows that the monotony of this heterogeneous drudgery will daily leave her too tired to go out, even if she has somewhere to go; and too destitute of initiative to seize upon any form of pleasure unless she has already a mind trained to find delight in books; and she sees no prospect of being able to gain the training that will open fields of intellectual enjoyment to her. She keenly feels the lack of recreation. She comes to believe that if she were in the city she would not have such late hours of labor. She does not see the twelve and fourteen hour days of work in that rosy dream of good wages and leisured evenings in town. On the farm it is from five in the morning till nine at night; the work is not only too heavy for her, but it is closely confining. She has not the strength for it; and the enforced toil exhausts her energy prematurely. She now sees that the methods used in her household workshop are laborious and out of date; her task is unnecessarily difficult; and who can blame her if under such circumstances her enthusiasm for her work fades away? There is resentment in the remark of the young girl who said: " If we always have to work in an awkward kitchen with rusty old pans, if we do not go anywhere and never have any company, we do certainly want to leave the farm." When the blind gentian speaks out like that the emphasis must be multiplied a hundred fold.

From the work of girls like these, incentive has been removed, or else it was never there. This sort of Country Girl may not reason it out to the point of clearness, but the lack of acknowledgment of her labor in the farmstead as an industry, as an essential part of the business, makes her toil seem hopeless; it renders her feeling toward whatever charm the country may have for her permanently callous; and it takes all the vibrancy out of her spirit. All this makes her alert to find deep-seated defects in rural life in conditions that, but for her disaffection would seem but difficulties easily overcome.

The look cityward is not always caused by the incitement of an uneasy, a commercial, or an ignoble impulse. It is sometimes the call of the best and noblest part of the soul. To such as recognize this higher purpose the passion for education, for free access to libraries, for association with intellectual people, form a part of the city's lure. They desire to see more of life, to have more and closer contact with one's fellows, to gain valuable companionship, to get more and broader pleasures, to have greater opportunities to make something of one's self. The young women who are thinking such thoughts as these are full of the energy of youth; they are at the moment of opening ambitions and developing personality; they are making plans for the future. They are not the women who in long years have grown accustomed to their burdens and have either learned how to bear them or have become sodden with the despair of ever finding any relief from their load. The brightness of young hope has not faded out, and the buoyant spirit still stands up underneath whatever is to be done or borne. Youth feels equal to anything. Therefore the slightest deflection of their courage from the norm should have the closest attention.

CHAPTER VIII

THE INHERITANCE

We men of earth have here the stuff
Of Paradise — we have enough!
We need no other thing to build
The stairs into the Unfulfilled —
No other ivory for the doors —
No other marble for the floors —
No other cedar for the beam
And dome for man's immortal dream.

Here on the path of every day —
Here on the common human way —
Is all the busy gods would take
To build a heaven, to mold and make
New Edens. Ours the stuff sublime
To build Eternity in time!

Edwin Markham.

CHAPTER VIII

THE INHERITANCE

THIS, then, is the indictment of country life as it now is, by the Country Girl who is now living in the midst of it.

It is depressing, it is terrible, that a concourse of country girls will stand up before The Fathers and declare that while they love the country, and prefer to remain there all their days, yet they cannot, because life there is intolerable to them. They say this in all sobriety; no one can accuse them of speaking in haste; their mood is most judicial. The young woman in the farm life of to-day has a deepseated love for country life; many things about it command her affection and give her delight; but there are also some things that she does not feel called upon to endure. If it were not for them, for these, and these, and lo! all of these, objections to it, she would be perfectly content and satisfied to live on the farm all her days; but as it is, well, she can only join that funeral procession of the nation cityward.

It is true that the Country Girl does not enjoy a house with no music under its roof-tree, a house where no games are played, where no stories are told or read about the lamp in the long winter evenings: a house, in short, with nothing she calls happiness in it; but this is a small part of her indictment.

She does not enjoy trudging back and forth a million times a year over the same square yards of floor-space; but that, too, is immaterial to her. In fine, she does not object to the work itself, but she cannot endure that heterogeneous, unsystematized, objectless drudgery, the enforced character

of the toil, the out-of-date methods, the absence of acknowledgment of any economic value in her contribution to the
business — this is what grinds her soul.

She is not wanting in appreciation of the possibilities in
farm life and the farming business; but, to quote with varia-
tions, she says to herself:

> If they be not fair for me,
> What care I how fair they be?

She sees the beauty of the changing seasons, and she enjoys the companionship of animals, naming them one by one
after all her favorite heroes and heroines of fairyland; but
the fact that she has nor chick nor lambkin for her own
is as

> The little rift within the lute
> That by and by will make the music mute.

If the struggle to pay the mortgage is long and the work
heavy, she does not especially enjoy spending days and
nights of toil with the rest of the family to accomplish the
desired end; but more than all this does she dislike having
the father keep all the trouble to himself; she wants a share
in the responsibility. She wants some acres of her own,
some stock of her own. She wants her personality as a factor in the business, which it really is, to be justly acknowledged. For without that, she reasons, what is there to look
forward to? Hope is the anchor of the soul; and without
something to hope for, how can one hope? She finds that
she has none of these joyous anticipations of the future that
every young woman loves and has the right to entertain.
She cannot look forward to the natural and normal life of
the home for her future lot, for the existing scheme of
country life does not provide her with a husband.

Therefore if the home cannot be made happy and the work
in the farmhouse cannot be made interesting, if her fair
share of incentive as a human being in the common round

The Country Girl takes a pride in her chickens that makes their
care a pleasure to her.

The Inheritance. The Country Girl working cheerfully beside her mother, will learn much that will be of value to her in her effort to make the housework of to-day a joy and not a burden.

of life cannot be assigned to her, if her part in the complex structure of the farmstead cannot be put upon an equitable basis, if the universal happy fortune of woman cannot be seen to shine as a goal in the long service of the farmstead, why, she will have none of it!

If this is the irrevocable decision of the farmers' daughters of the present day, it is a very serious matter. It means that the farmstead will have to be broken up, that the farm home must go out of existence, and the whole system of farm life must be revolutionized. What will happen then, it passes wisdom to prophesy! The Country Girl may well say, " After me, the deluge! " For if at any one point in the procession of the generations, the women will stand together and say " Thus far and no farther! " the procession must stand as still as the pillar of salt that commemorates the wife of the unfortunate Lot.

Can it be that the Country Girl has in some measure reached this point by doing what Lot's wife did — by simply looking behind her? Casting her eye along back over the generations, did she see anything that appalled her? May it have been something in the experience of her own mother that lent decision to her mind as she considered what she herself would choose for a life-path? Or rather, as she looked over the career that lay nearest to her, the life-struggle that was visible to her in her own homestead, did she see something that held up before her a warning hand?

There still lives many a farm woman who has to walk down a hill and carry up from a spring all the drinking and cooking water for her household and who gets it fresh for every meal. Her round of work may include all the house work with the washing and ironing, the scrubbing and cleaning. She sweeps all the rooms up stairs and down every week, covering all the furniture with sheets to keep off the dust that she flings into space with her besoms and brooms. She picks the berries for the table and they may have them three times a day. She gathers all the vegetables. If she has no cow, she goes for the milk and brings it home.   She is an expert cook, serving the meals in courses, carrying in and out the dishes, and providing ample quantities of everything.   She may can the fruit and make the pickles, jellies and preserves.   She will certainly take care of the chickens. In spite of all this she will never seem tired.   She will go to the woods and bring ferns and put them into pots to set about the house.   She will bring wild flowers and carry them with all sorts of dainties to neighboring houses where there is illness.   Her dress is invariably changed in the afternoon; and she always goes to prayer meeting.   She is a great reader and stays up after the family have gone to bed to read the church paper and the farmers' magazine. She is full of life and fun and can talk intelligently on any subject.   Every evening after her work is done she may walk to a neighbor's to visit, or if the village is near enough she will go every night to bring the mail.

This woman of the rural realm is a super-woman in the farm environment; her discouraging example cannot be taken as a rule to be followed by others, since few can equal her in strength of body or mind.   She is one who has in some way become possessed of a mental training above the average; her intellectual outlook has been brought to such a point that she can take pleasure in many of the resources of culture.   She has learned to read, — really read — a thing accomplished by but few of the many who can glibly reel off the words from the printed page.   This woman of the farm gathers the ideas and enjoys the fancies that lie behind the mere alphabetical letters.   She is one who can gain solace from her hour of reading whenever it is possible to have one; and this keeps her young and buoyant.   Then she has also a real interest in everything around her, the garden, the making of the jelly, the missionary cause, all the great wonderful world — everything has attraction for her. Moreover as a result of her mental and inner poise, she has the power to systematize the work of her home and so to get the best results in the shortest time. Does her husband appreciate what a wonderful woman fate has assigned to him? If not, if he never acknowledges the economic value of this woman's courage and gay spirit, as well as of her mere hand-work and its efficient system, then there may be a sore spot underneath that will never be cured in all her life. Many a farmer husband has said affectionately to his wife that he could never have made a financial success of his farm without her help. But it will take more than assurances like that to satisfy the mind and the heart of the Country Girl in the new era.

Going but half a generation farther back into the past one may find the woman who had not only all that has been described to do but the milking and the butter making beside. She worked up the wool and spun, wove, and made full cloth for men's wear, for flannel sheets and for all the flannel dresses, and she knit all the socks and stockings for the big family. She would rise at four, summer and winter. She would build her own fires, milk four to eight cows, and have breakfast at six. There would be a sugar orchard that made many hundred pounds of sugar, and she would make the syrup and care for it. The floors of her rooms would be covered with carpets of her weaving. The table linen and toweling would be both spun and woven by her hands. All the time she had for intellectual employments would be while some labor was going on. It is a tradition from the past in this country that if a woman can work with her hands or her feet and at one and the same time employ the eyes in some studious pursuit, she has a fair right to whatever intellectual attainment she may be able to gain thereby. Roxana Beecher in Guilford, Connecticut, a hundred years ago, had a volume of philosophy fastened to her wheel and read the book while she treadled and spun; and no woman was really accomplished in the old days unless she could knit and read at the same time.

Sometimes — but rarely — the women of past time in this

country took some part in the outside farm labor. The author knows of a woman who husked six hundred bushels of corn in one summer. The following season she piled up one hundred cords of wood and did all the housework beside. It would not be possible to speak of some pathetic cases of enforced toil lest some good men should be led thereby to fall from grace and wish they were non-combatants. The truth is that it has never been the custom in this country that the women should enter into the heavier farm work; from the beginning women were held so sacred that nothing must be risked that could injure their permanent strength. The men rolled in the logs of wood for the big fireplaces and did all the heavier work of the place. answering without a moment's demur the request of the women for help. Such a spirit in the men of America has crystallized in many laws more favorable to women than to men, and in many others designed to give special protection to women and to ward off the possibility of a failure in the persistence of their physical soundness. But clever bad men may break laws that clever good men may make; or good men may be confidingly inattentive while valuable laws and customs become obsolete. Yet the fact does stand out that the spirit of the republic does not favor anything that will dull the physical vigor of the women; and those who feel this spirit and are representative of its urgency — and they are, we must believe, the great majority — are the men in most danger of falling from grace in the manner referred to above. Moreover they are also the people, voters and what not, who will make an effective bar against the inroads of a certain disposition on the part of the foreigners who are, in the main beneficently, coming across the wide seas to find homes in our farming regions, namely, to place the women of their tribes in rows along the fields who bend their backs like the picture of " The Gleaners " by Millet, and to produce such descendants as Markham's " Man with the Hoe." A sight like this with promise such as this is abhorrent to the institutions of our country; the men of the republic, not to say the women, will not tolerate it.

But progress is made little by little. There are cases of arrested development and examples of retardation. There are places where backward-drawing influences have kept some groups from making the advance that other groups have made. If we could penetrate still farther into the past, we should find more reason for the drawbacks that we run across here and there in our own time. We have no histories of selected working days that the great mothers of times past wrote — they certainly had no time to count up calories and set down scientific records of their cookery and their collections of simples. There is a Journal extant which was written by one Abigail Foote in 1779. It goes something like this:

September	2.	I spun.
"	3.	I spun.
"	4.	I spun.
"	5.	I spun.
"	6.	I spun.
"	7.	I spun.

And so on, excepting, of course, Sundays.
About November the record is stated in this wise:

November	11.	I wove.
"	12.	I wove.
"	13.	I wove.
"	14.	I wove.
"	15.	I wove.

And so on, again. Certainly monotony could no farther go. If such workers had not fastened a book to the distaff, insanity would surely have set in. The weaving never could be quite so monotonous as the spinning, for there was necessary a constant watching of the web that effectually prevented any wandering from the business in hand, or any flashing of looks toward the window-sill where lay the volume of romance.

If however, a leaf from the daily life of one of our grandmothers were accessible, it would contain the story not only of the bread-making, but of the soap-making too. That good grandmother in her brisk and energetic days would kindle the big fire in the back yard, bring the large kettles up from the cellar, pack the barrel full of good hardwood ashes and set it on its supports, and then pour the water through it to make the lye. She would then melt up the bones and grease saved from the winter's supply of pork, and when the grease was tried out she would mix the lye and the melted grease with as nice an art and with an expertness as much the product of long experience as is the skill of the artist when he combines his paints for a masterpiece. " With what do you mix your paints? " inquired a young sprig of a great artist. " With brains, sir," was the answer. So might the housewife of a hundred years ago have said if she had been asked how she attained her ends in the soap, the candles, the dyes, the cakes, the baking of the beans — as critical a piece of business as ever a Parisian chef could attempt — the turning of the heel in stocking-making, the weaving of the colors in the carpet, the bleaching to snowy whiteness of the linen and the woolen blankets. " I mix all these processes with brains — with the results of experience bought through many decades of experiment by many costly mistakes and especially by a vivid and unfailing memory of what happened when it was done in one special way and what happened when it was done in some other way. By these means I gained the power to do these things and to gain these successes. It was not so easy as it may seem." Thus might the ghostly grandmother speak if she could come back and let her voice be heard and then she would point to the long rows of soap-bars, put away side by side, white or brown or yellow according to the purity of the grease that had been used, to become dry and fit for

household use for the next half-year. Meantime the tallow
would have been saved out to be used for dipping the candles
or for molding them out in the tin candle-forms. The cotton cord would be strung through the long tin tubes and
pulled out at the lower end for the wick end; or the strings
of wicking would be hung along a pole, to be dipped into
the melted fat again and again as fast as the grease would
cool on the strings and thus increase with every dipping the
size of the slender tapering candle. Between the intervals
of dipping, the little mother would hurry back to her chair
and there sit and cut long strips of cloth and sew them
together into carpet rags. When the piles on the floor at
her side would be high enough, she would run them off
around her elbow into a hank ready to be colored. The
little girls in the family would have peeled bark from the
butternut trees and gathered golden rod and other herbs and
these would have been steeped thoroughly for the magical
liquors which would be standing ready in crocks full of
dyes to give the brown and yellow and green and blue tint
to these hanks of rag-cord. Then the weaving loom would
be got ready in the attic and the shuttle would fly back and
forth and the rags would soon be transformed into a smooth,
well-striped carpet, which would come off in pieces several
yards long. Later on these would be sewed together into
a beautiful floor covering to be used for the parlor first,
afterward, when the freshness was somewhat worn off, for
the living-room; later for some hallway, and last of all,
what remained from many footsteps would be made into
little rugs to be put down extra in such places as needed
special protection.

The craftswoman who did all this was equally gifted in
making the cross-stitch initials for the corner of the bolster
and the knitted lace for its edge. She was master of all
tricks with the needle as well as with the shuttle and the
wooden spoon. Moreover, that grandmother was the
mother of fifteen children, and there was nobody but her-

self to make mittens and stockings for all of them for both winter and summer.   So her knitting-needles simply had to fly in all the interstices between tasks of weaving and spinning and dyeing and soap-making and candle-making and other work.   All this was to be done besides what the average women of to-day have to do and think pretty hard for them.

Edith Abbott in her book, *Woman in Industry,* mentions forty-nine different processes in the factory of to-day that now take the place of the work of one woman as she stitched a pair of shoes in her home, as women often did in the middle New England pioneering era, to accomplish the detail of all the industries that passed through the hands of that capable little grandmother of ours in, say, 1790 or thereabouts.

In still earlier days the women performed prodigies of heavy labor and bore a child a year while they did it.   History, however, grimly adds the illuminating note that most of these had a short career.   And it is just possible that the women of that earlier time went beyond their strength, exhausting their resources of vigor, so that the women of to-day have not their full share of energy for the tasks before them and therefore do not add to the sum of life in the same numbers that their foremothers did.

Such grandmothers, such mothers as those, were " the kind of mothers that men must worship," says Sarah Comstock in *The Soddy* as she describes the trials of women in present-day pioneering; and she adds, " worshiping mothers makes men great! " Is it not clear where the true greatness of America lies?   If there are old men living who are the sons of such mothers, though they may be worshipers of the memory of their heroism, if those sons have any spark of chivalry remaining in their bosoms, they will wish that their mothers had lived to-day instead of then, that their labor might be lessened by modern work-saving methods and their lives brightened by modern amplitude of resource.

The practical executive ability of those great women of one, two, and three generations ago should be the inheritance of the Country Girls of to-day, and their faithful examples should be an inspiration to them.   But the loyal descendants of those self-sacrificing and sacrificed women should say that they will do all in their power to make the time come swiftly when there shall be a new day in the kitchen, a day when the housework may be a joy and not a burden to press the strength and buoyancy out of the young spirits of those who prefer — if they can get themselves to be brave enough — to enter upon the long service of life in the environment of the open country.

CHAPTER IX

THE DAUGHTER'S SHARE OF THE WORK

THE KITCHEN

O little room, wherein my days go by
Each like to each, yet each one set apart
For special duties . . . nearest to my heart
Art thou of all the house . . . in thee I try
New issues when the old ones go awry,
And with new victories allay the smart
Of dismal failures; and afresh I start
With courage new to conquer or to die.
O simple walls, no pictures break thy calm!
O simple floor uncarpeted below!
The inward eye has visions for its balm,
And duty done is solace for each woe,
And every modest tool that hangs in view
Is fitted for the work it has to do.

Helen Coale Crew.

CHAPTER IX

THE DAUGHTER'S SHARE OF THE WORK

THERE is a doctrine held by some theorists that a people really needs now and then to be plunged into the struggle and stress of actual war in order to become inured to hardship, toughened and strengthened in nerve and fiber. In a memorable essay Professor William James proposed a "moral equivalent" for this discipline that he thought would afford a like toughening training. His suggestion was that there should be a military conscription of the whole youthful population; that they should for a certain number of years form part of an army enlisted in the fight for the conquest of nature, a campaign for compelling the forces of the material world to become subject to the needs of mankind. Definitely, Professor James' suggestion was that "our gilded youths" should be made to go to work in coal mines, on freight-trains, in fishing fleets in December, at dish-washing, clothes-washing, road-building and tunnel-making, in foundries and stoke-holes, and on the frames of sky-scrapers, in order that they may get the "childishness knocked out of them" and come back into society with "healthier sympathies and soberer ideas."

When the word "youths" was used in the last sentence it probably was not held to include, as it sometimes does, the young women as well as the young men. But the work of girls and women must have been in the mind of the writer when he said "dish-washing and window-washing," for these have been feminine specialties from time immemorial or at least ever since the days of the Amerinds when women were the bricklayers, builders and architects, and men were the weavers. Therefore by admitting these occupations it is avowed that the women may come in for some of the benefits of discipline that the struggle for the conquest of nature is to bring to those that take part in it. Does it not make the down-trodden woman feel more grand, does she not hold her head higher and stiffen her neck proudly, when she thinks that her melancholy and sickening work of dishwashing will stand for her in the place of that grandeur of the army going out to battle, that her humble employment may be invested with some of the heroism of the flag-bearer for his country's sake, that she may take to herself a little of the glory of the battle-scarred? If this may be so, there will be some comfort for the house-keeper in the farmstead on a rainy day when the wood from the pile outdoors is so wet that it will not burn, and the water is cold, and everybody in the house is cross!

It is not a matter to be treated lightly. Whatever burden there is to be borne falls more heavily upon the wife than upon the husband in the farmstead. If the farm is isolated, she is the loneliest person there. If there is poverty, she has the least to use or to spend. If there is lack of labor-saving devices, she has far fewer than the farmer has. If life there is monotonous, hers is the victim of the greatest sameness, the unending changelessness of three meals a day through planting and harvesting, through week days and Sundays, year in and year out.

Professor Fiske, author of *The Challenge of the Country*, takes a large view when he touches this phase of the subject. "The annual conquest of farm difficulties," he says, "makes splendid fighting. There are plenty of natural enemies which must be fought to keep a man's fighting-edge keen and to keep him physically and mentally alert. What with the weeds and the weather, the cut-worms, the gypsy, and the coddling moths, the lice, the maggots, the caterpillars, the San Jose scale, and the scurvy, the blight and the gouger, the peach yellows and the deadly curculio, the man behind the bug gun and the sprayer finds plenty of exercise for ingenuity and a royal chance to fight the good fight. Effeminacy is not a farm trait. Country life is great for making men; men of robust health and mental resources well tested by difficulty, men of the open air and the skyward outlook. Country dwellers may well be thankful for the challenge of the difficult. It tends to keep rural life strong."

This was written from the standpoint of the farmer himself and his business. A like account and with quite as much zoology in it could be made for the women that share his problems. Life under farming conditions is as likely to provide opportunity to develop character in the women folks as in the men; and the daughter in the house may receive some of the benefits of this developing discipline.

To have a joyous share in a useful work is one of the most satisfying things in the world. In such a joy as this, the daughter in the farmstead is, within the bounds of her working capacity, invited to partake. She may have the inspiration of work, the exhilaration of struggle, and the keen delight of victory in the solution of farm problems. There is much that she can do without injury, even if she is not very strong, and almost nothing that she cannot do, if she is robust and vigorous. If the housework seems a hardship, the matter must be attacked as a problem and studied into to see what can be devised to lessen the drudgery or re-adapt the burden. Invariably the parents should consider what is good for the girl, not what is good for the farm. Sacrifice the farm, if need be, but save the daughter.

The American Country Girl is doing her full share and often-times more than her share. In the majority of cases " shares " should not be mentioned at all, for each does all that is in her power more for love's sake than because the division has been allotted out by some technical rules of supposed right or law. The Country Girl of to-day can have nothing to blame herself for in the part she takes as first assistant to her mother in the home part of the farmstead. She is the vicegerent in a kingdom where the mother is queen. And if the mother falls behind in the race for the finish the daughter comes in and takes her place. She does this ungrudgingly. The daughter in an American farm home bestows liberally of her strength to make the housekeeping as nearly a success as under the circumstances it can be. Either she shares the work with the mother, or she works under the mother's direction, doing the heaviest parts; or she does all the work while the mother takes care of the chickens or carries on some of the business of the farmstead that presupposes experience.

For instance, a twenty-two year old girl who is a good helper in a house where the work is not overwhelmingly heavy may have for her " share " to do all the chamberwork, wash the dishes, do the sweeping, the dusting, and all the ironing; to rinse, starch, and hang out all the clothes; to bake all the cakes, the pies, the cookies; to help also with the mopping and scrubbing, and to have the loathsome duty of taking care of the kerosene lamps. And she may add the churning and much outdoor work beside.

Such a girl as this does not consider her work a stint; she does not say that she will do so much and no more: she helps till all is done. She is the crack-filler.

The Country Girl and her mother make some attempt to organize their work and to introduce some little system into the program of the day. Sometimes they will arrange for the daughter to be housekeeper one week and assistant cook the next. Sometimes they divide the work equally between mother and daughter; or two sisters take turns about doing the entire housework.

An arrangement like this affords to both mothers and daughters a rich opportunity. But a strange little paradox comes in here. If the daughters wish to give the greatest degree of reverence and protection to their mothers they should not pay too much attention to what the mothers tell them to do. In other words if they will follow the beckoning hand of progress and take up with the suggestions of modern invention in their further housekeeping, they must depart from their parents' advice and from the ways of the old folks. The oft repeated saying, "what was good enough for my father is good enough for me," should never again be heard without protest by any member of the younger generation — at least an inward protest that will rob it of its depressing influence. It is not a want of reverence toward the memory of our forefathers that makes us wish other and different conditions from what they had. It is not a disloyalty to the living mother for the daughter to say that she will not follow in her footsteps if she now sees better ways of doing things. Shall not the large-hearted mother wish that her child may have better and improved ways, greater conveniences, lighter burdens, machinery for making work less burdensome, more leisure for the higher life? She should — but does she? She often does not see the use for the new-fangled appliances. She is too stiff to change her ways, even when she sees that the new methods are an economy of time, labor and nervous force. As to such a farm woman as that, one who is so fixed in her ways that she will not listen even for her children's sake, to the voice of progress: why, there remains nothing for her to do but to pass on. Peace be to her! She has stood there for a life-time and drudged and submitted and has done nothing for household or community advancement. Some among the older women may awake to a new life; here and there one will step over the abyss that separates her from her daughter, will pass down and stand side by side with the younger woman. But as a general thing the abyss is too fearful and she lacks the energy for the leap. There remains for her only a martyr's crown and a harp.

The most isolated farm woman in the country of half a century old must have been touched by the edges at least of the wave of progress in social and home-making conditions that has swept through our life in late decades. Most of the dwellers on farms as well as townspeople have been profoundly moved thereby. Some strange new kind of utensil drifting to the remotest mountain valley and appearing in some neglected despairing kitchen, like a bit of flotsam floating across seas from richer lands, was a symbol of a reorganization as undreamed of as heaven will be found to our awakening eyes. That utensil was the call of a new era. The isolated farm wife may not have had her ears opened to know the sound, but that was what it was, for all that. It represented a new life, the making over of a whole generation.

Naturally the younger people are a part of this new life; naturally the difference between the wants of the older people and the wants of the younger makes a cleavage between them. The more swift the change, the greater the difference between the people of the two ranges of family relationship. This is the all-sufficient reason for the frequency of differences between the young men and young women of this period and their parents. In the country these differences have appeared with less frequency because the progress in those parts has been less spasmodic, more normal, more natural. This has been at least one good effect of the slowness of the countryside to take up with the new ideas. But the progress there has been fully swift enough to make a distinct divison between old and young, and this divison, the result of perfectly natural influences that do not by any means belong to the country alone, has been one of the causes why the young men and the young women have drifted away to the city.

A better way would be to stay and work out the problem. It would be wiser for the older and younger to attack it together as one. As for the Country Girl, we are far from suggesting a separation between the motherly and the daughterly ideals. We would wish rather to pour greater

tenderness into the relationship, already one of the dearest
of human ties.   Said one noble-hearted man, after giving a
full description of the work of his mother under the old
régime with soap-making, dyeing, spinning, and candle-
making, " Do we want to return to those good old times?
Not by any means! My greatest regret is that my mother
could not have lived to have some of the luxuries of the
present era."   This is the right spirit.   And the young
woman who brings her thoughts to her mother with the
brand of the later era upon them, must remember that she
is carrying out the spirit, if not the letter, of her mother's
life and character, her cleverness and her patience, her
adaptation to circumstances and her tact and perseverance,
when she takes the result of her mother's work and carries
it a step farther, adapting her hands to the use of the tools
that her time provides, even as her mother did in using the
tools of her own time and station a half-century ago, when
she exchanged her tallow dip for the kerosene lamp, her fire
place and crane for the cast-iron stove.

CHAPTER X

THE HOMESTEADER

What man would live coffined with brick and stone,
    Inprisoned from the influences of air
    And cramped with selfish landmarks everywhere,
When all before him stretches, furrowless and lone,
    The unmapped prairie none can fence or own?

What man would read and read the selfsame faces,
    And, like the marbles which the wind-mill grinds,
    Rub smooth forever with the same smooth minds,
This year retracing last year's, every year's, dull traces,
    When there are woods and un-man-stifled places?

Lowell.

CHAPTER X

THE HOMESTEADER

IN 1777 the famous ladies of Litchfield molded delicately the leaden statue of King George into bullets that their husbands might have the wherewithal to fight King George's men. To this day there stands along the edges of the West many a shack with chunks of lead imbedded in its walls where women still live who defended themselves there using bullets they also molded, not a century, but just a few decades ago. The pioneering era is with us still.

"Over vast expanses of America," says Dr. Albert Shaw, "the log-cabin period still continues." And if the log-cabin is found — or the tar-paper shack, or the sod-wall house, or the dug-out, or whatever device stands as an apology for a dwelling place while the claim is being "proved up"— then also the dolorous conditions of isolation and struggle, of overwork and wearing out and all that follows as a reprisal by fate for the inroad into a new world, are matters of present day experience.

There are unirrigated deserts where women wear out their lives in despairing labor. The unwatered soil laughs at the puny human beings, and human need and human desire do not easily learn the lesson that only by united effort, by community union on a grand scale, can conquest be made against that array of nature's inexorable forces.

Across prairie uplands on the slopes of the Rockies are vast stretches of level yellow soil where not a green speck is in sight in any direction. The gray-hued buffalo grass spreads everywhere and not a tree, rock or stone can be seen. In the widely separated farmsteads most of the houses are of sod.   The men are sheep herders: they start out with a collie and supplies for a three months' trip. When they come back they are startled at the sound of a human voice.   Often on their return they are disturbed in their mental balance.   The solitude has not been good for them.   Many go insane.

The women remain in the sod house and work.   In illness they have only the midwife to rely upon.   As a result they suffer from the effects of unskilful treatment.   They are all Eastern women, all homesteading; but they never can save money enough to go back East.   Hopeless of that, they lose impetus and all life descends to a lower key.

In this dark picture, from which some of the deepest shadows have been intentionally omitted, a definite region has been kept in view; but there are other places out on the edge of things that are like or similar to this.   Such conditions require the heroism of martyrs.   Noble martyrdoms pay well but reckless waste of life does not.   It cannot be said that any daughters born under these conditions have one-tenth of their rightful chance in life.

In other portions of the vast and but partially subdued West, conditions may be trying but they are not hopeless. Here, as we have seen in former chapters, life to the Country Girl may be buoyant and inspiring even though the eight hour day of hard labor may stretch out to ten or twelve or even fourteen hours.   The rest is sweet, conscience is crystal-clear, and " what one does is of consequence."

It is that ultimate possibility that lends zest to effort, the " consequence " that inheres in the task.   While the registry of cattle brands in the local western newspaper always includes among its symbols some three-ply hook or decimal fraction or swastika design that stands for the ranch of an enterprising and successful woman, there is always a suggested possibility to the mind of the young girl that lends fervor to her efforts.   It is not forbidden that she should excel and even have a ranch of her own.

The author knows of an efficient woman who owned and
ran for twenty-five years a ranch of fifty thousand acres in
the midst of the southern Rockies.   The place produced annually twenty thousand tons of hay; they had about ten
thousand head of cattle, three thousand head of horses, two
hundred angora goats, selling the wool for sixty cents a
pound; there were two thousand chickens, three hundred
head of hogs, and two thousand doves.   A stream ran near
the house from which a five-pound trout could be taken at
any minute.   In summer some fifty men were employed.
The owner had a son and a foreman with whom she advised,
but she managed things herself.   There was also a daughter, she sometimes put on a sombrero and drove one of
the two-furrow disk plows when ten in a line worked over
a field one mile wide by four miles long, following the big
irrigation ditch that ran along the side of the field.

Of course the woman's opportunity and will to own a
farm are not confined to the Western country.   Many a girl
in New Hampshire, Michigan or Alabama has saved the old
home for her disabled parents by putting her shoulder to the
wheel, bearing the disaster of the near-cyclone and the barn-
burning, the desertion of renegade " help," and the distrust
of old fogy neighbors.   A girl graduate of Wellesley has
hastened to acquire a farm in a lovely river bend in Central
New York before the price goes higher still, and one has
doubts of her success until one hears her at the telephone
arguing with a man who thinks he can go back on his bargain about her wind-fall apples.   Stories like these would
take us trailing across the country from Maine to California
and would leave us bewildered before the upspringing of
new life everywhere in the energies of the young women of
America.

To many of these younger women, the fact that in
America a woman does not have to be head of a family in
order to take up a claim seems a golden opportunity; the
struggle and privation inevitable in the years of proving up,

are not sufficiently appalling to prevent their attempt.   The
number is swelled by recruits from among the straight college girls, the agricultural graduates, those who have had
business training, some of the writing clan, some artists, and
some who are moved by a clear spirit of adventure.   Nothing daunts them.

To this energetic girl the business part is a mere detail.
She writes to the Department of the Interior at Washington, asking for full information about the method of taking
up land, about the unappropriated lands and instructions
for homesteaders.   These pamphlets are promptly received.
Or she applies to the Chamber of Commerce of the biggest
city in the State to which she wishes to go.   She carefully
regards the warnings set up along the path of the would-be
homesteader, which are these: see the land itself before de-
ciding; decide that the home you are seeking is to be a permanent one; be sure that you are adapted for silence and
solitariness; and finally, this all-important rule — have
enough capital for buildings, for cattle and horses, for
machinery, wells, cisterns and seed, and enough more to
carry you over a bad year or two, before you undertake
the great task.

Having met these requirements, she gaily packs her carefully selected goods on a gigantic prairie barge and con-
voyed by an efficient freighter (a freighter is a human
being), she rides the fifty miles from the last station out
to her claim, paying the freighter twenty dollars for his service.

She is very busy, that instinct for the practical that has
been developed in the ingenious American through centuries
of pioneering comes to her rescue now.   She resorts to all
manner of tasteful makeshifts; she works miracles with
hammer and saw; she makes easy chairs out of barrels and
dressing tables out of packing boxes.   As soon as possible
a piano is installed in the soddy.   The tiny shack becomes an
orderly little combination of laboratory, boudoir, and study.

The little house acquires a charm of its own. Wherever the American girl is, it is a home. She sits at the door of her soddy with her faithful tabby in her lap and is content.

She loves it all. The wild surroundings have a charm for her. Said one: "I certainly fell in love with life on the ranch. I still have my place and have bought more land adjoining it. I guess I am a sort of Indian myself. I love the big outdoors and I love every rock in our mountains. There is something in the somber green of the pines that creeps into one's heart and I am lonesome away from them."

A young woman in Wyoming writes: "This country is so different, so big, that the horizon alone seems to set the limit. I visited on one ranch that is fourteen miles from one end to the other. There are no green wooded hills here, but great rocky slopes and rushing water and great sandy flats with wonderful changing colors. . . . I do not think we miss the outside world as there is something about this country that, after a time, fills one's whole thoughts and it is hard to remember that there is any other world than this."

But do they not mind the deep changeless silence in those distant solitary places? "But there is no silence here," she answers, "except on the high places of the mountain tops. Here there is always the roar of the river at the bottom of the canyon and the wind in the cedars all about me."

But the Indians? Do you not fear that war-whoop? "It used to alarm me to meet an Indian out on the big flats, but I soon discovered that they will not even look at you as they pass."

But how about rattlesnakes? In answer came this: "I never had any rattlesnakes in my bed, though I fancied I had one night. I got up, carefully lifted off the sheets, and found — the comfortable under me wrinkled up! There are not many rattlesnakes now — you see, we kill them."

Another girl who taught in a sod schoolhouse told how one day she discovered a large snake coiled around the rafters of the little room. She and the larger pupils got

sticks and drove it out. She then modestly added, " We
certainly would have killed it had it not been a bull snake,
but bull snakes kill the deadly rattlers, you know, so we let
it live."

But are you not afraid to stay in your cabin alone on
your lofty butte? " No, I do not believe that I am afraid.
When I first came here the bigness of the hills frightened
me, but now some of the best times I have are when I am
walking over the hills and through the trees at night. I
have a bull terrier and a collie that are always with me so
I am not so much alone as it might seem. I have also a
beautiful big Morgan saddle horse; I ride over the country
alone and I have never been frightened."

Another homesteader girl has learned how to overcome
fear. She says: " It takes some courage to stay alone on
one's claim night after night. But perhaps that is a foolish
fear, for there is really nothing to be afraid of. I positively
love to hear the coyotes howling and barking among the
hills as I lie on my little bed in my little house. One night
last winter I heard the creaking and groaning of heavy
wagons laboring through the snow. I had been in bed for
some time and the noise of the wagons mingled with the
voices of the men awakened me. I rose, threw on a cloak,
and opening the door a few inches, I looked out. The fore-
most wagon had stopped just in front of the door. ' What
is it?' I called. ' Which way do you go to get to Grass-
ville?' I told him, he thanked me, and I shut the door.
The wagons creaked and moved away. *I had not been
afraid.* Perhaps it is faith in God which keeps us out here.
If that is so, then this life *is* favorable to moral development, is it not?"

" Homesteading," says one college girl and successful
homesteader, " is not simply one means for leisure, outdoor
life and freedom from conventionality — it is an opportunity
to test one's caliber in withstanding privations, in braving
blizzards, in conquering the fear of rattlers and that greater

fear of being alone on a seemingly limitless prairie. It is
also a chance to recognize in those sturdy men and women
of the West their big heartedness and clean mindedness.   A
girl too timid to stay alone over night in a city apartment
may feel a sense of safety alone in her shack in the West
that the civilized East would not understand.   It does not
take long to realize that the old cow-boy courtesy of protect-
ing women holds good still.   As a result of it all we might
say that besides gaining a new view point on life, besides
the moral strength attained in conquering that desire to return to the ease of civilization, comes that mental and physical vigor which seems to be inherent in the girl who has
held down a claim for fourteen months and who has successfully proved it up."

To take a place like this in the community such as homesteading involves, requires the assumption of responsibility,
and responsibility always develops.   Cases are mentioned
where a young woman has been strengthened morally by the
evident necessity for rectitude.   Young women who have
not before been interested in church work have been drawn
into it, for they saw that somebody must do this between the
times when the circuit preacher could come around.

A well-balanced judgment comes from Elinore Rupert
Stewart, whose homesteading experience has been detailed
in a delightful book and whose record of a working day has
been shared with us in an earlier chapter.

To her homesteading offers one solution of poverty's
problem; but she adds, if the would-be homesteader is afraid
of coyotes and work and loneliness, she had better let ranch-
ing alone.   Nevertheless, any woman who can endure her
own company, who can see the beauty in a sunset, who loves
growing things, and is willing to put in as much time at
hard outdoor labor as she has done over the washtub, will
certainly succeed.   Her reward will be in independence,
enough to eat all the time, and a home of her own in the
end.

This homesteader with her power of literary expression has given us vivid pictures of the possibilities in the cabin life of the new country.   Her claim lies sixty miles from a railroad.   There is no rural delivery of mails, no doctor, no preacher.   To the west the Rocky Mountains lift great gorge-scarred masses of rock and to the east stretch bad lands and desert and interminable uninhabited space.   Her "community" includes all the ranches for fifty miles around.   And how interesting are those neighbors!   So good, so queer, so like folks!   She has brought Christmas cheer into every camp of sheep-herders within reach.   She is nurse and doctor to every sick woman.   She has been guardian angel to the lone rancher, Zebulun, finding his friends for him "back home," and to a pair of abused young lovers, for whom she gave a wedding dinner, providing the elegance of drawn-work paper napkins and inviting the guests to wash dishes — a compliment that they did not in the least consider a breach of decorum.   She is community companion to her neighbors in hours of joy and in hours of sorrow.   A missionary could scarcely ask for a more needy, a more vital or a more responsive "field."

In the circle of her ministrations was found a young girl whom she calls Cora Belle.   This little person, half child, half grown woman, so unconsciously brave, so pathetically buoyant, asking little of Fate and receiving so little from the hand of that close-fisted autocrat — forms an appealing figure and may be thought of as the typical young Country Girl in the realm of the ranch and the cabin.

Cora Belle lived with her grandparents, two useless old people who drank up each other's medicines just to save them, and frightfully neglected the poor little granddaughter.   The description of the child brings her vividly before us.   "She was a stout, square-built little figure with long flaxen braids, a pair of beautiful brown eyes, and the longest and whitest lashes you ever saw, a straight nose, a short upper lip, a broad full forehead,— the whole face, neither pretty nor ugly, plentifully sown with the brownest freckles."

The child did all the housework for her rheumatic and ignorant grandparents and took care of the stock. From the big sheep men that passed their way, she begged the "dogie" lambs which they were glad to give away, and by tender care she preserved their lives. Soon she had a flock of forty in good condition and preserved from attacks by the wolves. The next step in her progress was that she began to help cook for the sheep-shearer's men in order that her sheep might be sheared along with theirs. The one to whom she appealed was kindly disposed and he hauled her wool to town, bringing back to her the magnificent sum of sixty dollars, all of which she soon had the hard luck to see paid out for more quack medicines. And Cora Belle went on wearing the poor gingham skirt that was so unskilfully cut that it sagged in the back almost to the ground. No wonder that this unselfish, hapless little girl touched the heart of the capable young woman homesteader so that she made a party all for her, giving her a few simple presents, some underclothes made of flour bags that she had carefully preserved, a skirt of outing flannel and a white sunbonnet built from a precious bit of lawn and trimmed with an embroidered edging.

Cora Belle came to the party driving her lanky old mare, Sheba, hitched up with the strong little donkey, Balaam, who balked every three miles and had to be waited for. The grandparents were in behind all wrapped in quilts, and they were as astonished as modest Cora Belle herself to find that it could enter anybody's head to appreciate and honor that small child. Now—good luck to all the Cora Belles! And may every one of them find such a friend as this girl has found!

While the brave people that have adventured into a new country will invariably be interesting to the seeing eye, it is the experience of many homesteaders to find in their expansive communities many who will surprise them by their ability and attainments.   This is not strange for a new country always beckons to the strong, the intelligent, the highly individual.   In one region the forest ranger had been a newspaper editor in Dublin; one of the hired men had been a photographer artist in Detroit; another had been a wireless operator in Alaska; another was educated in a German university, and an Oxford man drove the stage.   " Our neighborhood," says a college girl homesteader, who herself wears a Phi Beta Kappa key, " is as cosmopolitan as Ellis Island itself.   One family of three from Illinois are good neighbors and law-abiding citizens.   Another neighbor is a Mexican freighter.   Another is a Norwegian whose sole delight is to poison other people's stock and dogs and to read the *Appeal to Reason,* which he calls " The Apple."   Another lawless one hails from Denmark.   Would that he and his tribe had never left the Fatherland, if they will not become Americanized!   Another is a half-witted Bosco.   Another is a woman who has trodden the historic Appian Way and journeyed to world capitols.   Another is a sweet-faced teacher who is much in demand in higher circles of learning than we have here.   So there are Italians, Scotch, French, Germans, Swedes, and many Finlanders,— making up the good and the bad, the strong and helpful as well as the opposite."

Sociability and a community spirit of a kind adapted to the conditions are possible under such circumstances.   And there is probably no better field for the weekly paper, the woman's magazine and all the monthlies than in the dugout and the soddy.   " Any pleasures?   Heaps of them! " cried one of the homesteader girls.   " Visiting, horseback riding, parties, socials, dancing, camping, hunting,— all kinds for all tastes."   To be sure, when the ranches are ten to twenty miles apart, it is difficult for the people to get together very often.   But when they do have a dance they come from fifty miles around.   They come for supper, dance all night, and have breakfast together the next morning.

A happy homesteader in front of her "soddy." The vastness of the country does not daunt her. She learns to love the quiet, broken only by the roar of a river at the bottom of a canyon or the howl of a coyote on the great sandy flats.

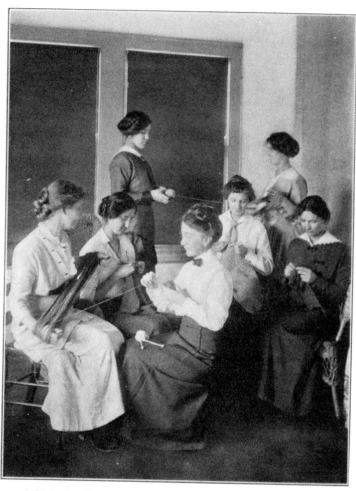

A Knitting Class at an Agricultural School. Note the splendid poise of the Country Girl in the background—how naturally and yet perfectly she is holding herself.

To a lonely girl on her claim it is an event if another girl becomes her next door neighbor fifteen miles away. Hence the newcomer no sooner arrives than an eager neighbor comes to call, and the call lasts the whole afternoon. They talk about the cabin and its fixtures, cooking and recipes, dress and styles, the family and the crops — and the neighbors. If the circle includes foreigners then the question of being neighborly is more difficult. It is also a problem when one finds one's self near a group who spend the whole time in playing bridge, for there is nothing more certain to asphyxiate intellectual intercourse or human exchanges of any kind. If the leader of the Four Hundred in a one-hundred-mile-square community cannot read or write but plays cards like a gambler, it is impossible to entertain a hope that true community spirit will flourish there and good works will be furthered. But the Country Girl who finds herself in such a place as that may reflect that perhaps her very reason for being is to provide from her abundant resources some offset of joy and entertainment and good will that will plant good community spirit and unharmful pleasure where evil things had sway.

Both the gay bravura and the sound judgment of the American college girl are shown in this picturing bit from Mabel Stewart Lewis, a successful homesteader of South Dakota. "It is such fun to go visiting the other girls, to taste their goodies, to sleep four in a bed, toast marshmallows, and make fudge. But these things are mere trivialities. The great and glorious fact of *being it* and *doing it* is the pleasure! What could be more delightful than owning one's own land, having one's own house, digging in one's own soil, and being one's own and only boss?

"Looking down deeper than the surface and out beyond my quarter section, I see that our life here is another part of the great feminist movement of the world, a real and very vital part for the young women who are fortunate enough to be classed among the homesteaders. And fortunate not only are they, but the country, a part of which they are building."

Pioneering life is a passing phase; the girl homesteader is exceptional.   But transitory periods may teach great lessons as they glide along before the glass of history.   And if the girls that brave the danger, endure the solitude, become angels of mercy in their communities, survive the bad years, and master the situation commercially, show that they can do this when the incentive that is rightfully theirs is given to them, they have performed a service worthy of their strenuous labor, their suffering, and even perhaps of their martyrdoms.

This chapter has spoken of an exceptional group; the following chapters return to the average Country Girl and her general problems.

CHAPTER XI

THE NEW ERA

It is especially important that whatever will prepare country children for life on the farm, and whatever will brighten home life in the country and make it richer and more attractive for the mothers, wives and daughters of farmers should be done promptly, thoroughly and gladly. There is no more important person, measured in influence upon the life of the nation, than the farmer's wife, no more important home than the country home, and it is of national importance to do the best we can for both.

Theodore Roosevelt.

CHAPTER XI

THE NEW ERA

THE mother of to-day is a bridge between two eras. Her mother had a wooden spoon and a skillet; her daughter has a dynamo. As for herself, she hardly knows which way to turn — whether to be loyal to the wooden spoon or to enlist her sympathies with the dynamo.

This is, by the way, the reason for many of her troubles, though she may not assign them to this cause. For the utensil is the symbol of a psychology, of a rationale of living, of an esthetic ideal, of a spiritual recognition. When the soap-kettle was carried for the last time into the back-yard to rust away forever in the weeds behind the barn, the New Era believed itself safe in the dining-room and made up its mind to stay there. Science riding on a gang-plow and scattering bulletins along the way, was making happy inroads on the farm; and the electric motor in the kitchen became inevitable. All that remained for us was to adapt ourselves to it, and that is what we have been doing ever since.

It was a revolution — this introduction of machinery; and it was none the less so because it came so gradually and with so little show of intention. No one noticed when Hannah found it no longer possible to sit by her window binding shoes. She then, however, ceased to look through the pane for her unreturning lover, but sorrowfully rose from her chair and walking out of the low door, she passed over to the factory across the street and there went on as before, binding shoes — but in another way. She simply became one of a hundred who gave their whole attention to one single element among the forty-nine different elements now made possible in the process of making a pair of shoes, and left the other forty-eight elements to be done by other industrious women working in groups of one hundred. The women were not driven out of their work; they did not crowd into the places of men in the manufacturing field. They simply took their long-accustomed work in hand and went into the factory to do it. So with weaving and many other kinds of industry. So is it now with canning. Women are the prehistoric caretakers of our foodstuffs. They still are this when in the factory they are canning pickles and green corn and tomatoes.

Strangely enough the same influence that took the industrial woman out of the home is to conduct her back again. It was Power embodied in the steam engine that wooed her away from the home; it will be Power expressed in the marvelous dynamo that will set her again by the hearthside. It will be a regenerated home, one in which the regenerated woman will be able to live, the woman that can think in terms of calories, who will act as quickly as the new mechanical force will demand, and who after a little will find the far more exact methods no strain upon her powers of adaptation and execution.

In the present era of transition loyalty leads her to make the best of her surroundings and to do all that she can to-day to ameliorate the difficulties for herself and her family; sometimes she does not know that a better lot should be hers; sometimes she is dulled by the care and the burden she bears. But the great upward pressing tide will reach every one in time — soon, yes, very soon! — and she will see that the new way is going to set her free for a better and a higher service to those she loves. The wonderful element of mechanical power embodied in the dynamo or in some kindred form, is to contract her working hours, as it has the stint of men, from ten hours to one, and will leave her with lightened hands to do other and more valuable things for family and community. Of course the old era and the new era are now seen standing side by side and will be for a long time yet. There are ardent unenlightened women who stand for old ways as if the new must have a sort of wickedness about them because they are expected to lessen the work. There are by this time also many who have experimented with the use of mechanical power in the household and have found this newly adopted servant of the Lord in that great laboratory of the Lord, the human house and home, to be a comfortable and loving companion; as at the beginning, this application of divine force to human happiness has been pronounced good.

As the old and the new stand side by side, they will be sure to clash to some extent. Every detail must be studied out and applied to various needs as they come up. Progress is being very swiftly made just now and every one must get in step as soon as possible.

The awakening that is proceeding along all the great channels of thought meets, however, at certain points a very definite obstacle. For instance, if one of those famous self-sacrificing housewives who survive from past times, should be asked why she did not have a certain convenience that would lessen her labor, she would say: "Well, I thought that over and decided that I could possibly get along without it." The answer would be typical. Whatever she could possibly get along without she ought not to have. Unconsciously the woman makes all things a matter of conscience. But the conscience is a creature capable of education as well as of ethical impulse and determination. The conscience should be more highly educated. The question should not be, can I possibly get along without that? — but, can I bring myself and my family to a higher degree of efficiency, to a state of more robust vigor, of more intense and joyous activity, by having the conserving appliances, by cooking more sustaining meals, by inducing them to wear shoes with thicker soles and coats of rubber, or to stop work sooner? Can I get a little more efficiency out of my-self and of my family and out of the workers in barn and kitchen by adopting these new-fangled ideas or devices? The new era woman will always give the new-fangled idea a chance.

A noble joke was played upon a woman of this kind by her modern young niece when she took an old barrel from the woodshed and with the aid of two old kettles and an armful of hay turned it into a fireless cooker — or rather into a "hay-box" cooker, for it hardly deserved the better name though it was built on the same principle. The girl had been bragging that she could cook potatoes for dinner in an old box out in the woodshed. The aunt, of course, thought her niece was joking. But she assured her aunt that she was in earnest and would show her. So she peeled the potatoes and bringing them to a boil on the stove at eight o'clock in the morning and whisking them, piping hot into the hay-box, she left them there till exactly twelve, the dinner hour, and then brought them triumphantly forth, still piping hot, perfectly cooked, perfectly mealy and delicious. The happi-ness point was reached for her when her aunt sank down in a chair absolutely nonplussed with this miracle that she had seen with her own eyes! — Or, better still, when the potatoes the aunt had surreptitiously prepared by her accustomed methods were refused by everybody, while the family par-took of those that were cooked by the miracle. Triumph could no further go! It cannot be said that old is old and new is new and never the twain shall meet, for old and new met here at that moment and old was demolished! The next thing would be for that identical very capable housewife to buy a good, first-class, durable and sanitary fireless cooker and use it habitually. But, alas! the prejudices of her hus-band prevented that desirable consummation. Progress was therefore stalled in that particular spot. But the valley where she lived had had one ray of light let into it; the thought of a possible relief had come. Let us hope that this may soon happen to every vale and corner, and kindle a hope in the heart of all farm women everywhere!

The light of this hope may not shine very brightly in the hearts of many women of the earlier training and habits. But for the young women, for the six million between the age of fifteen and twenty-nine, it is radiant and alluring. The present-day mother may still say that her mother's ways are good enough for her; but the daughter — as between the wooden spoon and the motor, what will she be likely to choose? Can any one ask the question?

She will ask that when her new house is built she shall have ample accommodation of cisterns full of soft water together with pipes to carry it to every part of the house where water is needed and an adequate accompaniment of drain pipes and plumbing. She will ask for an electric motor or a power-engine to run the washing-machine, to pump the water into the attic cistern, and to be the avenue of force to every activity, including the dishwashing.

She will plan to give thirty minutes every other day to that dreaded work that now takes an hour three times a day. She will make no provisions for carrying in coal and carrying out ashes, for her electric stove will not use that kind of fuel and will not produce that kind of waste.

There will never be a fly in her kitchen; the household laboratory will be as clean and glowing as the parlor. The floor will be as artistic as the tessellated pavement of a palace. The aluminum utensils will be always shining, for the material of which they are made will not tarnish. They will be light as feathers and never be a trouble to lift. Her hands will be neat and exquisite; her dress for the laboratory of the house will be tasteful and tidy and becoming, for there will be no reason why it should not be. She will be a joy to look at because she will be happy and because she will be adapted to her work.

If the Country Girl of the New Era is asked to go and begin her own home-making in the old homestead, she will ask to have the walls perforated and a large-sized vacuum cleaner installed in the cellar with hose connections on all the floors.   There must be slides and pulleys to let heavy things down to the lower floors, and to draw them up to bedrooms or storerooms above.   Room must be made for dust chutes from all floors above the cellar and heating pipes to every room.   One may think that the House in the New Era is to be all pipes, but this is the laboratory installation idea; this is simply applying the same principle to the house that men are applying to the office.   The telephone, the private wire, the repeating phonograph, the card system, the calculating machine and all the different kinds of recording and stamping machines — these are what the mechanical age provides for the workshop of the man.   Well may we repeat what has been said: " The workshop of the woman is the worst workshop in the world."   But it is not to be so very much longer.

The scheme above described is not by any means a dream of the far distant future.   No: here and there it is now being realized.   In many a kitchen in small villages and along the countryside where the distance is not too great to make electric connections from central plants, we may find installed the electric stove which with fireless cooker and scientific manipulation is found to be no more costly after the initial expense of installation than other forms of heating, and the dishwashing machine which reduces that part of the labor from three separate hours each day to forty solid minutes of one single morning.   We may find also the inlet of power by which many other household processes as well as such branches of the farming business as are carried on in the house, are turned from unbearable drudgery almost into play.   In such a kitchen the fittings will be exquisite; to work there a delight.   The housewife who has devoted so much money to mere machinery may have resigned the addition of a wing or a porch and devoted the two thousand dollars the enlargement of the house would have cost to the

installation of these expensive fittings. But it has richly
paid her. The whole field of family welfare has been lifted
to a higher plane and the happiness and health of all indefinitely increased. And the same fine experience will be
within the reach of all farm and village women soon.
Those that live in villages and closely inhabited country districts will get their electric power from streams and water-
falls, utilized for community service; those that live on
remote farms on the prairies and mountain-sides will have
their individual resources for power. For the most part
these are financially able to gain this, for if they were not
they could not remain in the regions where they dwell. A
comparatively small proportion of the population could not,
if they would, make use of some source of mechanical power.
If they would! What prevents them? It is this — only
this: the lack of community spirit! And since this desirable spirit is constantly increasing, since recruits are coming
to this new army almost daily, since students, teachers, ministers, philosophers, one after another are putting shoulder
to this wheel, and farm men, farm women, and farm sons
and daughters are coming forward with the new light in
their eyes to ask and expect the aid of machinery to make
their work more effective, it is not unwise to hope that the
people of the countryside are not going to be made to wait
many years more for the fulfilment of their dream.

The Country Girl of the New Era will ask to have a new
house, built to the highest ideals of sanitary living, and of
release from unnecessary, uncalled-for toil, or else she will
require that the old house be made over to the new mechanism. Which will be the most economical? Sometimes that
old place has advantages in the lines of its roof, the store of
its traditions, the love laid up in its cubby-holes; but then —
it will have to be torn out somewhere for the entrance of
labor-saving devices. Science will insist on some surgery
for cleanliness and deftness and the wisdom of the future to
enter in.

Whatever plan is made for the house of the future that its household laboratory may have the attention it deserves, the life of the Country Girl therein is to be set to a new rhythm, or she will be hopelessly left behind. Can any one doubt that she will ask for such things as she believes are necessary to her highest efficiency, and insist upon having them?

Various lists of essential labor-saving devices have been suggested. The one that follows was taken for the most part from an agricultural paper and includes most of the things now recommended by specialists in household economics. But it must be noted that the progress in the application of forces to needs is now very swift, and any day these devices may be superseded by more expediting appliances. It is the duty of every young woman to keep track of these additions to her repertory of activities. The various journals of mechanics constantly report them, and the wild frenzy of the advertisers may be turned into righteousness by watching what they have that will be of use to us.

A List of Labor-Saving Devices

Water system, including bath-tub, and all fixtures connected therewith.

Heating system.

Lighting system.

Vacuum cleaner.

Refrigerator, or a concrete cooler built near the well to take advantage of the coolness of the well water.

Sewing-machine with electric power to run it.

Washing-machine, do.

Wringer, do.

Dish-washing machine, do.

Cold mangle.

Alcohol iron or electric iron.

Carpet-sweeper.

Bread-mixer.

Cake-mixer.

Meat and vegetable mill.

Fireless cooker.

Coal-oil stove, three burner.

Dinner wagon or wheeled tray.

Ash chutes, to the kitchen for the range and to each room that has a fireplace; not needed if electric stove is used.

Cement walks — through the yard and garden to prevent wear and tear on floors of the house.

A scheme for the equipment of a modern kitchen follows, with, again, the proviso that the young woman must adapt it to her own needs by careful study of her conditions:

EQUIPMENT FOR A FARM KITCHEN

FURNITURE

Stove with water-back and boiler.
Kitchen table with drawer.
Kitchen cabinet.
Ice-box.
Fireless cooker.
Scrap basket.
Clock.
A revolving high-stool.
A magnifying glass.
A dissecting microscope.
A linoleum floor covering.
A double sink.
2 double wheeled trays.
A perfectly fitted wire screen for each window.
A wire screen door.

UTENSILS

Granite or aluminum

1 tea-kettle, 4 qt. and cover.
3 saucepans, 3 qt., 2 qt. and 1 qt.
3 double-boilers, 4 qt., 2 qt. and 1 qt.
1 pudding dish.
1 colander.
1 coffee-pot.
1 nest of mixing bowls.
A set of covers, various sizes.
1 stock pot, 12 qts.
1 salt dredger.
1 flour dredger.
1 garbage pail, with tight-fitting cover.

Wire-ware

1 toast broiler.
1 meat broiler.
2 strainers.
1 tea strainer.
1 flour sifter.
1 potato masher.
2 egg beaters.
1 soap dish.
1 dish drainer.
2 cake coolers.
1 soap shaker.

Tinware

4 jelly cake tins.
6 bread pans.
2 cake tins.
1 potato ricer.
1 pint measure.
1 biscuit cutter.
1 doughnut cutter
1 flour scoop

1 funnel.
2 dishpans.
2 muffin pans.
1 biscuit pan
1 wash boiler
1 quart measure.

1 apple corer.
2 graters, small and large.
1 steamer.
1 ladle.
1 sink scraper.

Ironware

1 roasting pan.
1 omelet pan.
1 griddle.
1 frying kettle.
1 coal scuttle.
1 shovel.
1 stove lifter.
1 poker.

1 waffle iron.
3 irons 8 lbs.
3 irons 7 lbs.
1 iron 5 lbs.
1 iron stand.
1 food chopper.
1 pancake turner.

Japannedware

1 bread box.
1 cake box.
1 flour box.
1 sugar box.

1 tea cannister.
1 spice box.
1 dust pan.

Woodenware

1 mop.
1 broom.
1 vegetable brush.
1 sink brush.
1 stove brush.
1 floor brush.
1 scrub brush.
1 stepladder and chair combined.
1 sugar bucket.
2 chopping bowls, large and small.

1 meat board.
1 rolling-pin.
2 small wooden spoons.
2 large wooden spoons.
1 work board.
1 boiler stick.
1 wringer.
1 ironing-board.
1 clothes horse.
1 pail.
1 ice-cream freezer.

Hardware

1 bread knife.
1 cleaver.
1 butcher knife.
2 vegetable knives.

1 heavy mixing spoon.
1 ice pick.
1 meat fork.
3 forks.

1 cristy knife.
1 palette knife.
1 corkscrew.
1 can opener.
1 scale.
1 coffee mill.

6 teaspoons.
6 tablespoons.
1 chopping knife.
1 pair heavy scissors.
1 set skewers.
1 knife sharpener.

Earthenware and Glass

1 bowl, 6 qts.
2 bowls, 3 qts.
6 bowls, 1 qt.
12 cups (custard).
6 breakfast plates.
6 fruit jars, 1 pt.
6 jelly tumblers with covers.
6 fruit jars, 1 qt.
1 baking dish, 1 qt.

1 baking dish, 2 qts.
1 teapot.
1 casserole, 2 qts.
1 bean pot with cover.
1 butter jar.
1 measuring cup, ½ pt.
1 pitcher, 2 qts.
1 pitcher, 1 qt.
1 pitcher, 1 pt.

LINEN

12 fine linen dish towels for glass.
12 coarser dish towels.
24 knit dishcloths.
12 hand towels.

6 coarse floor cloths.
6 dustless dusters.
12 holders, washable.
12 cheesecloth squares for wrapping lettuce.

MISCELLANEOUS

1 letter file for bills.
1 hook for business notes.
1 memorandum pad and pencil.
1 account book.
1 fountain pen.
1 pencil.
1 indelible pencil.

Supply of blocks, impression papers, pencils, erasers, blotting paper, ink, pens, pins, clips, etc.

Supply of cards for a card catalog for all household records.

It is not claimed that this list is imperative for each and every girl. She must adapt it to her special needs. It is merely a typical list. And if the young woman who reads and ponders it does not know how to adapt it to her own needs, she certainly is not fitted to undertake her own housekeeping. She should go to some school where young women are trained in household science and there study the science of utensils and the chemistry of cooking and cleaning, and the whole science and art of home-making.

The list may seem a long one; but when the appliances and utensils are placed before the adequately prepared young woman, she will have a sensation not of discouragement but of delight. To make every young woman realize that if she has adequate preparation she can feel perfectly at home in a house with an industrious little motor at its heart from which will go forth the miracle of an invisible force that will bring every part of the work to magical completion without any effort of ours and that thus what once was drudgery may be turned into a delight,— this is the problem that stands with expectant, perhaps ominous, eyes at our doorway; ominous if we show an unwelcoming look, expectant if we give it greeting and stand ready to take this friend to our heart.

Everything in this world is good. The great god Power led the woman out of her House and into the Factory. It was necessary in order that she should have a chance to learn the rules of the game. Now, her lesson learned, the same great god Power is quietly but firmly taking her again by the hand and leading her back to her House. There she will dwell; and there she will again attempt to create that divine reflection of heaven which we call Home. Now that she is once more allowed to undertake this task, let us hope that she will be successful in building up an institution worthy of the scientific age in which she lives, illuminated with electric beams that shall beat into every rat hole and every germ-protecting dark corner, and with every conceivable energy-producing and conserving device that can be planned by the human mind.

CHAPTER XII

THE HOUSEHOLD LABORATORY

VOICES IN THE HOUSEHOLD

Upon the shelf the clock ticks merrily;
The kettle sings his song in drowsy mood;
Within the stove crackles the fragrant wood;
The coffee-mill grinds out a cheerful lay.
Surely within the oven one can see
A roast . . . what else on earth would smell so good? . . .
And little globes of fat, all amber-hued,
Dance in the pan and sing with noisy glee.
Sweet sounds! Inviting yet another song;
And I will sing in unison with them.
Work brings the joy that helps the work along,
And so, harmonious, sounds the kitchen hymn.
While all about the ready dinner-table
The children's voices raise a merry babel.

Helen Coale Crew.

CHAPTER XII

THE HOUSEHOLD LABORATORY

THE kitchen should be a combination of laboratory, machine shop and studio. The work done there is just as complex as that! There are an almost infinite number of different things needed to accomplish the different processes that have to be carried on in this workshop. There must be a variety of mechanical devices to negotiate and subtly maneuver all the effects that are to be brought out to artistic and wholesome conclusions.

This is true to a great extent nowadays in all households whether in city or country. But the farm is yet, as it always was, a place where there is greater complexity to master because many more things are done there. The spirit of machinery has entered into the life of the city kitchen and eased the burden; it must now enter the country household and work the same magic there.

If the kitchen is to be a combination laboratory and machine shop it must look like one. It must be filled with appliances for every part of the intricate work of making ten thousand things that are needed for the family through the various seasons and changes of the year.

Imagine an exquisite room long and narrow. The walls are painted white or light gray — a warm golden gray for the relief and pleasing of the eye. The floor is comfortable to the feet, sanitary, easily cleansed and durable. There is an iron ring in the floor where the cover to the chute is lifted down which the dust is to be thrown. There is another for the ash chute, lined with metal for protection from fire by

137

means of the hot coals that may sometimes be left in the ashes.   One beauty of the electric stove is that it produces no ashes; one advantage of the vacuum cleaner is that it does away with dust.

The sink has two compartments — all enameled white — one for the washing of the dishes and one for the draining. In the second is the wire drainer.   The sink is placed at the right height for this particular housewife, be she a little treasure done up in a small parcel or a tall stately woman when standing very straight — as every one ought to, whether city or country bred.

At the right of the sink there is a table or shelf for the dishes as they are taken from the wheeled tray that has brought them from the dining table, and at the left is the draining sink or draining board or a shelf on which the dishes may be laid when they have been dried with the linen drying cloth.

There is a window before the worker and from it she can look out over the garden off to the fields, and beyond toward the village, following her thoughts now and then to the great big world outside.

When an ideal like this is held up before their eyes, the younger women see the futility and bad policy of the old methods.   For it is the worst policy to lay heavier burdens upon man or beast than he can carry.   It is better policy to conserve the strength of the beast of burden whether horse or daughter.   The farmer has found that labor-saving utensils and appliances are his best investment in the barn. Why not in the house?   Running water is needed for the dairy stalls; but it is more necessary in the pantry.   The live stock in the kitchen is of a fiber incomparably delicate and fine.   It will be good for the big brother to scrub that floor; and everything the father and the brother can do to sustain the struggle of the mother and the sister will come back to them with rich interest in the value of the product, viz., the health, happiness and vibrancy of the women in the home and the power to give out energy in their home life and to their children.

The young woman of to-day takes it into account that she will probably have to deal with a scheme of life that does not include service in the household laboratory other than that of her own hands. She realizes that there will never be a peasant class in this country; and she sees that housewives must take the consequences of this happy lack: namely, they must do their own work. Every woman will be always as good as every other woman and therefore there can be no servant in our kitchen; there cannot even be " help."

What then shall be done? There must be fit machinery. The drudgery point must be reduced till labor becomes a joy. The kitchen is not to be a place to which the housewife is condemned; it is a place she is going to love because it is a laboratory where science has sway, where aseptical cleanness reduces every process to a fragrant dream, and the laws of processes appear as miracles of nature controlled at last by the art of man.

Seeing all this clearly, it is not strange that the young woman decides to relegate the bad kitchen to the limbo of broken and disused furniture. This, to her, is the impossible kitchen: one that has no shelves, drawers, or cupboards, and no place where things can be put away; or if there are any shelves, they are made so wide that things have to be stored in behind each other so that the first row must be taken out in order to get at something behind. In this impossible kitchen the pantry is on the wrong side for the worker. By the arrangement of doors and windows light and air are shut out. The rotten old wooden sink is bad smelling, too low, and too narrow, and it is so far from the pantry that the worker will have to go back and forth ten times as many times to do a piece of work as she would if the articles were conveniently placed. The room is too large; there is many times as much walking as is necessary; it is as far removed as it possibly can be from the compact convenience of the ideal kitchen. The floor is uneven and there are broken splinters where the wood has worn. They catch the dust, and little bits of string drag along from them to catch more dust and dirt. It is impossible that this floor should ever be clean; the very thought of it is discouraging. The water must be brought from an outside well, and the wood from an outdoors wood-pile. If it is a rainy day, the wood is wet and takes a long time to get to burning in the range. It is not a range — it is only a stove and a poor one at that.

There are many other things that might be said about the impossible kitchen, but perhaps it is not necessary to go any further, for has not everybody seen one? The great majority of kitchens are now impossible. The great majority should be torn out before any more machinery is bought for the farm business, and a full kitchen equipment should be installed in the place of the worn-out floors, the ill-adapted furniture, the cracked and rusted hardware, the soaked and disease-laden woodwork, and the leaky pipes and shingles.

When the daughter in the country home sees that the father and mother are working together for one end, that they have for the good of all undertaken a task that is too great for them, and that they are oppressed and almost despairing in their fight against untoward circumstances, she is ready to join in the struggle and to give her sometimes slender strength to help in the lifting; but when it becomes evident that the old unsanitary kitchen of the average farm home could be renovated and made the workshop of joyous efficiency instead of the treadmill of despairing burden-bearing; and when at the same time she sees additions constantly made to the greater efficiency of the farming side of the farmstead business, the daughter feels with the mother that their work does not have the appreciation that it deserves. And this is what puts the one little drop of bitterness into the cup she has to drink. There is nothing like this to take the tuck out of one. To know that there exist means to reduce the time limit for a certain piece of work from four hours to twenty minutes and that these means are stubbornly and constantly denied to the worker, takes the poetry and the hope out of her heart and the buoyancy out of her joints more than anything else could. Especially is this the effect when the chains are being hung in the new barn to swing the feed along the passageway to every stall, all to save the strength of the men's arms, and no chains and pulleys are being strung in the kitchen to lift pails and swing loads for the mother and sister. To know that the time spent in dishwashing for a family of five could be reduced from six hours distributed through two days to forty-two minutes at one time in one morning — and then to have to go on interminably giving three separate hours daily to this loathsome, lukewarm, greasy, unsanitary, ill-assorted, deadening task — no, the next group of household administrators will not do that!

It is not that the younger women are lazy and inclined to shirk the heavy tasks. That is not their spirit. But they cannot keep up their fine buoyancy of mind and heart when better methods are constantly going into the barn and none into the house; when appliances are bought for cattle and none for the women. And they know that life will not be held up to its high level if they cannot command buoyancy of spirit.

Life is framed on a larger pattern nowadays; there is a greater demand for standard; there is a higher degree of intelligence required. All this the new young woman sees that she has to do and be. She springs to meet the situation — but hanging at her heels is a chain, the chain of old-fashioned methods. She must be free of this chain, or she will not sustain the burden of country life in the time to come. She thinks she sees a way out in the industrial opportunity of the town. It is a mirage — but she follows it. She follows it and follows it — and what is the end to be? Would it not pay us to give her the opportunity to put the housekeeping for the next generation of home-makers on a better foundation and thus keep these finest of the girls of the nation in the environment they love but now find unendurable because they cannot under present conditions have the help they need?

The papers and periodicals for women nowadays devote long columns to telling us how to make some kind of contraption that will take the place of a fireless cooker or of a movable tray or of some other new housekeeping device. It is true that woman may use her ingenuity to make something that will " do."

But we have been too long getting on with half-measures, makeshifts, contraptions of all sorts. The star we should now hitch our wagon to is an electric motor. The young woman who wishes to live on the farm would better enter some industrial field, make something commercially and with efficiency, sell it, and find in her hands the fifteen dollars for the fireless, the eleven for the double-decker wheeled-tray, and pretty soon the larger sum that will be needed to install a perfect kitchen, that will not only be a joy to herself but will be a lesson to her whole community, that will lift the whole region into a new realization of life, that will show how the time necessary to be spent on the drudgery of the household may be reduced from eighteen hours a day to two, and so release her energies as to give to the higher needs of the family and to the equally great needs of the community the services that she alone is fitted to give, and that are absolutely necessary to the well-being and the safeguarding of the life of the rural realm and therefore also of the whole people.

How can we get a kitchen like that? Well, that is the Gordian knot that the farm daughters will be able to cut. They can do it — they must do it. Every instinct of patriotism, every breathing of passion for the welfare of the future homes, every thought of affection for the home circle that will be theirs, calls for the most valiant struggle to gain the goal — a perfectly hygienic, perfectly fitted household plant, with all in it that can by scientific mechanism be placed there, to be the perfect working basis for that highest product, human happiness in a human home.

CHAPTER XIII

EFFICIENT ADMINISTRATION

Scientific management is the application of the conservation principle to production.

The time, health and vitality of our people are as well worth conserving, at least, as our forests, minerals, and lands.

When we get efficiency in all our industries and commercial ventures, national efficiency will be a fact.

Theodore Roosevelt.

CHAPTER XIII

EFFICIENT ADMINISTRATION

IF the Country Girl of the future takes her life in her hands and asks for a household laboratory such as has been described, she must make sure also that she will be able to work in that place in such a way as to get the most good out of it and to prove its value to those that have installed it for her. This presupposes a high degree of efficiency in herself as well as in the tools she handles.

Never has young womanhood been so fortunate in opportunities for preparation as is the girl of this day. The very minutes seem to bristle with the word "efficiency." On every side she may receive suggestion and instruction as to how to make herself consonant with her era. Scientific management is being carried out in every sort of factory, workshop, studio, regiment,— everywhere,— with the one exception, perhaps, of her own, the household workshop. Therefore it is for her to see what scientific management means to all these other institutions and to apply the lesson to her own realm, and make that factory of hers, that workshop, regiment, and studio, into the most efficient place upon earth!

The great movement in the interest of efficiency has its origin in the desire to get just as much result as possible out of the labor of the workers. Their strength must be conserved, not because of any philanthropic feeling for the man, but because that strength is needed for further use, in order that a greater output of the product may be gained. The method employed is to consider studiously the movements made in carrying on any one part of the work. They separate this operation into its elements, and then they determine upon the best motions to make to accomplish the end, and upon the exact order of those motions, shaving off a part of a second here and there by the careful choosing of motions and the surest order of them.   The motions the workman makes, whether with eyes, fingers or arms, are thus economized.   The bricks for the building up of the wall are conveniently placed, and all the details in following any pattern are fitted together so as to make as few motions as possible, to use as little energy as possible, and to reach the end as quickly as possible.   This is, says one, " the application of the conservation principle to production."   " The art of management," says another of these experts, " is knowing exactly what you want the men to do, and then seeing that they do it in the best and cheapest way."   In order to accomplish all this in, say, the business and work of a factory, there must be an efficiency engineer, who shall spend days and weeks and months in finding out what the right order of motions is, what the best arrangement of the tools and materials shall be, what elimination of unnecessary acts and things can be made in order that every possible waste of energy may be pared off and the path to the end may be absolutely, sternly direct.   Then there is the route clerk, who sees that this order is followed by each man until he is able to do it involuntarily and as if by instinct.   To make definite record of the success of this work, the time-and-cost clerk will keep track of time and per cent. items, and make known exactly what are the results of doing things in one particular way.   If not satisfactory, another way must be chosen.

It is the belief of the advocates of scientific management that if we thus make the individual efficient, his productive capacity will be raised twenty-five or fifty per cent., or even sometimes doubled.

Scientific management calls for a careful study of the surroundings.   The appliances must be adequate, comfortable,

handy, and such as require the least percentage of rest.   The
scaffold or bench must be the exact height to make as little
strain as possible on the worker.   The table must be made
at the right height so that the worker will not have to stoop
over for his tools.   If he works on his feet, there must be
something for him to stand against so that he may have no
fear of falling.   To get the full output, the right appliances
must be devised, standardized, used, and maintained.   The
worker's clothing must not be ill-fitting, or it may restrict
the movement of his arms and hands.   It must be of such
material that he will not be in constant fear of ruining it.
Everything about him must be such as to increase speed and
not restrict motion.   Nothing that will affect the eyesight
unpleasantly is to be tolerated.   There shall be no reflecting
surfaces from which the light may shine into the eyes.   The
colors that will help the eyes are to be selected for the room,
those that are pleasant, that will induce a happy mood and
will therefore decrease irritation and help the spirit of
energy.   He must take up the nearest tools first; the pockets
and containers to hold tools must be placed so that the least
and shortest motions may be made in handling them.   And
so on.

There are several reasons why the work of the kitchen
has not been more promptly attacked by the believer in scientific management.   In the first place, the business of the
home laboratory is of so complex a nature that no factory
can compare with it in difficulty of analysis.   Efficient
housekeeping is a combination of many factories.   The scientific expert can far more easily separate the making of a
single pair of shoes into its forty-three acts than he can
analyze any one of the processes of the home laboratory:
say, for instance, the making of a frosted layer-cake, the
assembling and concocting of a mince-pice, or the infinitely
complex business of washing dishes.

In the second place, men have been fairly busy putting
this matter through in their factories.   They have natur-

ally studied out the processes nearest to their own hands. They are not to be specially blamed for inattention to the woman's realm. That will come next. Now that their attention is being called to the need for expert management in the other department of life, they are recommending in many books and lectures what should and must be done to put housekeeping on a basis for efficiency. So if women do not standardize their work, men will do it for them, and that will not be so well for them as if they did it themselves.

The woman who is administrator in the farm home must be equal to several women. She must be master in the difficult art of cookery, adapting her menu to the welfare of a group of people of all ages and with all kinds of needs. She must be washwoman and laundry woman, cleaning and scrub woman. She must know all the proper chemicals to be applied to the cleansing of different kinds of metal, cloth, wood, and every sort of surface painted and unpainted. She must be food expert, and textile expert, medicine and poison expert. Besides all this, she must be teacher, instructor, and entertainer, the encyclopedia and gazetteer, a theological and philosophical professor. And all these separate functions must do their work together within the one personality, the administrator, the little mother of the home, the companion of the kitchen, the parlor and the bedside.

Translated into technical engineering language this women in the heart of the farmstead is her own route-clerk, and order-of-work clerk; she is her own instruction-card clerk, time-and-cost clerk, gang boss, speed boss, repair boss, and inspector. All these and much more must she be in order to gain the effects of scientific management in that factory which is her home realm.

Theodore Roosevelt said, " When we get efficiency in all our industries and commercial ventures, national efficiency will be a fact." Does he include the farm laboratory among the " industries "? The farm home is producing (or ought to produce) the most valuable product that can be found in the country — the man and woman of the future. If these men and women are to be efficient, the home from which they are to come must certainly be a model of efficiency. We have to pierce through the crust of our national conceit and find there the truth that our people are painfully in need of more efficiency and that therefore it is a matter of the most vital concern that we should put the home in all its phases into a condition more adapted for producing the perfectly efficient human product.

The Gospel of Efficiency has reached the farmer; he finds that with three men he can do the work that fifteen men did forty years ago. He realizes that the efficient farmer progresses, the inefficient falls behind.

Will not the same thing be true of woman in the farmstead?

To see how the principle of efficiency may be applied in the work of the farmstead, we have but to look, for instance, at that task of dish washing. Suppose that the worker were piling the dishes at the right of the dishpan and also trying to drain them at the same side. The efficiency expert would promptly decide that this arrangement would cause a waste of time and energy, for while the right hand was ready to lift the dishes to be washed into the pan, the left would have to move back and forth in many unnecessary motions to put the dishes back into the draining rack which was also on the right. The efficiency clerk would demand that the dishes be drained at the left. If there were some article of furniture at the right, so that the dishes could not be placed there, say a pump or a door or a cupboard, that would have to be removed. If the time and strength and nervous energy of those workers were to be conserved and the product to be put forth with the least expenditure of mind and nerve, such changes would have to be made as would make labor-saving motions possible. Not to make the changes would be bad policy, because these conditions would be constantly causing waste of time and strength; and that time and that strength would be of pecuniary worth to the business. What business? The important business of administering the affairs of the home!

Every Country Girl should experiment to see how she can economize motions and save time. She should make a study of every part of her work and see where she can by forethought cut down useless movements and intensify energy. If at first she finds difficulty, she should persevere; she will master the task in time. There is a knack about it that she must master before she can become adept.

If, for instance the hair is being done up in a new way, it takes a longer time than usual the first day, less time the next, and after a few more days the new way takes no longer than the old. Some natural motions have been found out that economize the time and effort, that introduce convenient moves, that shake off awkwardnesses, and set the whole into a rhythm of motion.

Josephine Preston Peabody has written a lovely poem about a child watching her mother as she braids her hair. The child is delighted with the deftness of her mother's hands, and with the perfect rightness of the braids as every loop comes into its place and all of them are so quickly and so beautifully fitted about the head. That mother had by long practise found the exactly right way to manage that complicated piece of human industry, the "doing up" of a mass of long and wavy hair. She did it almost without thought. Her "motions" were perfectly smooth, exquisitely graceful, and adapted absolutely to the end desired through a series of separate acts composing all together a whole scientific process. And she was so accustomed to it as a whole and to all the separate details, that she could do it with a rhythm that was like music. When it was done she could give one little final pat and say, "There!" with a slight thrill of delight.

Just so should it be with any of the intricate operations

of the household laboratory.   Just such a thrill of delight should be possible when the complicated piece of hand-work and machine-work called washing the dishes is finished.   At the end one should be able to express a delighted " There! " — not because a dreaded and abhorrent quarter-of-an-hour was over, but because a piece of work necessary to human welfare has been turned off with firm conclusiveness and dispatch.

The inefficient way of doing things is a too frequent experience.   A farm housekeeper will bring a dish of cold potatoes from the kitchen, carry it all the way through the dining-room, set it down on a chair while she opens the door to the cellar, carry it haltingly down the stairs, and then set it down on a box because it is too dark to place it in the cupboard where it belongs.   She does not want to take the pains to get a lamp, but she has to.   She carefully lights the lamp, carries it down the cellar stairs, places it in a safe place, and then takes care of the potatoes.   Then she comes back and carries a little plate of bacon that has been left and deposits it in the same careful way.   Then follow the bread, the milk and the cream in pitchers; follow the cake, the jam, and many other things in little precious bits too good to be thrown away, all requiring a careful passage, each one at a time.   It is good that she has so many beautiful and promising things to put away; but how different it would have been if she had been able to load all these things on the dummy and with one stroke of the arm to move it all downstairs.   Then, O joy! if she had had the electric light to turn on in the cellar-way and down in the cellar cupboard, she could have gone downstairs with perfect safety and without fear, and she could have returned with a light heart, swung the wheeled tray into its place, and all would have been over in three minutes at the most, instead of taking twenty-five and being accomplished only by a vast expenditure of effort and nervous fear.   The money that woman wasted in reduced energy and nervousness causing doctor's bills, would have bought her a wheeled tray, put in a dummy with pulley, rope, and weights, and paid the family doctor's bill besides! Nothing can be done hygienically that is done in the dark.

The Country Girl may practise for efficiency while she is waiting for her perfect kitchen to materialize, by doing all in her power to make herself save steps.   To learn to make no useless passages across the floor is to begin a conquest of one's own mind, to establish self-control, and to utilize forethought.

"Think twice and step once," was a good motto.   There is a one best way to do all things.   Why not search for it?

CHAPTER XIV

AN OLD-FASHIONED VIRTUE

Ill Housewifery pricketh herself up with pride;
Good Housewifery tricketh her house as a bride.

Ill Housewifery lieth till ten of the clock;
Good Housewifery trieth to rise with the cock.
                              Penny Magazine, 1798.

CHAPTER XIV

AN OLD-FASHIONED VIRTUE

THIS may be considered a brief for the " old maid " of olden time; or rather for the quality that she stands for in our dream and story life. We have not given this so-called " old-maidishness " its rightful place among the virtues. The quality deserves to be classified among the highest expressions of the intellect. In the olden time, when the mother was busy with her family of from two to twenty children, the mother's unmarried sister was the " efficiency-clerk " of the big household. She was the motor, the balance-wheel; she knew where everything was, to the last sheaf of catnip; she put everything in its place and could go and get whatever was wanted. Behind all this was her classifying mind.

That " old-maidishness " was composed of three elements: a fine discrimination of values, an appreciation of little things as pivots for greater things, and a love of orderliness. To her the first law of heaven was her first law. Heaven never had a law till it had order; and when the stars found that there was to be something more than a fortuitous concourse of atoms in the universe, we know what they did: they sang. In any house there will be more singing when orderliness reigns there. But the household is a concourse of myriads of parts. We cannot always sing that the house " is so full of a number of things " that we think we " should all be as happy as kings." It is only when we can keep good track of these things that we can be " as happy as kings." This was a large part of the mission of the invaluable old maid in our early centuries.

There was a great deal of system in the housekeeping

of our ancestors.   Bags, basket and bundles were trained into the service of good order.   They cross-stitched numbers on the pillow-slips and on the sheets and on the rare napery they had spun and woven with their own capable hands and had bleached on their own soft grass-plots. They kept their " simples " in carefully protected and distinctly labeled sheaves.   Their piece-bags were innumerable.   They could go in the dark into the storeroom, put their hand in behind things, feel unerringly for what they needed, and find it there.

The burden upon the memory that this elaborate system of old must have entailed is now transferred to the card catalog.   This invaluable modern device is a system for recording upon cards of a certain uniform size the items and lists and notes to be remembered and preserved, and of classifying them carefully for ready reference.   These cards are stood up in a closely packed row, in a box or drawer, or in a compartment made especially for the purpose, where they are arranged alphabetically or by subjects, in such a way as to be easily run over by the finger till the desired card is found.   The cards must be made of stiff paper or card-board; they must be accurately cut to a required measure, usually five inches wide by three inches tall, and they must be fitted exactly into the box, with " guides " to aid in finding the main subjects.   The " guide " is a card of a different color from the others, usually yellow, and has a little top extension, so that when the guide is put in its place in the row of white cards, this top extension will stand up above the others so as to catch the eye readily.   On this little bit of the guide that stands up above the rest, a main heading is written very clearly in fine lettering, — or, better, printed neatly — and on all the cards that are selected to be slipped in behind that guide are written the notes or references on subjects that belong under that heading.   For instance, suppose the main heading, written on a certain guide, should be this: " Recipes."   Then each card that folows that guide would have written on its face the details of some recipe — one recipe to one card. And all the cards on which the housekeeper had written the recipes she wished to preserve would be placed behind that guide. Then whenever she wished to use any one recipe, she would open her drawer, look along the tops of the cards until she found the guide extension — the little projecting piece that had the word " Recipes " on it. Behind that guide she would find all her recipes; then it would be but the work of an instant to pick out the one she wanted. On each separate card would be written in the upper right-hand corner, the name of the recipe on that card. If the housekeeper had a great many recipes, she might make more guides: one for cake recipes, one for bread, and so forth.

Then there would be still other main heads. One might be marked " Inventory." One might be called " Clothing." Records of music, of engagements, of books, and so forth might be set down. Any subject that needed to be kept track of could be thus securely noted in the card catalog.

Under the heading " Inventory " a most useful record might be made. Subordinate headings on cards of some other color should be used. The first of these would be " Parlor." Behind that would be placed the cards that told all the articles of furniture or decoration that that important room contained. " Dining-room," " Kitchen," "Pantry," etc., would come along in order and all items considered worthy of note would be put on their proper cards. Then there would be other cards entitled " Linen-closet," " Sideboard," " Old Bureau," " Old Chest," " Black Trunk," " Brown Trunk," " Old-fashioned Deep Basket," or other containers of clothing, silver, bedding, linen, utensils, or treasures of any kind. In case of fire, the card catalog, along with the locked document box or safe, would be one of the things to be sought for first and rescued from harm. In fact there should by rights be two copies of any household inventory made, so that in case the inventory in the house should chance to be burned with the house, there might still be a careful record preserved in some safe place for future reference, for purposes of insurance or for historic archives.   Every one of us should think of the family as an institution of dignity, one whose smallest doings have importance, because we belong to a great human family, and because we are bearing on the touch of life to future generations.   We are now making history.   And we should see to it that our link of the unending chain should not break for want of a sensible and accurate recorder.

This description of the card catalog is given with so much particularity because it has been proved by long experience that it is a very great saving of trouble to have it exactly right.   The making of the cards is a matter of the nicest care.   This exactitude is essential to the quick movement of the fingers and is therefore a saving of time in hunting for the one card desired.   The jelly may be almost ready to " jell," and one may run to the catalog of recipes to find what is the matter; one must not be impeded an instant at that critical point.   Time is always precious, too, to the housekeeper, and the orderliness that makes it possible to find things quickly is one of the most important elements in the success of the new housekeeping.

Whatever part the daughter in the farm home may have in the business of the farm, she will find the card catalog of the utmost value to her in making herself useful and in placing her results on the basis of authority.   In such a system of records she can always find what she wants on demand; the various accounts can be added to and taken from and corrected to date at any moment without recopying the whole.   So the records of the daily egg-harvest can be kept, the in-come and out-go of any of the products of the farm, the weighing and testing of the milk, the mending and making of fences, the apple harvest, the dates for putting in crops, the dates of payments to the men and the number of their days' labor, and many other items that belong to the business of the farm.   Of course when the farm business becomes very large and intricate, an elaborate system of bookkeeping is necessary.   But for the myriads of little things that belong to the home side of the farmstead, this ingenious system is especially adapted.   Here we may advantageously keep our records of such memoranda as specially concerns the family, the household accounts and receipts; inventions we may hear about and new devices in which we may be interested and that we may sometime want to find out about or make our own; contents of the tool chest, dates of repairs and memoranda of things that need to be repaired about the house; cans of fruit and other things stored away on the shelves and in the cupboards of the cellar and in the cold room and elsewhere — a valuable record to check up against another year's yield of these treasures; doctor's visits and prescriptions, notes of symptoms, together with dates and any circumstances that may need to be accurately remembered; music, victrola records; Christmas and birthday gifts given or received; dates of events, the coming and going of guests at the home; personal items such as the size of shoes, gloves, collars, hats, etc., for the different members of the family; books we should like to have; newspapers and magazines taken or desired; records of the magazine club or of the book loan club; correspondence, letters received and sent; patterns, clippings, quotations.   For remembering all these things the card catalog will prove the unfailing helper; and all and many more will be the care of the Country Girl when she becomes administrator of a household in the new time.

A simple bookkeeping may also be recorded in the card catalog.   The monthly or seasonal or annual statements of expenses may be recorded here, however, and may be kept for comparison with other seasons and years.   These records may be placed under the following heads:

Food (including meat, groceries, milk and eggs, green vegetables, and fruit, ice, and fuel for cooking).

Shelter (including rent or purchase money, taxes, insurance, interest, repairs, fuel for heating, furnishing).

Clothing.

Education (including papers, books, school, lectures, concerts, art).

Benevolence (including church and charity).

Recreation.

Transportation (including expenses of travel).

Health (including doctor's bills, and medicine).

Savings.

Labor.

Sundries.

This scheme is designed to be used for the budget of a family; but it is most important that every young girl, whether in city or country, and whether her purse be a long one or a short one, should know each year whether the demands upon her cash account are exceeding those of the year before, and that she should make up her mind whether there shall be any change in that regard during the year to come. This is a training that every girl should insist upon giving to herself constantly. If she finds herself called " oldmaidish " therefor, she will know that she cannot have earned the name, since there are no old maids any more! The same sort of person must now be called " efficiency administrator."

In suggesting this form of self-discipline to the Country Girl, we know very well that the girl that determines to keep accurate records of her expenses has a good fight before her. Women seem at present to have a preternatural disinclination toward keeping their own accounts, and nearly every girl inherits this bent. In canning clubs for women it is found that the members will do all the delicate measuring accurately; their sense of taste is unerring; their judgment of results is perfect; but they just will not render an account of their work!

That women are not by right of their sex incapable of

mathematical processes is shown by the fact that so large a number of women attain distinction in the higher fields of that study, becoming astronomers, computing eclipses and ranging the outer realms of the sky with great telescopes. The rather general dislike of women for the simpler forms of computing probably has grown up in the financially irresponsible state that has become a part of woman's very bone and marrow during late centuries. But it must not be so any longer. Too much depends upon orderliness in finances, for the Country Girl to neglect this means of becoming efficient in her life-work.

All of these card-catalog and other "devices" are a part of a great movement to put efficiency into every human industry. And this movement, again, is a part of the upward striving of mankind. The "industry" that is to be the life-work of the Country Girl must not be behind.

It is claimed that the average farmer puts more thought into his work than the average woman in a farm home puts into hers. This is partly because the seasons make less change in her work than they do in his. But they do make a very great change in her work; and the difference between her work and his in this respect ought not to make the great difference that exists between the amount of foresight he shows in his planning and the dim irresolute bungling that is so often the characteristic of hers. We cannot say that we have an ideal unless we contrive a plan to express that ideal. Something luminous and startling may glow before our eyes and flatter our self-conceit with a hope that seems like a resolution. But without a definite plan, the glow soon vanishes and we are no better for having had it. In fact we are worse. It is a real injury to our soul development to entertain an unfounded ideal and then allow it to fade away before we concentrate it into purpose; for we have deceived ourselves and we have weakened our will.

Now and then we read of some woman of olden time who thought out her plan for the next day after she went to bed at night. She was a prophecy of the present; or rather, of the time to come. Too much cannot be said to the young women of to-day about the necessity of foresight. Foresight is the great bulwark of efficiency. Hurry, they say, is only poor planning; and we know what depredations hurry is making upon our fields of life. The Country Girl, if she wishes to help in the upbuilding of national character, must drive hurry from her field, and this she can do by efficient planning. She must now adopt the systematic spirit in order that when she has a farm home upon her hands she will be ready for the simplification that alone will make her work under the new complications endurable and easy. It will be necessary for her to reduce all to a definite scheme. She must then plan her work by seasons; she must plan it by days, and by hours in the day. She must make records of the time it takes for each part of the work, and she must think out a way to do it in less time. It will be well if she can arrange it so that different kinds of work will overlap, in order that one thing may be preparing while she is doing something else. And if she finds it a weight upon the mind to keep track of so many things at once, she must yield herself to this discipline, knowing that she is thus training her mind for better service and that she will be more fitted to use to good advantage the extra hours that she will thus gain. She will come to the new cultural duty of the hour she has thus wrung from the working period with increased joy and with new powers gained by the strenuousness of the hour's work that went before.

The administration of a house is to call for a higher training in mechanics. Education is giving much more of this now than formerly and will answer the demand for still more. The girls of the country, where this education is needed far more even than in the city, must be prepared to answer this need.

We cannot be expert in the new housekeeping unless we have some comprehension of the chemical processes that constantly go on under our hands. One young woman took for her master's degree a study of the bacterial flora found in spoiled canned peas and string beans. She found that there are some organisms that only grow all the better after they have been boiled one hour. She found that the strongest acids do not inhibit the growth of some other kinds. She has been a good year working on that theme. If she should include one or two other kinds of spoiled foods her work would extend over another year.

How many kinds of bacterial life are there? How many fruits, vegetables, foods of all sorts, are made the home of these various kinds? What processes will protect each kind from becoming harmful to human life? How many hours will it take to show that certain processes will render each variety a safe food? How many young students must give years to the business of finding out what we may use and what we may not? How long will it take us to realize that the detail of preparing the food for the table is a great scientific study, one deserving our highest expertness, meriting our highest honors, to those who work in the laboratory of the university and to those who labor in the laboratory of the house? Every young woman should consider herself a licensed observer; she should watch every process to see what she may learn of nature's secrets, that she may compare it with what she has read and thus make additions to the sum of knowledge that may be beneficial to all.

It is not alone because foods have as close a connection with our well-being that we should study them. They have in themselves an extraordinary fascination. The daily and hourly companion of the worker in the household should be the magnifying-glass. The dissecting microscope is a form of magnifier that is especially adapted for household use and should be within the reach of every one. To get into the habit of putting all foods to the test of this infallible little instrument gives one a great feeling of safety and comfort. Every bag of oatmeal should be examined, all cereals, especially cornmeal, all products that have been kept in any storehouse, should be thus tested. If all the women of the country would use the magnifying-glass on everything that comes into the house, and promptly reject what is not perfectly clean, the level of good health and long life would rise suddenly by perceptible degrees among our people.

If the prospective household administrator cries out that she cannot be bothered with such little things as these, she will be one of those that will be left behind. Those that *can* be bothered are the people that are to win. The value of the little thing, when it is the pivot for greater things, is one of the discoveries of modern science; and, strangely enough, there is no little thing that is not a pivot for greater things. Our part is to train ourselves to realize this. In the household of the future there will be nothing that the microscope can reveal or the card catalog record that will not be of importance to the success of the whole.

It would be amusing — if it were not so tragic! — to see the utter serenity with which some of the older women will say, "But I have no scientific turn of mind, I do not care for the microscope!" It is as if they said: "But I prefer to murder the members of my family; I do not care to give them the key that will let them out of imprisonment where they have been carelessly but dolorously confined; I have no predilection for dashing away the poison from their lips when unwillingly they are about to drink it!" To such a woman either the word "duty" has no meaning or else she is lacking in instruction as to what duty is. But the coming Country Girl will avoid the mistakes of the past; she will do everything in her power to gain the training that is necessary for her to meet successfully and inspiringly the duties and privileges of the new era.

CHAPTER XV

HEALTH AND A DAY

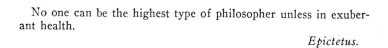

No one can be the highest type of philosopher unless in exuberant health.

Epictetus.

CHAPTER XV

HEALTH AND A DAY

"GIVE me health and a day and I will make ridiculous the pomp of emperors!" cried Emerson.

The ultimate use of health is to make us happy, and the deepest hurt of sickness is that it destroys our power of enjoyment. Moreover, since our happiness when we are at our human best, consists in adding to the welfare and happiness of others, our highest in life is sadly crippled when we allow disease to get the better of us. If we desire to be happy, we should, as the Camp Fire Girls' law says, "hold on to health" and with a tight grip.

It used to be thought that health was a gift of heaven bestowed on certain of its favorites. You had it or you did not have it: that was all there was about it. By pious behavior and prayer perhaps we might gain this benefit from the partial hand of heaven — perhaps not! And if you did anything to help yourself directly to a larger portion of vigor, ate heartily, or took an invigorating walk, you were in danger of indulging a selfish spirit that should be curbed.

We have now changed all that belief. We do know that we may inherit certain disproportions, certain maladies, that interfere with our soundness; these we have to fight against. Knowing them, we can fight intelligently. Our duty lies in taking the resources of strength that we possess, and making the most of them. We are to give ourselves the largest opportunity to make ourselves useful to our friends and to our world in general as much as we may with the portion of vigor that we receive by inheritance, and we are to develop that portion as much as we possibly can. Doing something for ourselves will sometimes be the greatest un-selfishness.

This teaching the Country Girl should take to heart. It is her duty to recognize the great value of her physical vigor to the life of her realm, and to do all in her power to conserve it and to increase it. She should think of this not only because she is of tremendous importance in the home of to-day and because its happiness depends in large measure upon her buoyancy and cheer and hopefulness, which may so easily be increased or diminished by her physical state, but also because she has so great a part in bearing the torch of life to another generation. Let me repeat the words — it is her duty; and again, and yet again let me say it — it is a duty!

It is a duty to exercise every part of the body, the hands, the wrist, the fingers, each finger! Every part of the body has a function and should be prepared for its uses. The lifting muscles, the straightening muscles, the apparatus that pulls and that pushes, that bends and that twists; the machinery for stepping with vibrancy, for going uphill, for going downhill, for walking on the grass, on irregular stony paths, on cement walks; every kind of movement has its special apparatus in this wondrously varied human body and all should be developed and rounded into perfection.

Housework affords a training for more of the body's needs than perhaps any other occupation. The household administrator has an advantage there, and the physical vigor of women in this country ought to increase as they more and more have the opportunity to take up this work in their homes. Probably when every house in the country has mechanical appliances so that there will be enough work in the household and not too much, the health of the nation will increase by leaps and bounds.

At present housework, especially in the country, affords wearying labor which is not so well adapted to the development of physical strength as it might be because it is not systematic. Certain parts of the body are overexercised and certain parts are neglected. The result is frequently a body with a semblance of strength but with, as you might say, strands of weakness, rendering it liable to fall at the least onslaught of infection or unusual strain. These lacks should be made up for by consistently arranged exercises, by carefully studied diet, and by proper sleeping plans, so that there may be rightly developed muscular force — not too much and yet enough; so that there may be perfect circulation; fat enough and not too much; and that there may be a full supply of energy. If the young woman is vain enough to wish not to be portly when she is forty, she must not wait till she is forty-five to go to work at it; she should begin at twenty to train for that special form of beauty; if she does this she will soon express it in trimness, in an energetic and graceful step, in the exact curve of the spinal column at the small of the back, the right lift of the chest beneath the neck, and the perfect position of chin, elbows, shoulder blades, hips, feet, and all the parts of the body, for walking, sitting, standing, running, sleeping, and for every possible activity. Beauty is a thing to be valued and worked for; but a greater motive for the attention necessary to the full development of our physical powers is that we should be able to give to our children the greatest allotment of beauty and vigor that we can possibly command.

Miss Goldmark in her valuable study, *Fatigue and Efficiency,* says that the results of overstrain in the labor of women are manifest in a heightened infant mortality, in a lowered birth rate, and in an impaired second generation. We should take this to heart. Not to make a struggle to increase our store of vigor for the sake of the children that are to be is to do them a great wrong.

For girls under twenty the responsibility of the mother is greater because so much depends upon the establishment of the daughter's health during these earlier years. But girls themselves should take it upon their own responsibil-

ity to a large extent also.   In the appendix to this volume
will be found a bibliography where among the works published by the Young Women's Christian Association, the
girl may find some that will answer many questions that
perhaps have puzzled her in the period of swift growth between fifteen and twenty.

Every mother should be in her daughter's confidence in
regard to all questions of health and physical wellbeing.
And now and then the father should stand his daughters up
in a row before him, look them over, and see for himself
whether they are sound, blooming, well developed and rosy.
Do their chests stand up good and strong?   Is the chin well
down and back?   Are the shoulders well back?   Can they
take full, deep, long breaths?   If they were set back against
the wall, would the hips be close to the wall, the shoulder
blades nearly flat against the wall and would the girls be
perfectly comfortable in that position?   And can they then
walk off, holding the frame in this way, and keep the position firmly and gracefully?   How hard can they hit, how
fast can they run, how high can they jump, how much
can they lift, how free are they from pain, and how happy
are they?   If the answers to these questions are not satisfactory, that farmer's crop of humanity does not take a
prize!   And he should try to know the reason why.   It is
not a lightning streak of divine disfavor that has destroyed
this crop.   It is just as impossible that a woman should have
a beautiful child if she has been the victim of overstrain for
ten years before that child is born, as it would be to get a
good crop from absolutely untilled ground.   The home is
the field for the harvest of children.   That ground must be
cultivated as carefully and assiduously as any other, or the
harvest will bring no honor to the family.

If the young girls in the farmstead do not measure up
to the standard, will they try to do what is in their power
to make themselves more strong, fit, and beautiful?   It will
take six weeks of hard, unremitting work, by night and day

and every hour in the day, to turn a round-shouldered girl into a well-shaped, straight-shouldered, elastic figure. Is it worth while? The result will be a girl with better breathing capacity, more vigor, more beautiful carriage, and in every way better prepared for a happy life. There are some wrongs that are done to the young people by neglect of the laws of health that never can be made up to them. But there is much that can be done, and perhaps it is not too late to correct some errors and to make up for some losses. Health conditions on many farms are not up to the mark and among the causes of this the Report of the Commission on Country Life mentions the too long hours of work. There are of course other causes. Three meals a day of pork and bread, seven days in the week, fifty-two weeks in the year, year in and year out the same, will never produce blooming youngsters, especially if we are speaking of the delicate constitutions of girls. Nor will bedrooms hermetically sealed from air during half of the breathing time, favor development of lung-capacity.

Theoretically, the farm should be the most healthful place for the growth of human beings; and wherever sanitary conveniences are installed, health conditions need no betterment. The point is not that the rural people have declined from a former better condition, but that they have not gone forward so fast as they might. While the residents of cities have at the command of new science been making swift progress in sanitation, working vigorously on the problems of pure food, good water, the suppression of tuberculosis, pellagra and other diseases, the country people have not so swiftly answered the call.

Such movements as, for instance, the one to provide pure milk for babies, lower the death rate in the cities, while the health rate in the country has not shown a corresponding rise. This is simply because the country towns have not waked to the importance of these endeavors toward betterment. The country may be the home of abounding phy-

sical vigor; but many an unsanitary farmstead and many
an unregenerated village is still in a decidedly unmoral state
of ill-health.

In this matter a recent investigation in New York State
has aroused serious apprehension. Statistics were made
public showing that the death rate in so-called rural districts
was increasing as compared with that of the large city, New
York, the conclusion being that the country would have to
give up its world-old claim to being a supremely healthful
place to live.

If, however, we look into the matter more closely, we may
find a ray of hope. The investigation included under the
word "rural" towns of over eight thousand inhabitants,
the divison being no doubt made because of the fact that
the United States reports were, up to 1810, made on a like
basis, and other statistics could be more conveniently compared if these were included. But the census of 1910 makes
the word "rural" cover towns and villages of 2500 and
under, and what we understand by rural conditions pertains
to this smaller grouping. The larger grouping includes a
number of towns that are manufacturing in character, that
sometimes contain a large foreign element, that have the
beginnings of congestion without the open air to offset them,
and that have notoriously not followed in the steps of the
larger cities in sanitation. Thus these very unrural towns
bring down the average.

We feel, then, that we have a right to take heart of
grace and tell ourselves that the open country is as good for
health as it ever was. Moreover, farm houses are rapidly
acquiring the principal appliances for sanitation. The wells
are being looked out for and the pure condition of the
water supply being insured from contagion; and the level
of education in regard to sanitation is being rapidly lifted.
At present, the small towns and the larger villages are about
on a par in regard to indifference to the laws of health, and
to the necessity for framing new ones to meet new demands.

But in the smaller villages and in the open country the necessity is not so pressing because the congestion has not been so immediate as to cause depression of the death rate there.

Therefore we may say that the girl who is born in the open country or in the small village is more likely, all other things being equal, to keep her hold upon life than any other girl in the land.

It is said that sixty per cent. of the school children in the country suffer from removable physical defects. The countryside has its share of these. Fortunately for girls, life force is more persistent with them than with boys, and women are longer-lived than men.

Sometimes fate deprives the home of the mother, and then heavy burdens fall to the daughter, too heavy for her young and undeveloped body. It is then that the young girl feels the necessity for a better understanding of her physical needs. Wanting this, life-long suffering may be the result of undertaking severe labor ere yet her health is thoroughly established or her maximum growth has been gained.

There is much, then, for every young woman on the farm both to study and to practise. The following code of rules is suggested as an aid and as a reminder:

Code of Rules for Maintaining Health

Bodily carriage

Hold the head erect.
Keep the chest high.
Hold the abdomen in.
Rest the weight of the body on the balls of the feet.
Keep this position constantly, by day and by night.
When lying down, stretch out; do not curl up.

Exercise

Make a special study of the proper times for exercise and take a normal amount of it at those times.
Let nothing induce you to undertake severe bodily work or strain when the body is not in a condition to sustain the strain.

When all conditions are right for it, take a good deal of joyous exercise. (No one can regulate this for any girl but the girl herself.)

Learn some systematic exercises and practise them every day.

Systematize the exercise in housework as far as possible and supplement it when needed by long walks and hill-climbing.

Correct breathing

Take long breaths of fresh air on rising and frequently through the day.

Breathe always through the nose and from the diaphragm.

Keep the air in the room fresh by day and by night.

Breathe deeply to keep the mind clear, the blood pure, and the spirits buoyant.

Clothing

Let the weight of clothing hang from the shoulders.

Have the clothing loose enough to allow free play of the diaphragm in breathing and of the limbs in exercise.

Protect the feet and ankles from exposure to wet and cold.

Keep the chest well protected but do not over-wrap the neck.

Food and eating

Have meals absolutely regularly and at proper intervals.

Choose foods adapted to present needs. Study adaptation of foods so as to know how to choose.

Drink at least six glasses of pure water daily, between meals.

Always think and speak of something pleasant while eating.

Elimination of waste

Free the body from poisonous waste by keeping the bowels active.

By keeping the pores of the skin open.

By using a great deal of well-planned, vigorous exercise.

By general cleanliness.

Cleanliness

Take a cold tonic sponge or shower bath every day when in good health.

Take a warm cleansing bath once or twice a week.

Keep the mouth and skin free from dirt and germs.

Give perfect care to the hair and the finger nails.

Wash the hands before eating or serving food.

Brush the teeth at least twice every day — on rising and on retiring; after every meal is better still.

Avoid gathering or spreading disease germs through any form of contact.

Amount of sleep

Ten and one-half hours (8:30 to 7:00) for those 10 to 14 years old.

Ten hours (9:00 to 7:00) for those 14 to 16 years old.

Nine and one-half hours (9:30 to 7:00) for those 16 to 18 years old.

Eight hours (10:00 to 6:00) for those 20 to 30 years old.

Lost sleep must invariably be made up.

Try to go to sleep happy.

Rest

When you work, work efficiently; when you rest, rest efficiently; whatever you do, do it with all your might.

When resting, relax perfectly; let go.

Stop worrying; think of something else; think of something cheerful.

Do not yield to impatience or to anger; they shorten life.

Think pure and beautiful thoughts; learn the beautiful thoughts of others and say them over till they become your own.

Cultivate a well balanced mind; preserve courage and cheer.

Prevention of illness or of a depressed state of health

Study the laws of hygiene and of sanitation.

Avoid patent medicines of all kinds.

When ill, consult a reliable physician.

Prevent illness by following the laws of health and by regular health examinations.

CHAPTER XVI

THE COUNTRY GIRL'S WAGE

" To preserve as things above all price
The old domestic morals of the land,
Her simple manners and her stable worth
That dignified and cheered a low estate,
. . . the character of peace,
Sobriety, and order, and chaste love,
And honest dealing, and untainted speech,
And pure good-will, and hospitable cheer;
That made the very thought of country life
A thought of refuge, for a mind detained
Reluctantly amid the bustling crowd.

Wordsworth.

CHAPTER XVI

THE COUNTRY GIRL'S WAGE

A VISION had certainly visited the soul of a certain fifteen-year-old Country Girl of New York State who claimed that the girls of the present day have a progressive spirit, and that if this spirit of progress is not found on the farm, they will seek it in the city. The bearing of this spirit on the question of the Country Girl's wage has made her think more deeply and feel more keenly than words can express. She cannot resist the conclusion that unless the young people are paid definite wages for the work they do on the farm, it will not seem to them that they are getting on so well as they might in a city office. This is a delicate diagnosis of a very painful trouble.

Many of the girls realize that the tenure of industry in the city is light for the person that comes unprepared for it; many realize that the dangers are thickly set about her path; many know well that the lure of the city is to be valiantly resisted; but the majority, being but little accustomed to the handling of money, and having sadly little instruction as to real values, cannot see why eight dollars a week gained in some city industry does not represent a fortune. In making her budget at home the cost of rental and food have not been taken into account, and she has never been made to realize what these items mean in the new environment. Parents and teachers and ministers and all sober people in the farming community are cruelly to blame for the ineptitude of their neglect in leaving these things unimpressed upon the mind of the young women in the community and for not watching out for the strangers who may fill their minds with glowing descriptions not founded on fact about the abundant opportunity and the free and enjoyable life to be found in the walks of city work and play. " Let the child earn money, have money, spend money, save money," advised a country mother; and if this were done, wisely and all the time, from earliest years up, the boys and girls would not come to the age of question and desire with so little preparation for its responsibilities.

From a wide correspondence with Country Girls in many parts of America, the conclusion is forced upon us that very few of them, even when mature and hard-working young women, are receiving definite pay for their service to the household. They are doing a wage-worthy work but they are not paid for it. Instead the fathers think their duty is done when they give to the daughters as a benevolence what they, the fathers, think the daughters should have for their needs and pleasures. Meantime there is a new thing under the sun, namely, an awakening of the desire for economic independence in the soul of woman, and the younger women on the farms are partaking of this spirit. Result, the cityward procession! Some medieval daughters have not heard of this new spirit, but they will hear of it and they also will be stirred with a divine discontent.

Many girls gain time and permission to enter into some earning work outside of the home. The money that they thus gain they generally feel that they may lay claim to and use it as they think best. At any rate, the fear that it will not be understood that they do have what they earn leads them sometimes to emphasize the fact that they do positively consider what they earn outside of the home as their very own. Public opinion is ahead of law in this respect. A father who took legal means to take the earnings of a son under age, was quietly told that the village would be too small for him hereafter. Perhaps we have not come to the point where this would invariably happen in the case of a daughter.

The daughter as she grows up should have a reasonable

sum of money to spend as she likes; this is essential as a matter of education, to prepare her for the responsibilities that are to be hers as one of the great body of spenders. She should grow up with a fully trained power to spend money wisely. And when she becomes mature, if she is strong enough to do a full-grown woman's work, she should have her self-respect educated and cultivated by receiving the sum of money that would be her fair wage if she were not a member of the family. Moreover, a father may attach his children to himself in a very real and spontaneous service, if he will allow each child, including the daughters, to be responsible for some part of the farm business, to own a piece of land or some of the livestock, and to control the produce thereof. This will be the best way to train them not only to understand the problems of the farm but to feel that interest that comes only through possession and responsibility. The daughter will be as keenly responsive under this method as the son.

Dr. Anna Howard Shaw in a recent address made a good point. It was in effect something like this: She said that if the farmer gave his son a colt, not a scrub colt but one of the very best on the farm to be all his own and to do with as he chose, that colt would tie the boy to the farm as nothing else could unless it was a share of the farm itself. The same, she said, was true in regard to the girl who went out to milk the cows because that was part of her duty, without having any heart or interest in the result of the milking; but if she were given a cow, one of the best of the herd as her own, she would not only be interested in the milking of that one, but all the cows she milked would give more milk — she would do all her work better because of the interest she took in the work.

This is not saying that either the girls or the boys are unconscientious in their work and will not do well unless they have a selfish motive; it is only to say that they are human beings and all the more like grown-up people. Dr.

Shaw added as her opinion that the ownership of the boy
and girl should not end merely with the colt and the cow.
Each year they should feel that a certain percentage of the
net profits of the work should belong to them, and that
they were having a chance to accumulate, even though it
was only a very small part of the income a year.

"If I had a farm and had sons and daughters on it,"
said Dr. Shaw, "I would sit down and discuss the whole
matter of the work of the farm with them, and agree upon
a certain share of the net and then let each one have his or
her share, and encourage them to invest it, but leave them
free to use their own judgment as to the investment. Until something of this sort is done, I am afraid that the boys
and girls more and more will turn from the farm to the
city; and who can well blame them, even though it costs
them more to live in the city than they can make? Sometimes one feels happier in spending every dollar he has
merely to live, if he is free to spend it as he wishes, than
he would to save if he were not free."

This wisdom may sound a little utopian, at any rate as
far as Country Girls are concerned. Very few girls are
assigned any pecuniary share in the farm. Now and then
one remembers that she once had several calves that were
"called" her own; but she does not remember ever receiving
any money from that stock. A mother will share the precious egg-money with the daughter. One girl confessed to
owning a tree, and one a canary. Another mentioned as
her pecuniary share in the farm the fact that she helped
milk! Nearly all would agree with Dr. Shaw that having
a share in the ownership would make them more enthusiastic
for the success of the farm.

If the young woman in the farmstead would be more systematic in the use of what money she can command, perhaps she would the sooner be trusted with greater financial
responsibility. It certainly is a motive in many parental
minds that the children—they still seem to be children in

the thoughts of some parents even when they have reached years of discretion — are not wise enough to use money discretely. Often they are not, but whose fault is it? If children were trained in the use of money from childhood up, they would not be so foolish when the time comes for putting this discipline into practise. Parents should remember that they are sure to wish some time to have a wise, careful son to lean upon. Then they will wish they had trained the child properly. The same is true of the daughter. There is nothing more certain than that the daughters in the wide countryside are being brought up in the main with very little inkling of business. Now any girl that has gone as far in her education as to spell and to compute fractions is quite far enough to be taught the meaning of a deed. And not long after that she should know the force of the little word "warranty" or "full covenant" or "quitclaim" written before the word "deed." She should understand something of the meaning of the fell term "mortgage"— something besides the fact that when it is mentioned everybody is expected to weep. If young women grew up with a more common-sense attitude toward this vital subject, the word would be robbed of some, at least, of its terrors. In just a few years those young women will be the distributors of the income for a whole family; they are to be the conservators of the saving for the fatal day of interest-paying. If they understood more of the practical working of the matter, the saving would be approached with less dismay.

Does it not seem reasonable to suppose that if a girl is made to see the relation of "overhead charges" to the "cost of living," if she has been taken into family confidence with regard to the business of the farm, and has been made to understand the difference between the basis for a girl's wages in town and that in the farm home, she will not run away under a fatal misunderstanding of conditions there?

Moreover the girl of to-day is to be the home-conserver of to-morrow.   Since the woman is the fore-ordained overseer of the whole business of spending, we may say that her failure to save and to plan and to adapt, has been the cause of all our trouble.   It makes no difference to the women of the countryside that the women of the cities are more culpable in these things than are they; their affair is their own, and their duty is to attain not some one else's ideal, but their own.

The model home-conserver will have the budget for the year put into shape; she will know all the items of rent, interest on mortgages (if the family are so unfortunate as to have these troublesome things to look after), the dates when the fatal inroad has to be made into the cherished store of savings, the days when the various taxes are due — the inheritance, county, village, water and other special taxes — and all other payments that belong in the system of support that the farm or village home requires.   She must know that the thing to be aspired to and looked forward to is that at the end of the year the financial income and outgo should accurately balance.   The young woman who neglects her own small account will not be preparing herself for these larger responsibilities; and she must be able to make this small one balance if she expects to do the same with the greater one.   The comfort of having it come out right once will be an incentive ever after; and the effect upon character of compelling one's self to keep steadily to the task of mental accuracy, of remembering each item and of putting it down quickly before it has escaped, will be incalculable.   It is not a matter of mere idiosyncrasy that a young girl may say, " Oh, I cannot keep my accounts and make them come out right — it's too much trouble for just me! "   To have to confess this should be considered a disgrace.   One should conceal the disinclination to this duty, as one should conceal a disinclination to give one's hair the thorough weekly washing which that passion for cleanness that is the mark of the true lady calls for. It is impossible for a young girl of right instincts to say, " Oh, I would just as lief be an unclean person! " So it should be impossible for the young girl of right feeling to say, " Oh, I would willingly be a lazy, ineffective and partly dishonest person in my understanding of business! " — for slackness and inaccuracy in business are the next door to dishonesty. In all finances, to the remotest penny, the rightly constituted girl will be accurate. If necessity compels her to borrow a small sum, she will repay it at the earliest possible moment.

It is not the mark of a fine woman to be careless in spending; quite the contrary. The young woman who has intellectuality and training and taste to compute her expenses carefully, to use the money to good advantage and to the best purpose, is the young woman of higher grade, not the one who wastes, who scatters carelessly and purposelessly, and who indulges in things costing much and affording no permanent good. Our ideal in these respects needs some right-about-face orders from our conscience. " Saving," says Professor Martha Van Rensselaer at Cornell University, " cultivates self-control, imagination, resourcefulness, character." She continues: " It is quite right to economize on some standbys and then spend more for some esthetic object, if the esthetic better satisfies a real craving connected with the higher life. . . . It is not meanness to study economy; it is not ' near ' to avoid waste. To work out new uses that may be made of every particle of food, to get the full food-value out of every bit of it, is scientific exactness instead."

It is possible that all the skill of the woman in the farm home will be needed as time goes on to keep the financial foundations of the farmstead firm. A long look forward seems to discern on the horizon a rising necessity for greater care, and perhaps for all the skill that the farm women and other women of the next generation can master. Why should Nature go on interminably caring for a people who indulge themselves so heedlessly, so criminally in waste, cutting away their forests, throwing away good food, refusing to use the supplies of electric power in their rivers? Of course she will not. Disciplines are before us. It is the part of wisdom to use greater stringency and more scientific exactness in our household systems, that disaster may not come upon us unprepared.

Some prevision of this may be in the minds of women when they endeavor to give themselves a bit of training for direct money-earning business. For them, and especially the younger women, openings are being made in almost every direction. A woman is no longer to be accused of a tastelessly commercial spirit if she desires to know through actual experiment the value of her labor in the commercial rating of the community. It is only by trying that she can thus standardize her labor. If she offers cabbage plants from her growing patch, honey from her bee-colonies, wild fruit that she has gathered from God's free gardens, if she takes boarders, weaves hair, embroiders, or mends, if she takes advantage of postal service and builds up a business in fine lace-laundering, or silk and lingerie waist cleansing, whatever she takes in hand, she is not only earning a little money, but she has gained skill in manipulation, developed taste, compelled herself to seek excellence, and strengthened her character by putting her work — and that means herself — to the test of comparison with the work of others to stand or fall by the decision. If she has failed in this test, she has the chance to try harder and gain more character in further struggle.

All this should be looked upon as a part of the girl's training for life. When parents have presented to the human family a highly developed and trained young woman as their contribution, they should expect her to desire to be a worker and to take up some form of activity as the beginning, in turn, of her personal contribution. Professor Nearing says that every girl should occupy the years between the latest school days and her marriage in some wage-earning pursuit.   There should be two or three years there that she could spend in this part of her education.   She should thus learn business law, the stringency of markets, the balance of purchase and sale, the interchange of commercial motive, and the art of salesmanship.   Here will be a great field of training for her, and every part of it will be useful to her when she enters upon the duties of her own house and home.

The best way for any girl to start upon this means of discipline, is to think over what she can already do well. What have you been praised for doing?   Take that and try to do it still better.   What you best like to do will be the easiest to start with.   Do this so well that people will desire the product.   People buy what they think is most excellent: therefore make something so excellent that people will want to buy it.   And remember this principle: the *appearance* of anything offered for sale has a great deal to do with whether people will take a liking to it or not.   Do up all things nicely; make all packages neat and shipshape; use color if possible; have the box and the cord match in tint; humor the fancy of the buyer.   At a certain country fair the girls in one particular booth had great success.   Why?   Their voices were sweet and they themselves were neatly dressed. But above all, the packages were done up so deftly and looked so beautiful when they were handed out that it was not difficult to understand the success of this booth.   Buyers want a good product, but they do like it in a fine package.

A beautiful enthusiasm for Canning Club work comes from the South.   Joined with many other good things that come inevitably with the organization of young life, it has enriched and blest the girls incalculably.   Writing to me of this, one woman said: " It has done more to stir the Southern girls from the lethargy into which so many of them had fallen than anything else I can think of."   In reply to an inquiry, Mr. O. H. Benson, in charge of Canning

Club Work for the U. S. Department of Agriculture, wrote: " During the present year there are about 250,000 boys and girls enrolled in club projects in the United States who are receiving special follow-up instruction and who are organized on the federated basis, making them members not only of their own local community but of the State and national movement.   About half of these are girls who are doing work with poultry, home gardening or the canning club project work."   Mr. Benson was kind enough to lend me the photograph of the young lady with the two Jersey calves.   She is Miss Myrtle Hardin, of Camden, Tennessee, a girl fifteen years of age, who has been a member of the Gardening and Canning Club of the State for four years. The two Jersey calves were won as premiums for having the best records for Club Work in the State Fair for 1912 and 1913.   Mr. Benson gives a list of the prizes she won, and of the educational trips she has taken, and adds: " Besides this, she has earned from her work several hundred dollars which she deposited in the bank and will use to pay her expenses to attend college and take a domestic science course."

This efficient girl so interested me that I wrote her and asked her to tell me herself something about her achievements that I might hand it on as an inspiration to other girls.   She wrote me this delightful account:

The Tomato Club has meant more to me than I am able to tell. My two years' experience has taught me how to prepare nice things for the table, how to beautify the home, and how to make life in the country attractive and happier. Nothing has done more to train my mind than our Club work. I have read bulletins, cookbooks, books on home-making and domestic science, and dozens of different papers and magazines in the two years' work. I have written histories of my crops, and compiled " Tomato Recipe " booklets, and " The Life History of the Tomato "; and have drawn the plan, complete, of my home and grounds. On all of the above I won First Prizes in my State and County.

I have as a result of my two years' work two Jersey calves, 17

This Tennessee girl is a member of a Gardening and Canning Club. She won the cow and calves as premiums for having the best exhibit at the State Fair.

Springtime in the country. City children may well envy their little country cousins the free life in the open and the companionship with animals.

Indian Runner ducks, raised from a pair I won last year, a pen of thoroughbred chickens, a fireless cooker, a cut glass bowl, and a great many small prizes, as well as some cash which I won at different places. I love best of all my calves, ducks and chickens and hope to tell you some ups and downs with them some time.

I have always been a " Benton County country girl," and love the farm and its life. I had been out of my county but twice when I became a Club member. In the last two years I have traveled in ten different States — but still like Tennessee best of all. I have also visited a great many large cities, our National Capital being one.

Last year, Miss Moore said I could go, as First Prize Winner, with four other girls to the National Corn Show at Columbia, S. C. We spent a delightful day in Atlanta, a week in Columbia, and two days in Charleston on this trip, besides stopping at several other cities for a few hours. O how grand the Atlantic looked and how majestic its ships ! I thought then that a Tomato Club girl could be no more highly favored than I.

But this year when Miss Moore wrote me that I had been selected to go to Washington it seemed too good to believe. What a delightful time we had, girls and boys from Michigan to Florida and from South Carolina to Oregon. The greatest people in the land showed us that they thought we too had some degree of greatness because we were " Good Farmers and had a purpose in life." We were not ashamed of our work, either, for I presented " The Highest Lady in The Land " some of my canned goods, and she very graciously accepted them and told us she was proud of " her girls." As a final treat Miss Moore carried me to New York where we met some lovely people and spent two days full of interest and sight-seeing. Then home in time for Christmas.

Some have asked me how I won. I don't know, but my County Agent says, " It's because you TRY to do everything you are told to do in the work, and do it like you are told." That may be true. I advise every Club girl to do no less than this anyway.

Full information about the work of Canning Clubs for girls may be obtained by any one who will write to the Department at Washington or directly to Mr. Benson, and ask for circulars on the subject. Many of the State Agricultural Colleges, also, have bulletins on the subject.

In all these wage-earning endeavors there is but one caution to be thought of beforehand. We should remember that when a young woman is working in the kitchen of the farm home, she is doing a wage-worthy work fully as much as when she is offering to some outside market. Now if she undertakes to make use of some by-product of the farm, if she cans the waste vegetables, reclaims them to common use, and standardizes the product, will not this new industry march into the factory as the others have, and will not the woman in the home be left without her wage as before? Unless the right principle underlies the business of canning, this will surely come to pass. There is no reason why the housework should not be standardized and brought under the law of economic production; there is no reason why a new sort of canning should be left in the unregulated realm for the benefit of the woman's whim for a work of her own. It shall surely not escape commercialization. The rag carpet, now a cheapened factory product, should be a warning to women. What we should work for is not the enclosing of a certain piece of work with bars that we may get our hands upon it, but the establishment of economic laws that shall make women free to work wherever their taste and abilities incline them.

For the Country Girl in her plans for a future life of healthful, satisfying labor, the pathway to this better order lies over the rocky pavement of household systemization and scientific budget-making.

CHAPTER XVII

THE DRESS BUDGET

There is that scattereth and yet increaseth; and there is that withholdeth more than is meet and it tendeth to poverty.

Proverbs.

Except a corn of wheat fall into the ground and die, it abideth alone; but if it die, it bringeth forth much fruit.

St. Paul.

Even the Son of Man came not to be ministered unto but to minister.

Jesus.

CHAPTER XVII

THE DRESS BUDGET

THE Country Girl has this advantage — the business of the farm and the home are so closely connected that the work she has to do can be carried on without separating her from her home. This would not be so in any work she could undertake in the city. She would not have a great big house to return to from her store or factory, but some little upstairs room, the " hall-bedroom " of that tragic book *The Long Day,* which so painfully portrays the conditions of work for girls in a great city. The Country Girl in her home with her housework about her is in a paradise compared with conditions such as these.

The " home " means rent, board, general living expenses — all these are looked out for in the scheme of life for the Country Girl. Why, then, does she feel so great a need for sheer money? The reason is partly this: she has the dress problem on her hands. She is scantily supplied with a bit now and then when she asks for a cloak or some other garment; she is not assigned a certain sum a month, as her self-respecting spirit demands, and left free to use it as her judgment directs. She has not been trained to do this and the fear that she will not do it wisely keeps the father from inaugurating such a system. In the long run, after the daughter has gained wisdom from a few mistakes with the suffering resulting therefrom, the outgo from the parental pocket would not be much increased by adopting the educative method of letting her have the personal management of her little budget. Few fathers can bear to see a daughter really suffer; most fathers will not let her even foolishly think that she is suffering, and a plea from her will generally bring an indulgence in some unnecessary purchase.

The problem is intricate and has many sides; but we believe the best way for the father to take would be to place a set sum at her command with the injunction that she is to plan and use it carefully — and make it do! If the parent is able to go so far in the process of education as to start her on a cash account and oversee her as she tries to carry it on, especially if he will initiate her in the mysteries of a small bank account, he will in the majority of cases be richly repaid in the development of an ability to manage and to save that he did not suspect the daughter to possess.

The father himself, in the happy-go-lucky method of most fathers in their financial relations with the women of the family, does not know what the daughter's dress budget for a year ought to be. The following lists of items for a country girl's dress budget are presented here as much for the father's sake as for that of the girls. The lists have been drawn from various sources and they represent the thought of many students of country life conditions and of some country girls themselves.

The first list was made by a wide-awake Country Girl in the State of Idaho:

LIST OF CLOTHING FOR A YEAR, FOR A GIRL IN HIGH SCHOOL

1 suit for best for 1 year, coat for best 2 years	$15.00
1 winter coat	6.00
1 winter hat for best	2.50
1 winter hat for school, a felt knock-about	1.00
1 spring coat or party wrap	6.50
1 summer hat	3.00
1 pair gloves, seldom worn here except on Sundays	1.50
1 pair golf gloves	.50
4 pairs shoes	10.00
8 pairs of stockings	.80
2 pairs rubbers	1.30
2 suits underclothing, winter	1.80
2 suits underclothing, summer	.70

3 underskirts, white	2.25
1 underskirt, knitted	.50
1 silk underskirt	1.98
2 pairs corsets	3.00
6 corset covers	1.50
4 waists (not worn much)	3.00
1 worsted skirt	1.98
1 linen skirt	.98
2 gingham wash dresses	2.00
1 princess slip	1.00
Miscellaneous, per year of nine months	9.00
	$77.79

She adds this note: " Some figures are guessed at, for I make and remake my clothes always. Note that the suit is not necessary. Needless to mention these figures are doubled and even trebled by some thoughtless girls of poor but long-suffering parents. I earn my own money."

The following meager list represents, I am sure, the thought of a girl who has been accustomed to the least that could possibly be got along with:

DRESS FOR A VILLAGE GIRL GOING TO SCHOOL

2 woolen combination suits	$ 3.00
1 corset waist	.50
2 flannelette petticoats	1.00
1 black petticoat	1.50
1 waist	3.00
1 dress skirt	3.00
1 woolen dress	3.00
1 winter hat	3.00
1 pair gloves	1.00
6 pairs of stockings	1.50
2 pairs of rubbers	.80
2 pairs of shoes	6.00
1 winter coat	10.00
1 spring coat	7.00
6 handkerchiefs	.99
	$45.29

The following is quoted with permission from a valuable little leaflet prepared by Miss Caroline D. Pratt, of Hampton Institute, Hampton, Virginia, and shows what the prices would be for a girl in the southern realm:

SUGGESTIONS FOR CLOTHING FOR SCHOOL GIRLS

6 undervests (summer)	$ .60
4 undervests (winter)	1.00
4 pair drawers, homemade	.80
2 white petticoats, homemade	1.00
3 nightgowns, homemade	1.65
4 underwaists, homemade	1.00
1 gingham petticoat, homemade	.40
2 short flannel petticoats, homemade	.70
6 plain shirt waists, homemade	2.40
1 white percale dress skirt, homemade	.55
1 gingham dress, homemade	1.00
1 muslin dress, homemade	1.50
4 gingham aprons, homemade	.72
2 white aprons, homemade	.60
4 pairs stockings	1.00
1 pair low shoes	2.50
1 pair high shoes	3.00
1 pair corsets	.50
1 hat	2.00
1 wool skirt	3.00
1 suit	12.50
1 rain-coat	3.00
1 pair rubbers	.60
1 umbrella	1.00
4 collars	.40
12 handkerchiefs	1.20
1 pair gloves, lisle	.25
1 pair gloves, wool	.25
Belts, neckties	1.50
	$46.62

This list has been very carefully thought out, it is evident; but while the sum is small, we believe that it would be difficult to get clothing of good material at these figures. For instance, the corset. A fifty-cent corset cannot easily be made to last a year; and it would probably be of such a shape that it would be injurious rather than helpful to the wearer. Perhaps something else could be substituted for that, however; that should be studied out by the Country Girls.

To this budget Miss Pratt adds a page of suggestions that are so useful that we are glad to have more girls read them. Here they are:

WHAT A WELL-DRESSED GIRL WEARS TO SCHOOL

Neat, plain, shirt waists.

Plain, well-made, cotton or wool dresses.

Plain, short, wool skirt. Good material will last longer and prove more economical in the end.

Clean, plain, well-mended, durable underwear. If trimmed, use cambric ruffles, lace, or embroidery of good quality. Torchon lace wears well and is cheap.

Clean collars and neckties.

Neckties and belts should either match or harmonize with skirt or waist.

Hair neatly and becomingly dressed, not extreme.

Clean hands and finger nails.

Plainly trimmed hat.

Plain, serviceable coat.

Neat, comfortable shoes.

Neat gloves.

Old gloves and shoes are neat when clean and carefully mended.

WHAT A WELL-DRESSED GIRL DOES NOT WEAR TO SCHOOL

Elaborate shirt waists or dresses.

Jewelry.

Low shoes and thin stockings in winter.

Bright, gay colors.

Petticoats longer than dress skirt.

Dusty, spotted clothes.

Fussy neckwear.

Soiled shirt waist and collar.

Dresses or underwaists cut too low.

Short sleeves in winter.

Coats, dresses, skirts, or waists whose buttons or hooks and eyes are lacking.

Holes in stockings.

Safety-pin showing beneath the belt.

From a report by Miss Caroline Gleason, Director of Social Survey for the Consumers' League of Oregon, is copied,
with permission, a carefully made list representing conditions in the Northwest:

1 winter coat	$ 15.00
1 suit	18.00
1 extra skirt	5.00
2 dark waists	4.00
4 white waists	4.00
2 dark underskirts	2.00
4 suits summer underwear	2.00
3 suits winter underwear	3.00
1 dozen pair stockings	3.00
2 pair corsets	3.00
4 corset covers	2.00
1½ dozen cotton handkerchiefs	.90
4 pair gloves	4.00
4 pair shoes	10.00
1 pair rubbers	.50
1 umbrella	1.00
3 hats	6.00
1 party dress	10.00
3 white underskirts	4.50
2 summer dresses	10.00
	———
	$107.90

Miss Gleason adds: "In making out a budget for the
cost of the Country Girl's clothes, I would feel it necessary
to consider whether they were procured in the city at city
prices (through mail order houses) or in the country store.
My reason for saying this is that, judging from my slight
experience, country prices are higher than city prices even
with postage attached."

These Western and Southern reports may be supplemented
by two that come from New England. The first of these
is made by Miss L. G. Chase, Social Worker in Providence,
Rhode Island, and represents a great deal of thought and

experience. It may be called final for that part of the country. It is as follows:

Underwear —

Winter — 3 union suits at 75c (cotton and wool) ....$ 2.25
Summer — 3 shirts at 25c .... .75
    3 pair drawers (made at home) at 25c .... .75
Two outing-flannel petticoats, 5 yds. at 11c .... .55
Two outside petticoats, 5 yds. at 9c .... .45
One ferris-waist 1.00
One pair garters .... .20
Four nightdresses (estimated) 2.00

Coats, hats, gloves —

Summer coat 6.98
Winter school hat 1.50
Winter hat (best) 4.50
Summer hat (every day) 3.50
Two pair gloves 2.00

Rubbers, shoes, stockings —

One pair rubbers .... .75
One pair high shoes 3.75
One pair low shoes 2.50
Repairs to shoes 1.20
Eight pair stockings (estimated) 1.63

Dresses —

Summer — 4 yds. gingham at 50c — Trimming 23c (best
    dress) 2.23
  Gingham dress, 6 yds. at 9c — Trimmings 23c .... .77
  White middy blouse and skirt — 5 yds. material at
    12½c .... .63
Fall and winter
  Blue ratinée — 4½ yds. at 25c, trimming and girdle
    65c 1.78
  Brown corduroy — 6 yds. at 50c, trimming $1.00 .. 4.00
Three shirt-waists — 2½ yds. each at 12½c .... .94
One pongee waist
  (Made from dress of mother, estimated value of waist
    to take its place) 1.00
Handkerchiefs, collars, ties, etc. (estimated) 3.00
                                                    ————
                                            $50.61

Left over for use for another year —

Winter coat,
Sweater,
White panama hat,
White dress,
Princess slip,
Corset cover,
Blue serge dress,
Black and white check dress,
Gingham dress,
House dress.

The second New England budget was prepared by a group of girls at the Agricultural College of Connecticut, most of whom came from the country. The scheme is made for three years' wear and is given with the caption that the girls themselves chose.

A THREE-YEAR BUDGET

SUITABLE FOR A SIXTEEN TO EIGHTEEN YEAR OLD GIRL LIVING IN THE
COUNTRY AND ATTENDING A NEIGHBORING HIGH SCHOOL, WITH
THE ADVANTAGE OF SHOPPING IN THE CITY.

To be attractive is not to attract attention. In choosing her clothes, a young girl at school must consider style, suitability, durability, neatness, and cost. Cheap materials should not be chosen merely because they are cheap, for in the end a high-priced material is often cheaper than a low-priced one.

8 light-weight unionsuits at 25c ....$	2.00
5 heavy-weight knit unionsuits at $1.00	5.00
8 corset covers (plain) at 25c	2.00
4 corset covers (fancy) at 60c	2.40
1 princess slip	1.25
3 white petticoats at $1.50	4.50
2 dark petticoats at $1.00	2.00
4 summer nightgowns (of long cloth or nainsook) at 85c	3.40
3 winter nightgowns (of outing-flannel) at 62c ..	1.86
6 pairs corsets at $1.00	6.00

4 waists (made at home of material easily laundered) at 50c 2.00
4 waists at $1.50 .... 6.00
1 heavy skirt 5.00
5 cotton dresses at $1.25 .... 6.25
1 dress (silk) 8.00
3 dresses, woolen material at $3.50 .... 10.50
1 suit (coat and skirt) 22.50
1 heavy skirt 5.00
1 sweater 5.00
1 heavy coat 18.00
1 light coat 6.00
1 raincoat 5.00
4 winter hats 11.50
4 summer hats 15.00
2 pairs silk gloves 2.00
4 pairs heavy gloves 4.00
4 ties at 25c 1.00
24 handkerchiefs 4.25
9 pairs stockings at 50c 4.50
18 pairs stockings at 25c 4.50
8 pairs shoes at $2.50 .... 20.00
6 pairs overshoes at 70c 4.20
Extras: hairpins, tooth-brushes, shoe-polish, various toilet articles 6.00
Extras: ribbons, velvet, collars, etc. 12.00

Dress budget for three years $218.61
Dress budget for one year ....$ 72.87

These various budgets are given that we may be sure to have some approach to a standard for each part of the country. But it is of course possible that none of them will meet the case of a great many of the girls. However, the hope is that they may at least give the suggestion that it is a useful thing to make such a list in order that a girl may thus be able to see at a glance what she is doing with her money; and when she is looking forward into the year ahead she may feel an inspiration to plan beforehand and thus forestall the disaster that so surely follows poor investment. The first principle of efficiency is to put in a pin, as it were, at a certain point, so that one may see what point has been reached and so be helped to decide whether it can be surpassed another time.

Let this chapter be a help to put in such a pin, to set something like an ideal of what is possible in the matter of reasonable dress. It may also aid the daughter to know what she may fairly expect her father to supply for her needs. It may help the well-meaning father to realize what he must do if his children are able to hold up their heads in the community. The rank of the head of the family is often reckoned by the appearance of the wife and child. Some of these lists are evidently made for a girl whose father may be marked by the daughter's dress as a man of less position and generosity and fairness than he imagines himself to be. That state of things can easily be corrected. On the other hand, the girl that has time for sewing, and the cleverness and training to do it, should take delight in making her clothing for herself. Given those antecedent conditions, the Country Girl's dress will thus be not only less expensive, but also better adapted to herself, and more charming because more individual.

CHAPTER XVIII

FOUNDING A HOME

The woman that can in the midst of her rigid daily duties fall on her knees and thank God for the dim, black forests which are the eternal fans of nature, for the rain that appeases the thirst of the birds of the air, and the newly sown seed in the fields, that can feel amid these natural objects awe, admiration, a sense of infinite force, of boundless life, of duration that is eternal in its broad and human sweep, leaving her stunned with the realization of her pigmied self in the presence of these veritable facts, and at the same time filling her with a deep, maternal pride that she, too, is a living, necessary factor in God's world of Rural Life is the one that possesses the power to rise above the common drudgeries of daily existence. She knows that the secret of the beautiful and simple life is to make oneself a symbol of heavenly life.

— Sigismund von Eberstadt.

CHAPTER XVIII

FOUNDING A HOME

THERE is one thing that may not be mentioned by any Country Girls even in their dearest confidences, but that we may for a surety know: it is that every one of them looks forward to the making of her own home. Yes; every one has her dream of a " hope chest "; and as she wanders about her home community she is looking here and there to see what hillside or what sightly place on the plain will be the destined location for her home. Like the wise woman in Proverbs, she, in imagination, buildeth her house beforehand, and thinks it all out according to the scope of her ideals.

These ideals that are cherished in the thoughts of the young woman are her most valuable possessions. They are the blossoming of the best that she has received from her education, her surroundings in the home, the advice of her elders, the influence of the books she has read, the music she has heard and has made, the plays she has seen and the poetry she has learned. They are the inherited result of long years of experience on the part of the race; and perhaps in no place is the best that past centuries have garnered to be found more assimilated and concentrated than in the country home in America.

In the history of the evolution of society we recall that woman was assigned no small place. In those early eons of the long slow growth of society, she was the creator of the home; she was the master of the mysteries of fire and of household devices; she was the carrier, the lapidary, the builder, the inventor, the harvester, the tiller of the soil;

she was the weaver, the skin dresser, the maker and mender of clothing, the hewer of wood and the drawer of water; she was the linguist and instructor of girls; she was a prophetess and a founder of religion; she went into battle with the fighting men and she deliberated in the council of the tribe. She had her full share in the creation of a social order.

To dwell upon the history of domestic evolution will perhaps encourage the young woman of to-day to step forward and shoulder the responsibilities that belong to her. But the young woman in the rural field has at present a special difficulty. If the better and more adventurous among the rural young men withdraw to the city, the choice of the young women that remain is restricted. Indeed many may continue unmarried because of the lack of companionship of their own caliber. This situation should work several ways; to the young men who are tempted to run away to city life, it should be an incitement to stay where their true home is; it should also be an inspiration to the youths remaining in the home village when the less loyal or the more enterprising young men have departed, to build up efficiency in every possible way, so that they may make themselves more acceptable and successful in the social field of the community.

But as to the girls themselves — ay, there's the rub! Difficult as the problem always is for any young woman, it is doubly so for her in the country to-day. Under these circumstances, what the dignified position for her to take is hazardous to say.

There is no use in trying to minimize the great importance of the problem. The advance or the deterioration of the community depends on the mental and physical health of the race. In order that a home may be successfully founded; that it may carry on the best traditions and improve upon them, it should be made by the best possible choice of each other on the part of those that form it.

Back of these best possible choices must lie the highest ideals and the courage to demand the fulfilment of these ideals. For the characteristics of the children in any home will be formed by the characteristics of both the parents. Therefore, the quality and character of both parents will determine whether the race shall ascend in the scale of being or shall decline and deteriorate. The young may not choose for their own pleasure alone; they should choose also for the sake of the whole race and its hopes and aspirations. They must develop themselves; they must make themselves and keep themselves sound and well-trained and in good trim not for their own joy in living, not even solely for the benefit of those about them, but for the strength and success of those who are to live after them.

It is for this reason that the choice is so momentous. And it is not to be wondered at that many young men and young women find the years of youthful decisions fraught with an almost tragic significance.

In the present state of social evolution, the burden of choice seems to rest chiefly upon the young man. But is it really so? Professor Scott Nearing asks the question and then makes the suggestion that though the conventionally modest young woman of to-day may shrink from the thought that she should take the lead in this matter of selection, still she may unconsciously and instinctively do so after all. The same suggestion is strongly urged by another educational authority. One of the wise men of Illinois, a man of culture, an educationalist and a close observer of life, writes as follows: " What the country girl most needs and wants is a larger opportunity for social development. Her life is isolated, her friends limited. She has little choice when she selects a husband from the home community. I almost wish custom would permit her to make the proposal, for I feel sure that she could do so more intelligently, and better results would obtain." We have indeed a mighty precedent in the earliest days of our national story for the initiative of the woman. "Why don't you speak for yourself, John?" has been said once, and it can be said again.

But then again, would the state of things be bettered if this important initiative were placed equally in the hands of women and men? Would the young men suffer themselves to be ensnared by the unbelated suggestion, remain in the rural environment and found their homes there? Would they allow themselves to be tied down in a place where they do not desire to be? And who would want to tie them down, anyway? The wings of Lord Love are tremendously energetic, especially when bound by artificial cords. In questions like these we must wait until we have seen what the young folks have done before we make up our minds what is right to do; and especially to-day when the boys and girls are suffering from the neglects of the last generation. The people who have just passed off the stage allowed education, science, recreation, good times, hospitality, and spiritual life to drag behind; now the younger farm people of to-day are feeling the results. We must look to the new life, the new methods, the new community spirit of to-morrow to make things over so that there shall spring up perfectly balanced homes all along the countryside with such attraction in home and community that no one can possibly be lured away. In this reorganization of community life, as we have seen, the Country Girl has a great share and duty. And one of the greatest services she can perform will be to cherish in her own heart the highest ideals as to the right and necessary construction of a home in the character of the parents, and to hold everybody on whom she has any influence in the community to those ideals as strictly as she possibly can. For it would be indeed far better for her and for her part in the onflowing life stream of racial progress if she should dwell unmarried, run her own farm, and fill her house with the laughter of some unmothered and unfathered children who would no doubt repay her with love and service and honor as devotedly as if they had been children of her very own, as if she should unite in a family plan that by carrying on impure or diseased influences would contribute to the degradation of the race, and increase the misery of the world.

Though hampered with some disabilities, the Country Girl of to-day has one great advantage. She was born after the time when it was settled conclusively that there was nothing in her sex alone that ought to hinder her mental growth and her opportunity for activity. In her time woman has come to realize that when she believes in her own inferiority, in the possibility that her sex may be a handicap, her nature will be restricted, and she will not be able to develop the powers she does possess. She sees that the obsession of this thought has tied down the woman in the past and has impeded her development. She is now wakened from this daze.

What barrier can there be to a woman's progress? Truly life presents many. For instance, her idea of what would for her be progress, may not be the right idea. There are many stern duties that sometimes seem to impede progress; duties to parents, to family, or to the social order; duties to religious forms that have become woven into society and could not be drawn out without too much sacrifice of what is good and necessary; duties to common legal form that has dominance and is the result of centuries of experience, and that could not be taken exception to without too great risk — these and many other things may form barriers to the desire of the mere individual. But, these being granted, the woman can have a free chance for growth and development only when she believes that nothing coming out of the mere fact of sex has a right to hamper her growth or restrict her activity, and that no one shall have the right to say what is best for her or what she ought to wish for herself, in matters where she alone can have the means for understanding the situation.

These principles intimately concern the question of marriage. George Meredith said that to a woman marriage should be a platform from which her soul may take a new flight. How wonderful! A platform from which the soul may take flight! — not a black cage in which the soul of woman must crouch, to which her soul must fit itself, moving cramped, and slowly, and at war with itself; not a cage in which a caught and imprisoned canary bird must sing for the amusement of its owner. No! a platform from which to take flight, with sunlighted realms to investigate and new skies to discover, with wings growing ever stronger for more daring ascensions into still clearer light.

Let every girl make sure that that is the kind of platform that is being built for her in the character and in the attitude of mind of the destined lover. And let her make certain that she also is building and developing in herself a character that shall be worthy of her high mission, that shall be sufficient for all its needs, and that shall merit the deep reverence that all hearts give to the mother and homemaker.

In order that the founding of a successful home may be the Country Girl's happy lot, is it too much to ask that she should cherish for herself the ideal of a nature clean and pure, with so high a reverence for purity that she shall demand it in her lover as in herself? And that she shall recognize no difference in her standard for the morality of both the young man and the young woman? Should not her ideal include the fact of established health, both physical and mental, with a physician's certificate for both young man and young woman as to this, and include also a good inheritance of health in both families together with absolute freedom from alcoholism or other death-dealing diseases? Moreover, no marriage can be quite happy and successful that is not based upon the principle that each shall respect the personal rights of the other; and this should include, not only matters of income and property, but of tastes and opinions, and of all personal relationships. Both should have a good common school education and as much more as circumstances will permit. If he is a college graduate, she should be one also; and she should never be asked to leave her college course in order to marry. A wise girl will frown upon the young man who makes plans for marriage before he has gained a thorough training in some good bread-winning occupation and also developed a fair money-earning capacity. The Country Girl may be reminded again that she herself should have the thorough training in the science, art, and business of the household that will make her a perfect house administrator and homemaker and leave it possible to adapt some part of this varied work to money earning should occasion require. The ideal for two who are to found a home together should certainly include a genuine love of home life, together with love of children and a capacity to become a wise, efficient father and mother. A home will be more interesting and therefore more successful, as years move along, if the founders are people of growing nature, if they have a disposition to keep in touch with affairs, if they indulge themselves with an avocation, something they especially like to do, something that will carry on their education to farther heights. There must be courage,— home-founding calls for heroism — there must be fortitude, reserve force, patience. Ordeals will come, and trials: a buoyant faith in the spiritual realities alone will bear us through these. Then it must be remembered that we live in the community. It is well to select a socialized nature, one having ability to live among people and to meet them successfully, one that knows the give-and-take of social life. Both the young man and the young woman must be good citizens in the community.

Now what has been forgotten? The great thing that perhaps with most young people is thought of first, namely, the question as to whether these two young people like each other or not. But the phase being presented here concerns

not so much the choice of a particular one who shall be companion in the founding of a certain home, as the qualities of
the group of people from among which that choice shall be
made.   Certainly it is of the greatest importance to decide
whether the two young people do really like each other or
not.   It would be blasphemy to enter into the relationship
without that satisfaction in each other's society that alone
gives promise of happiness.   There should be a strong,
deep affection and love for each other; they should have
a mutuality of interest, tastes and ideals; they should enjoy each other's society; and these points should be put to
the test of time and absence — but not too much of either!

Homes founded by members of groups who hold ideals
like these and live up to them, will be certain to carry on
into the future the best the race has attained and to add to
the stores of happiness and wellbeing of all people.   Into
such homes it will be the best possible fortune to be born;
and if these homes are set against an unspoiled country
background, they will be the places where children will have
the best chance to develop to perfect human height.   It
should indeed be a part of the ideal cherished in the depths
of every country girl's heart, that she will, if possible, make
to the world a contribution of children, the most perfect
that she can compass, the most complete in all their powers,
the most invincible in their strength, mental, physical and
moral; and that these shall go forth into the world trained
for the most distinguished service among the world's great
needs.   This should be her ambition; and I believe that it
is the desire and the ideal of the great majority of the girls
of the present generation.

To present a completed, fullgrown, thoroughly efficient
man or woman to the world, is a contribution to the world's
storehouse of power.   But how much more that means than
simply to bear the child!   The right direction of the baby-
hood and youth, the full apprehension of the value of education, and the entire dynamic encouragement to both the

sons and the daughters, the example of industry, the inspiration to work, the enthusiasm and self-sacrifice to help in reaching high ideals, the wisdom to guide these endeavors — these are the things that belong to the contribution of the woman. Whether or not a woman has made her due contribution is bound up in the matter of what her sons and daughters actually do for the community and the world, how wide their influence is, how serviceable they are to the general good. The mother of Edison, for instance, made a great contribution.

Let every young woman take this point of view and consider what she is now doing, even while yet only a girl, to make it possible for her children that are to be, to have large lives, useful to the whole community.

In olden time the family numbered fifteen to twenty children. Then, indeed, there were things happening in the farm home! Then was there companionship under the rooftree! The evenings were merry about the fireside — and, by the way, there was a literal as well as a spiritual fireside for the children to be merry about! Then, too, there was hospitality, the Thanksgiving dinner, the Christmas home-coming for all the cousins! In those days life was worth living and there was no country life problem.

We must look forward to larger families. The next row of fathers and mothers must live for this, plan for it, trust for it, and educate themselves for it; for only thus will the farmstead be at once a place where rafters shall ring with jollity, and the complex life offer dramas enough to be interesting. In this way we shall save the country.

The story of the home life of the Beecher family, a typical large family of old New England days, touches a high-water mark of vivid home life. There was a perfect furore of intellectual excitement going through the house all the time. Every topic of public interest was brought to the home circle. Books were read aloud continually. Excitement of all kinds was going on in the evenings, discussions of all sorts at the table. The children were not invited, they were required, to argue. If they did not do it cleverly the father would confound them with ridicule, or he would say: " Now present this argument and you will be able to down me." And then he would tell them just how to manage the point in order to show up the fallacy and gain the right conclusion. So the wise father trained their minds in a sort of play.

People have talked a great deal about the value to a child of a noble mother; let a word or two be said for the value of the father in the training of the home. It should be thought of both after the home is established and before. Young women should think of this in making the choice of a partner and the young men should know that they are doing so. In fact, this may be actually happening already. Two little boys were talking in the playground not long ago, and one said to the other: " You mustn't do that, for if you do, you are not training for parentage." The new era has certainly begun!

But there is a still larger view. The Country Girl should also consider what she is now doing for the community to make it one in which her sons and daughters shall, twenty years hence, have a chance for clean, wholesome and inspiring lives. If she now forms a society for the girls in her village so that the strength of each individual girl will be multiplied by the braiding together of their efforts, to the end that better social enjoyments and more intellectual and more ethical ideals may become habitual, it may be that the years filled with these high activities will result in a state of things in that community that will make higher things the rule and lower things impossible. Then her village will be a safer place for her children when they come than it could have been without her own girlish endeavors.

The country child starts out with a better physical development than the city child. Our countryside from the

Atlantic to the Pacific is full of children who are especially endowed for the highest attainments. May not the Country Girl of the next generation be expected to do something adequate and wonderful with these good gifts of heaven?

CHAPTER XIX

THE FARM PARTNER

Efficient housekeeping is the beginning of good citizenship.
— *Professor Martha van Rensselaer.*

CHAPTER XIX

THE FARM PARTNER

THE Country Girl of to-day may look forward to a life in which she shall serve in a double capacity. She is to be a farm-woman and she is to be also a wife-mother. The farm woman may do what she can in the work of the farmstead, but her occupations there must be in abeyance before the vastly greater importance of the work which is specially hers — the conserving of the best and highest interests of the family. She is, first, the head and link of the family. If after she has finished her contribution to the work of discipline, education, inspiration, reading and story-telling, spiritual and esthetic guidance, mending and making, and placing food thrice on the table daily; after she has supplied her own needs in self-education and self-inspiration, in recreation and social satisfaction, so that she may come to the tasks mentioned above with spiritual and mental energy and alertness; and if then she still has time, strength, patience, will, energy and taste, left for still greater demands upon her resources; then she may help in the things that concern the farm business. She may do whatever will be a joy to her to do, whatever she can do buoyantly and with enthusiasm.

No doubt in the new era this will be possible. But the woman of the next generation is going to insist upon being happy, and her happiness is to consist in maintaining efficient working power and in having her work appreciated. Her work in the home must be thought of as having the same value as any other earning work. It must be acknowledged in the home of the future that woman's skill and woman's power to save are both business assets.   It should be acknowledged in the home of to-day both for the wife and for the daughter.

One may say that all business is carried on by men in order that the home — which means the wife and the children — may be sustained and that its happiness and its outlook to the future may be made to prosper.   All men work for this end.   The love of a man for his wife and for their children is the inspiration of his daily toil.   But with all other occupations save the farmer's, the business is one thing and the home is another.   The woman and her share of world's work, namely the making and the keeping of the home, are a thing apart.   They are placed in a little coop by themselves and there treasured as a shrine.   Sometimes, to be sure, the little coop where the woman plies her work is in the mind of the man quite other than a shrine. But in the majority of cases it is this, and we are speaking of the law and not of the exception.

But with the wife of the farmer, the woman's laboratory-machine-shop-studio is not a little room by itself.   The home is a business center; it is a dynamo from which goes out the power for the whole machinery; it is itself a piece of elaborate machinery without which the rest of the cogs and bands and phlanges would all go awry and break into pieces, doing damage to the whole farm-factory.

It is because of this that the woman in the farm home is so essential a part of the farm business; it is for this reason that she is to be thought of as a partner.   It is for this reason that the farm woman may have the satisfaction of knowing that she contributes more of constructive value than do the women of any other group.   From these conditions farm women gain a training that no other women have.   It is claimed that suffrage was carried in the Northwestern States by the weight of the women of the agricultural regions; they had been trained to the new point of view by their position in the farmstead.

Students of the conditions of living in the homes of both city and country have proposed various schemes for the practical finances in the home. An excellent scheme for a household budget appeared in the *Journal of Home Economics* for June, 1914. It provided for three separate accounts, one called " The Man's Personal Account," one " The Woman's Personal Account," and the third, " The Family Account." Into the first went the man's clothes, traveling expenses (carfare, etc.), charities, amusements, society dues, dentist and doctor's bills — all personal expenses. Into the second went similar items for the woman, except that the bills connected with the birth of children were not recorded there. These went into the third account, together with the running expenses of living, and all expenses connected with the children, their clothing, amusements, instruction, etc. A weekly sum came from this account for the use of the wife for the household; what remained there after these depredations, composed the mutual savings, and this sum belonged equally to both husband and wife and could be used for any purpose only by consent of both. This scheme in its general features is adapted to any family, but might of course, after discussion and consent, be altered to suit circumstances.

Every difficult question in the apportionment of these separate accounts should be talked over thoroughly. Each member should endeavor to see the question in the abstract, pure from every selfish impulse. Each should try to see it from the other's standpoint, freed from prejudice, and in the dry light of reason.

By working out these problems for several years, it may be possible to bring the sums set apart for certain purposes down to fixed amounts. But it must not be forgotten that the general cost of living varies — who does not know that, alas! — from year to year. We have green years and slack years; therefore we are not to be blamed if we do not always live up to an ideal standard. Besides, we need a new cloak one year and do not need one the next. New-cloak-year cannot be always last year or always next year; it sometimes must be *this* year!

The comfort of a family budget can hardly be imagined by those who have a family to plan for and have not tried this system. You know what you have to do with; you can plan and thus reduce expenses where they can most conveniently be shaved off and not feel it so much. The husband will have the comfortable assurance that he is obeying that great principle of efficiency that calls for a "square deal" in the human group with which he has most to do. The wife knows that when she is taking a sum of money to use for herself or for her family she is not asking a favor; she knows that she will never hear the dire question, "Where is the dollar I gave you last month?" Immense quantities of self-respect are carefully preserved by a methodical arrangement of the home budget, and happiness is laid up for use both here and hereafter.

We may then ask how this general scheme may be adapted to homes in the countryside. The financial plan for the farm home ought not to present any difficulty, but it seems to, and for two reasons. In the first place the money generally arrives in bulk in connection with harvests, not scattered along through the year as in most other forms of business. But one would think that this peculiarity would aid system; to know all in a month what is to be available for twelve should be the most effective basis for a wise plan.

Second, a large part of the supplies for the farm home come directly from the farm without intervention of butcher, baker or candlestick maker. This, again, ought not to prove a difficulty. Why not record the farm-supplies on the day book at market prices, as if they did come from butcher and grocer? This is the normal, systematic and efficient thing to do. It is only the close interweaving of farm and house functions, that makes it seem difficult;

but in spite of this a carefuly worked out and closely followed system of bookkeeping will give aid at nearly every point.

May we, however, ask a further question? In trying to make just and equitable plans in the unique structure of the farmstead, how shall we place a value upon the labor of the house administrator? The farm home is an absolutely essential part of the farmstead, its heart and focus. The business of the home is a part of the business of the farm. Whatever the woman does to fulfil her duty in the home, to make the output of the home a real productive contribution, is of actual economic value to the farm business, and should be appreciated as such. If by specially good management, by industry and thrift, she can make an unusually good showing in her administration, lessen expenses by saving, increase energy by a studied dietary, make children more efficient and the family happier and healthier, she should be the more appreciated as a business partner whose service is invaluable and who is well worthy of her share of the profits.

If, then, besides these duties that are the normal work of the home-maker, she is able to add such work in the farmstead as belongs to the farming business, such as the care of the cream and butter, providing meals for the farm hands, care of stock, chickens, bees, lambs, or the garden, she takes the part of a farm hand or a farmworker, she is a unit in the farm business as well as a partner, and should have the value of the service she performs paid to her in wages. Of course we hate the word. We want at least the mother in the home to be the final unmerchantable thing there. But there are families in the country scattered here and there who painfully need some such planning of home affairs as this. If the happier women would move on lines of economic system, even though they do not themselves feel tragic need for it, but just in the interest of scientific accuracy and efficiency, the other wives would be happier and all life in the home realm would have a better adjustment. As long as the farmstead is a combination of home and farm business, the presiding genius in this combination may work for love many hours in the day; but where work is done by the woman administrator that a house servant, if one were employed, would be doing and would be paid for doing, the woman administrator, the mother in her function of housekeeper, should be paid in money at commercial rates for those services; and this should be accurately recorded day by day and week by week and taken full account of in the budget.

The spirit that will uphold the mind and heart during the instalment of such plans is the desire to know with scientific accuracy what the annual budget of the house is and likewise what the budget for the farm business is, and what each contributes toward the success of the other. That each institution will be more efficiently run under such a system, and that the elastic interplay of the two will move more harmoniously, with less friction, and with a larger output of happiness for all, admits of no possible doubt. Also that the Country Girl of to-day will be anything less than fitted, disciplined and willing to act well her vigilant part in this plan is equally inconceivable.

In order to meet this situation the average Country Girl no doubt needs training in system and in bookkeeping. She needs to adopt a point of view. She must take into account two things: first, every item, however small, is important; second, every item, however small, must be recorded. The apron-pocket should have pencil and tiny pad in it all the time, except that every few minutes it must come out to receive a record. One of the most important principles of efficiency is that we should record our daily or momently efforts. We must know exactly what we have been able to do before we can take a long breath and try to do more. All this the Country Girl of to-day may do for her present home; and in her future home, if she does not do it, she will be completely out of tune with her time.

In a thoughtful and courteous book on rural conditions in the United States, by a distinguished English observer, the suggestion was made that the woman in the farm home is the fitting person to keep the accounts. The author decides this by her leisure (save the mark!) and by her well trained faculty for detail.

This statement of opinion aroused a storm of comments in other books, chiefly by American gentlemen, claiming that the farm woman lacks the training for keeping accounts and the large comprehension needed for that part of the business. But this training is now accessible to the Country Girl, and we believe the "large comprehension" will come with experience. At any rate this will come to her as easily as to the unwilling agriculturalist himself, and the leisure (in a new era) and the faculty for detail will remain her valued assets. It is idle to say in this day and age of the world that the woman has no mind for the keeping of accounts when women are bankers and millionaires and managers of large business enterprises by myriads.

It is a simple matter for the girl to take charge of the butter and egg accounts, and also of the bookkeeping for the whole farmstead: she will be all the better mentally and morally for attending to this duty. Mentally she will improve under the discipline of exactness and promptness; morally she will improve under the discipline of the strictness and definiteness required by the responsibility. The reason why so many women have been so irresponsible in money matters is because they have been treated as children and therefore have adopted the habits of children in their buying and selling.

There is a telephone girl who can tell the 'phone number of nearly all the houses in three large cities where she has worked in the hotel 'phone booths. There are a good many things she cannot do but she can do that. The person at the head of the department for receiving payments at one of the largest department stores in New York City is a woman. She takes in all the bills and makes change on the charge slips and the checks, and estimates all the details of the accounts. She puts her mind completely upon the papers in hand, so that while a set of these are before her she is so absorbed in them that no question put to her by any one standing at the door of the cage would any more reach her mind than if she were dead. In a moment she hands the papers to the proper person with the correct statement; then that is over and she is ready for the next. She has done this work every day for sixteen years, and she looks young and blooming. This woman is working for herself; but she is doing her work so excellently that it becomes a universal benefit, inspiring us to imitate her efficiency.

As the home is the reason for being of the farmstead, the woman therein is making good her partnership if she is taking care of her housekeeping and family duties. Her contribution is being made. But the farm and the home are so closely interwoven that she is of far greater importance than this shows. She is a true partner and is worthy of all the rights and duties that this indicates. If the woman is not the keeper of books for the farm business, it is at least her right as a partner to have the books of the business always open to her. To see the books would be the first request of any partner.

One of the best farmers, who was also one of the best of men, affirmed that he was not in the habit of confiding his business matters to his wife. She on her part was one of the most loyal and most refined of women, the mother of wonderful children, and the very effective though unencouraged worker by his side for many years. His thought was that he would take the whole responsibility for the support of the family; he did not want to bother the rest of the household about details of business. One summer he lost a thousand dollars through the bad outcome of a bargain, but he did not tell his wife of this. Then after a while he made five thousand dollars more than usual — but neither did he share this news with her. Do you not think that if that wife had known that summer that there were four thousand extra dollars that might be depended upon for the use of the home, she would not have used two of them in the development of an efficient kitchen, placing a set of machines there that would have given her hot and cold water at hand, some form of power for the washing-machine, dummies, dust-chutes, ice chests, fireless cookers, lighting, wheeled trays, and all the necessary paraphernalia to put her household on an efficient basis — by this means not only lifting her own work up to the place of a scientific laboratory but raising the productive level of the whole valley where she lived and helping to lighten the burdens of a hundred farm women who were having not even so comfortable a time in their life plans as she was?

Now if this woman had had a little more business sense she would have realized that she had begun wrong years ago. It may also be that, if she had understood the whole situation, she would have approved of leaving the money in the bank for a time: it may be that she would have devoted it to sending a daughter to college. But, other things being equal, and if to her marriage had been a platform from which the soul of woman takes a new flight, we may believe that she would have devoted some of the money to better equipment for her own workshop.

But all these things are aside from the point, which is that she had earned the money as much as he had, and that she should have had as much to say as her husband had about the disposal of their joint savings.

The Country Girls of to-morrow must profit by experiences like these in the families of the generation now passing, and make certain that the efficiency principle of the square deal and the basic principle of a true partnership shall be established in the home-plans they are making.   If they cannot assure themselves that conditions satisfying to their self-respect will prevail for them in the farmsteads of the future, they are justified in rejecting the countryside for their home and in leaving it to wither away in its lack of their dynamic and rejuvenating presence.

CHAPTER XX

THE COUNTRY GIRL'S TRAINING

Here in America, for every man touched with nobility, for every man touched with the spirit of our institutions, social service is the high law of duty, and every American university must square its standards by that law or lack its national title.

— *President Wilson.*

The object of all education is to fit men for service.

— *Edmund Janes James.*

CHAPTER XX

THE COUNTRY GIRL'S TRAINING

IT would indeed be fortunate if every young woman who has been raised in rural surroundings could go to some educational institution where there is a department of home economics, and there prepare herself by a thorough four years' course for a life of service in her home and community. One could hardly ask for a more ideal life than a Country Girl prepared in that way would see before her, a life that would be joy-giving not only because it would be efficient, but because it would be inspired throughout by the noblest motives. There is, in fact, not an hour of the day that may not be full of joyously productive labor, if the Country Girl can take advantage of her present opportunities; and there will soon be no excuse for her, since it is now becoming the fashion in many States for most of the family to leave their farm for a time in the depths of the leisurely winter and to hie away to the university where the men listen to conferences on problems of business and produce, and the mothers and daughters hear lectures on the industrial and other features of the home.

Of this and other methods of special training for special work, some thousands among the millions of country girls must avail themselves if they will do their duty by their generation. At the basis of success in any field lies the drudgery of preparation; excellence and reward are beyond. The task of the household administrator is no exception to this law of efficiency. The work is no haphazard matter, no question of luck; housekeeping is emerging from the realm of medieval magic now.

Other things being equal, the one that has been trained

for a work invariably commands the higher salary. An investigation made by the Department of Agriculture in the States of Indiana, Illinois, and Iowa, showed that the men with no schooling had an average annual income of $301, those with a common school education earned $586, while those that were college-bred received $796. These figures tell the story and impress the lesson that these sweet fruits grow high and that the ladder to reach them is a superior education. If the Country Girl really is in earnest in asking for further appreciation in the farm budget she must train for the responsibility.

But where shall she begin?

The work of caring for and building up a home is so complex, there is so much to it, that it is difficult to pin it down into a curriculum. It really fits into every department of education. It is science — chemistry, physics, mechanics; it is art — pictures, sculptures, architecture, costume, color, form, proportion; it is pageantry, drama, music; it is history — the family, law, records, relationships, eugenics; it is literature — poetry, story, myth, folk lore, epic, expression, drama; it is philosophy — conduct, the ends of effort, the individual; it is religion — the mission of love, the ultimate things in life, the use of training, the ministry of discipline; it is mathematics — accounts, percentages, adding up, and also (save the mark!) dividing and subtracting; it is economics — averages, outgo and income, the wage, the unearned increment, the community; what, in fact, is it not?

Such a calling of the roll gives us some hint of the scope and range of the work that makes the dignity of the woman's duty and privilege — of her " sphere." It is truly a " sphere," for it rounds out in every direction. There is not a single part of education that may not be useful to the home-maker. There is no least strand that will come amiss in her day's work when she is mother and overseer of the destinies of the family in her household.

A review like this makes it clear how little the education attained so far by the world reflects the whole of life when the needs of the woman in her so important rôle as nearest helper to the next generation of human beings finds in none of these mentioned subjects the aid she needs for her part — her half, shall it be said? — in the work of bringing forward those who are to lift the race into a larger life in the ever receding, ever growing future.

In the schools of to-day the education is modeled upon the needs of the man. In this country especially, when schools of the higher kind began to be built, the need was for emphasis on professional education. To prepare men for that need was the aim. This was what women found when they began to enter institutions of higher education: they found a system adapted for men's needs, and especially to prepare them for the professions. At first it seemed strange to many men that women should desire to gain this kind of education. But there were other men who saw that the path toward their own needs was through the well-paved avenues of education as it then existed. So women went on; they felt that their first duty was to take the training that men were taking, if for no other reason than to show that they could. They did this. They showed it abundantly. Then they began to philosophize on the situation. They saw that they must have a system of education more adapted to their own needs. Hence the rise of courses of study adapted to the immediate needs of women in their work as home-makers and household administrators. So far these courses of study are usually found in the agricultural colleges or in institutions formed for the special purpose of training women for home-making. This is because the agricultural college has been founded in the main since the new vision of the relation of education and the work of women has touched the eyes of educators. The old-line colleges preserve the ideals of decades ago. They are hopelessly masculinized and professionalized.

There women will perhaps never find a natural normal education. At all events they will not find this until it is understood that psychology must as thoroughly prepare the young women to understand the development of the child's mind as it does the business man to understand the principles of advertising, and that chemistry should fit the housekeeper to gain aseptical cleanness in her household laboratory as efficiently as it does the manufacturer's expert to find a use for the by-product and turn it into money value. That the woman has a right to expect her college education in all its branches to prepare her for the duties that are hers, has not yet seemed to enter the minds of educators. She should no longer be required to go to a special institution for this. She has shown that she can undertake the severest strains of educational training; she no longer needs to keep that purpose in view. What she now needs is adaptation for her own work. The highest institutions that exist should give her what she needs. Until this comes along in the natural course of educational development — as it surely will — she must gain the training she needs in such ways as she can.

Nearly all the agricultural colleges now have courses of study in home science and art. For the benefit of any girls who may not be in the habit of studying the catalogs of institutions and who would like to know what subjects the university considers to be of educational value in household economics, I give here some outlines of courses of study pursued at certain typical institutions.

Home Economics Department, Cornell University, Ithaca, New York.

A Course in Household Sanitation. A consideration of the sanitary conditions of the house and site; the relations of bacteriology to the household in cleaning, in the preservation of foods, in diseases, and in disinfection; personal

A lesson in household economics, at Cornell University.

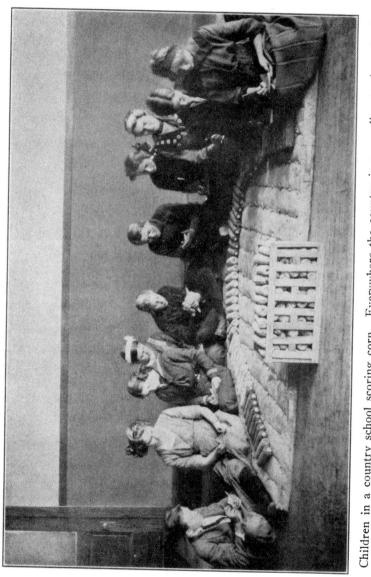

Children in a country school scoring corn. Everywhere the country is responding to the call of Progress, and these members of a new generation are striving to reach the best.

hygiene, including the care of the body in health; heat, light, ventilation, and the disposal of refuse; general lectures by specialists, giving a survey of the field of sanitation.

Teachers' College, Columbia University, New York City.

A Course in Household Management. Application of scientific and economic principles to the problems of the modern housewife — with discussion of them from both the ideal and the practical point of view, taking up such problems as: income as determining the type of household, the budget and its apportionment; the choice of a dwelling, moving, and settling; house furniture, utensils, appliances, decoration, supplies, the menu, clothing, maintenance, cleaning, repairs, household service, apportionment of time, household accounts, home life.

Home Economics Department, Connecticut College of Agriculture, Storrs, Connecticut.

A Course in Laundry Work. The principles and processes of laundry work; equipment and materials required to do good work in the home laundry, and the use and economy of labor-saving appliances; practical work in the processes of laundering, sorting, soaking, removal of stains, etc.; special methods of washing different fabrics; starching, ironing, and folding; experiments with hard and soft water, soap making, and composition of bluing.

Simmons College, Boston, Massachusetts.

A Course in House-planning. The designing and construction of the modern house; study of the plans and specifications in order to train the student to be able to read drawings, and understand the items of foundation, walls, plastering, heating, plumbing, roofing, and finishing; the history of furniture, color, and interior decoration; a consideration of fabrics, and wall coverings.

A four years' course of study may be arranged as follows:

First Year: Hygiene, biology, chemistry, household administration, cookery, physical training, and some electives.

Second Year: English, French or German, biology, nutrition, cookery, chemistry, physical training and electives.

Third Year: History, economics, household administration, clothing, textiles, nursing, and electives.

Fourth Year: English, administration, hygiene, social science.

The elective studies in this general course may be taken from among such titles as these: Dietetics, household sanitation, eugenics, sewing and embroidery, textiles (woolens, silks, cottons), clothing, laundering, landscape art, plant breeding, poultry husbandry, bee culture, pomology, vegetable gardening, meteorology, rural economy, marketing, cooperation, organization, rural education, citizenship. Such courses as these are given at Cornell University, at Simmons College, Boston, at Connecticut Agricultural College, at the University of Chicago, and elsewhere.

Correspondence courses are offered in many colleges. The names of many such courses have already been given in the report of one of the girls who took such a course under the direction of the Pennsylvania State College, Center County, Pennsylvania.

The young woman in planning to go to the university for a course in domestic science must take into account the benefits that she herself will gain from the association with the other students in the classes and in the various college exercises.   The educational influence the student-body as a whole will have upon the development of the individual has been already mentioned.   There are two things that no young person can gain without going away from home to some educational institution.   They are these: contact with the great teacher, and contact with the great fellow-student. The first she can make up for to some slight extent in the reading of books; for the loss of the second, if absolutely deprived of it by the lack of companions in her own community, she cannot be reimbursed in any way.   And there is nothing quite so inspiring as the personal contact with the revered instructor, nothing so entirely vivifying as the group of fellow-students.   Deprived of all this, however, the girl in a lonely life must make up for it as best she may, by books, by personal experiments, by keeping a buoyant and cheerful spirit, by seeking excellence by all means that are attainable.   In this endeavor she may approach heroism, and in doing this she may well attain the supreme ends of life without the help of schools, or of machinery, or of any human aids whatever.

CHAPTER XXI

A GREAT OPPORTUNITY

The mission of the ideal woman is to make the whole world home-like.　　　　　　　　　　　　　— *Frances E. Willard.*

CHAPTER XXI

A GREAT OPPORTUNITY

IT is possible that a good share of training for her profession will be brought right to the door of the Country Girl's future household laboratory. This she may look forward to as an assured hope.

It is to come about through the fulfilment of a plan which was the outgrowth of the Commission on Country Life, and which has been worked for by many students of rural conditions and lovers of the countryside. The whole scheme sets before the Country Girl of to-day an open door and gives to her more hope of relief from the unfortunate results of the unscientific farming and unbalanced conditions in the country homes of the past than any other one thing that has been devised.

But what is this Open Door? To explain this, we must start in by a sort of detour, with the Boll Weevil. His Imperial Highness was a fiend incarnate; yet his coming was not all a misfortune. For to rid the land of this depredating buccaneer among the Southern domains, demonstration farms were established, and these led to a more adapted form of conveying help to the distressed and threatened farmers in the cotton belt by means of instruction carried to the individual farms themselves. A wonderful degree of success attended this work, and the Western farmers, seeing this, called to the Government for aid of the same sort against their own special difficulties, an assistance which was generously given. Funds were distributed through the States by the Federal Government, and by means of demonstrations, the Government sought to give to all the States the benefits that had been proved so helpful in the

South. Meanwhile the States themselves were carrying on many projects of their own for the advancement of the farming interests within their bounds. There was likelihood that there might be duplication of effort, that there might even be waste of means and of energies. To make sure, then, that this should not happen, the Government has now devised a new measure, a bill for the inauguration of Co-operative Agricultural Extension Work, known at present as the Smith-Lever Bill.

The passing of this bill was an item of the 1914 national budget. Before the eventful thing happened many processions of women protesting their desire for more formal acknowledgment before the law and in the privileges of the vote had walked the length of Fifth Avenue, and in these processions many men of the highest stamp had taken their chivalrous place. By the time the bill was being framed the woman side of things for city and for country had begun to hold a far different position in the public mind than it did in the days of Thoreau or Horace Mann. It was not just as a slip of the tongue that the words " and home economics " were placed by the words " subjects relating to agriculture." No: the concurrence of the phrases came about as a natural outcome of well-considered belief, as indeed a testimonial to the fact that in the mind of the framer of the bill the two matters were of equal importance and were to be logically united in the minds of the people. At any rate, the fact that the phrase " home economics " stands at the head of this bill represents an incalculable leap forward of public opinion in the direction of betterment for the home and all that it contains of influence on our well-being. Let it be deeply impressed, then, that the two words, " Agriculture " and " Home Economics " stand together at the head of a bill that is to provide for instruction on a vast scale for all the rural districts of this land.

In a letter to the author, the Honorable Asbury F. Lever, the framer of the Smith-Lever Bill in its present form,

shows a full appreciation of the claim of the countryside
to a fair share in this distribution.   The letter by kind permission may be quoted here and is as follows:

COMMITTEE ON AGRICULTURE,

House of Representatives, U. S.

WASHINGTON, D. C., August 20, 1914.

MRS. MARTHA FOOTE CROW,
  Tuckahoe, New York City.

My dear Mrs. Crow:

Responding to your letter, permit me to enclose you herewith
a marked copy of my report which accompanied the bill from the
Committee on Agriculture.   I say unhesitatingly that the problem
of the farm wife is one of the most vital of all of our rural problems and when this bill was drawn, I had in mind the use of a reasonable portion of the funds for the amelioration of her condition.
I think the exact division of the funds should depend upon conditions in each individual State and may be increased or decreased
as seems wise to those charged with the handling of the funds.   I
believe that the home economics feature of this bill is one of its
most important features.   In my own State one-fourth of the funds
are to be used for the teaching of home economics by means of
the itinerant teacher.   This may be found to be insufficient and if
it is the ratio can be changed.   I would feel greatly disappointed
if those who use these funds should in any manner get it into their
minds that the home economics feature of the law is not regarded
by the author as important.   Trusting this will be of service to you,
Very truly,

A. F. LEVER.

When Uncle Sam starts out on some great endeavor, he
does so with a wide scope and plans on a magnificent scale.
And wise he is, too.   The universities, through their agricultural colleges, where, as Secretary of Agriculture Houston says, information has been "reservoiring" for the last
half century, will be made the effective means for the dis-
tributing of the wealth of the scientific knowledge and re-
search they have garnered.

Through men and women trained in these special schools
where all details of farm business and home economics are

now accessible to everybody, the demonstration of these forms of scientific knowledge will be carried out to the farms and to the homes on the farms directly. And Uncle Sam will pay for it. Ten thousand dollars is directly appropriated to each State annually, beginning in 1914. The next year after this another sum of approximately the same amount will come to each State according to the percentage of the rural population in that State, counting by the Census of 1910. In each year following, the same sum is added to that of the year before, until 1924 is reached, when the sum becomes a fixed annual appropriation of three million, paid according to the percentage of the rural population at the time. To show that the individual States appreciate all this, they must add to these appropriations in a certain ratio. Will any States fail to show their appreciation, and to meet the offer of the beneficent Uncle Sam? If they do, they will be standing in their own light in the most darkness-loving way.

Now this wonderful bill says distinctly nothing as to how the vast hoard of money shall be divided between the two departments, " agriculture " and " home economics." Perhaps it may be half and half; then again perhaps it may be in a ratio of ninety-nine per cent. to the first one named and one per cent. to the second! Here then is the crux of the matter. Would the young woman on the farms of this country like to have a good half of this sum devoted to her needs that she may carry out her ideals for rural betterment?

Then let her think and talk about what she wants. Let her discuss it in her ·house and among her friends. Who knows but one young woman may devise some new thing that will not be thought of anywhere else in all the world! Every new idea has to start somewhere; it must be born in the midst of the needs of some one person or family. It may be merely two crossed sticks rubbed together, yet this may light the fires for a whole world. And suppose that the one person who thinks of the one best thing should be too timid about the value of any idea of hers, should have so humble a mind about her own mental product that she will name it to no one and so let the thought fall to the ground and go to nothing! Do not let this happen: let every happy idea be talked out in a letter to the Secretary of Agriculture, stating the need and making the suggestion.

The young women all over the country are showing a keen interest in the outcome of this project.. The universities that receive Federal aid, who are to have charge of using these moneys, are setting apart the share that is to go to the home economics work; sometimes it is one-half, sometimes only a fifth; but every State must make some generous assignment or it cannot live with itself in the future. Women have but to make their interest known and — talk about it! to gain attention to their wish. Bret Harte has somewhere made a character say something about "poor lovely helpless woman." Another speaker answers, "No, she is armed to the teeth — she has her tongue." This primordial weapon of woman's — a far better sword than the man's — can be used to good effect now; and if she does this she may see some of her dreams fulfilled.

For instance, suppose the household adminstrator should look out over the piles of work to be done before nightfall and should say to herself, "Oh, deary me! I wish some one would just come along and tell me how to do this so that I could get it done in shorter time!" She not at all realizes that she has struck a very great idea. This is the thought that came into the heads of agricultural committees in several States and countries. In our land only it remains till now to hear it imperatively voiced. Perhaps we may understand this better if we recall that American women, because of the chivalry of our men, the freedom of our institutions, and the high standard of our domestic morality, have been more advanced in personal liberty and efficiency than the women of other countries, have been far more ready and able to cope with the difficulties of life on the farm, and therefore have not had the depression and the weakness that have taken the light out of the eyes of women in the rural parts of other lands.   Moreover, in our country, the pioneering period is not so very far back of us. We are still near to the effects of that discipline, which developed in us the hardiness that makes it easier for us to bear the burden of work and the strain of the struggle than women not thus developed could sustain.   For all this we should be properly grateful and forget as soon as may be the losses that we have been obliged to sustain while we were gaining this hardihood.

To return to the need for a wise helper and adviser. That efficient person coming along the road to tell the woman on the farm how to arrange her work so that its burden may be lessened, would in one or two European countries be a well-known figure in the farming community.   She would be welcomed and would take her place in the family for a time till she had filled the minds of the members of that family circle with much wisdom from her well-filled stores and had shown them by practical demonstration the " why " and the " how " of many a new method of making ends meet, of making long hours short, and of turning off work.   After supper she would be with the children for a time and let some light in upon their puzzles; then when they had gone to bed she would talk every difficulty over with the farm wife and the husband too; at least we may be sure that she would do this if she were in this country, though perhaps she would not in the Land of the Hausfrau; and being thoroughly trained in gardening and in the treatment of all the animals that may come under the care of the woman on the farm, whether pigs, lambs, bees, or chickens, as well as in house sanitation, the care of the sick, laundry-work, needle-work, embroidery and crochet, she can come very near to the heart and the hands of her attentive hostess in the farm home.

In this country the woman who is trained to perform this service will be called a Farm Bureau Agent. According to a late letter from the Secretary of Agriculture to his Crop Correspondents, it is the intention of the Government to have in time such agents as these in every county in the United States.

It is such a service as this that the so-called Smith-Lever Bill now projected by the Federal Government would provide for — that is, if the young women of the country will show that in their future homes they would like to have a distinct advance upon the homes of the past. To establish a faculty of trained women to go from home to home all over this land, making periodical visits and putting the results of their training at the command of the women everywhere, is the ideal dwelling in the minds of the workers for this form of instruction. Hundreds and perhaps thousands of women will be needed. They are now preparing for their work, not in sufficient numbers as yet, but soon there will be many who are prepared and willing and glad to lay their ability and their expert skill at the feet of this service.

Let another possibility be suggested. Suppose that a distracted young housewife on some prosperous farm will sit down among a great pile of women's papers that she takes out of the abundance of her means and the activity of her imaginative idealism, and cry out as she reads the many articles and the innumerable columns of suggestions, " O I should like to have a perfect house and a wonderful system of housekeeping! But all these things confuse me — there is really too much to do. I wish I could see just one perfect house, right down in the village there, where I could go and see for myself how it all ought to be done." She again, has little idea that she has hit upon a great discovery, a very great idea. She does not realize that the House for Demonstration of Home Economics is entirely within possibility and is a thing that ought to be within the reach of every woman in the land. Such a House should be in every village and town and within " team-haul " distance of every farm. It should be a social center where every week in the year the women of the region may come and meet one another and talk over their problems. It should be in charge of a scientifically trained woman whose sole business should be to stand there and be a help to every woman within reach who has a single question in home economics to ask. She should know the best ways to do everything about the farm home, the best ways to do them with the machinery at hand, and also the best household machinery to get and the most advantageous changes to be made for the sanitary and artistic and health conditions in each individual home. It is a large order, but the young women who offer themselves to be prepared for such work must and we believe will measure up to the need. Here is indeed a mission for the trained Country Girl.

Although the words " home economics " have not heretofore appeared in papers set before our legislatures, our Government has been for years giving aid to the farmer's wife through many pamphlets on subjects related to her work. From the Bureau of Animal Industry we have advice concerning the health of the farm animals, concerning meat, butter, eggs, wool, leather, diseases, meat inspection, — all of which are matters of vital importance to the home; in the Bureau of Chemistry studies are made on the composition of many things used in homes: sugar, bread stuffs, preservation of fruits, pure food laws, storage, and other subjects of value to the household administrator; the Bureau of Plant Industry gives us information regarding crops for food for animals and humans, protection of plants from injurious diseases, how to domesticate plants and how to secure variety in foods; the department of Entomology aids us in our warfare against flies, mosquitoes, ants, moths, etc.; the Agricultural library sends us bibliographies; the Experiment Stations investigate in every direction; the Office of Public Roads tries to bring markets and farms closer together; and so the work goes merrily on, full of beneficent endeavor. Does the Country Girl sufficiently appreciate our Uncle Sam? Does she make the most of his efforts in her behalf?

Any girl that has learned to take pen in hand and can command the value of a postage stamp can send a respectful request to the Department of Agriculture, Washington, D. C., asking for the list of bulletins on the farm home and on problems connected therewith. When she has received this and has read it carefully, she will be full of thoughts no doubt on subjects about which she would like help. She can then write again to the Department at Washington asking for the bulletins on the particular subject that interests her. For instance suppose she is interested in the subject of bee-culture. She should write and ask for a bulletin on that subject. One girl on a Western ranch is very much interested in the subject of — what do you suppose? It takes a keen, unprejudiced mind to show this interest; — it is nothing more than weeds! Studying into this, she finds that all the books she can get hold of give her very little help because they do not refer to the conditions in that part of the world where she lives. So she is going to study the divergencies she sees between books and facts. She has sent everywhere for bulletins and books, and has now a considerable library on the subject; and she has gone vigorously to work to mark out all the differences between her own experiences and those that are recorded in the books. In time her records will be added to those, and she will have been of great service to the world by giving new knowledge that may be used for the benefit of her whole region. In this way the Country Girl, however lonely the farm where she lives, may feel that she is in touch with great movements, and can believe that her life is of especial use to the world.

CHAPTER XXII

THE ILLS OF ISOLATION

The fruits of modern inventive skill and enterprise have enriched country life and have banished forever the extreme isolation which used to vex the farm household of the past. The farm now is conveniently near to the market. The town, churches, and schools are near enough to the farms. The world's daily messages are brought to the farmer's fireside. And the voice of the nearest neighbor may be heard in the room though she may live a mile away.

— *Professor G. W. Fiske.*

CHAPTER XXII

THE ILLS OF ISOLATION

ISOLATION" is a word that the Country Girl does not very much use, but still she feels the meaning of the word. This note sounds in the unusually frank answer of one who did not speak for herself but said that she really thought some of the other girls went away to the city because there was no one in the village for them to marry, and in the naïve words of the girl who stated that she always said a club was a very good thing. Where the community does not afford the social life they crave as a part of their development, as the natural normal state for their self-expression, and as a part of their plans for life, it is no wonder they seek it elsewhere. This is one of the chief causes of the cityward tendency. For this reason the girls are willing to exchange the pure air of the country for the close atmosphere of the town; the safe and kindly surroundings of the rural home for the dangerous conditions of the city, its unregulated contacts, its promiscuity and its perils, and its loneliness in the midst of the indifference of strangers. There is a forbidding solitariness in the city that is to that of the country as a desert to a garden. This misery attacks one even more virulently on the noisy boulevard than along the whispering country lane. But this the Country Girl does not know, and she seeks relief from a woe that she does understand.

Perhaps the young woman on a lonely farm in some remote region does not realize this. She may be too dulled and discouraged by the effects of isolation to know either what is the trouble with her or even that there is any definite thing the matter.

The lack of companionship is indeed a very real hardship; for companionship is necessary to our growth as well as to our happiness. The solitary girl on the remote farm or in the obsolescent village has small share in this form of education and remains with her resources undeveloped. For her natural and normal education she needs a great deal of association with other young growing human beings; something therefore must be devised to supply this need or the Country Girl will not have the happy and well-rounded life on the farm that is her right.

One woman in giving reasons why she preferred the city said she would " rather have folks than stumps!" Truly. Very few farms, however, consist solely of what is represented by the expressive word " stumps "; and as for " folks," it is possible to have in city life a plethora of social contact so that leisure for thought, reading and study, or for any form of self-development, is unknown. Besides there are " folks " and " folks "; and a neighborhood full of cousins and friends is an unsurpassed shelter for the favorable growth of the young human being.

But ah! there is the very point. A neighborhood! If every Country Girl had a neighborhood to grow up in, a group of homes about her to afford her companionship, she could ask nothing better. But there are many girls living on remote and lonely farms far away from any neighborly environment; to such as these the isolation is a very real sorrow. It falls as heavily upon the farmer's daughter as it does upon the farmer's wife — even more heavily if possible, for she is generally led to realize her need at a time when her social instincts are most insistent. To make for the young woman in the farm home a life so interesting, so fascinating, so full of purpose and of the possibilities of self-expression, that the loss of " folks " will to some extent be made up to her, and to give to her as much companionship as possible and the effects of companionship through all known means that can be devised, should be the object of an earnest and widespread effort.

A visit made to a country girl who lived at a farm that was on a steep hillside in a lonely part of the world far from any town or village, left a very deep impression. I was riding through that region with a cousin on my way to the railroad twenty miles off.

" In that house," she said, pointing to a dilapidated farmhouse nearly smothered in greenery and totally unkempt in appearance, " lives a relative of ours, a second cousin. We must stop and see her."

" Oh, no," I cried out, for I was then young and selfish; " don't let me have to see any more relatives to-day."

" Yes, we must stop," said my firm cousin. " She is a good girl and will remember it always if you stop, and will be bitterly disappointed if you do not."

We drew up; a figure promptly appeared on the rickety porch and came down between the tall grasses that almost obliterated the path to the torn gate.

" How old is she?" I whispered.

" About twenty-eight; yes, twenty-nine next December."

" She looks forty," I said.

" You must remember she has had a hard time on this farm — it's no good, the farm, and she and her father live here alone now."

Cousin Artemisia — for that was her ironical apportionment as to name — came down to the buggy and stood between the wheels and reached over a long slim hand in greeting to my companion. I thought she would never let go. Then I was introduced. Cousin Artemisia stood back and looked at me as if she would read every thought in my whole soul. The most devouring curiosity, the most rapt wonder, the still, thunderstruck, hypnotized look of absorbed contemplation, were in her eyes. All my features went, I am sure, into her memory's irremediable printing, to stay there forever. All this — more shame to me! — was only a bother to me, for I did not at all understand what it could mean to a poor lonely soul to have a vision of a young relative from the great big outside world. I will not accuse myself of cruelty — only of ignorance and carelessness; but that, of course, is bad enough. To pay me for this, and as a perpetual punishment, I have the memory of her last look. After some suave and polite nothings from my lips I nudged my driver cousin and we went on over the hill, leaving Artemisia alone with her solitariness, stunned, it may be, for the moment by our swift passing, as a prisoner might be into whose dark cell a ray of light had penetrated and then been quickly withdrawn, making the darkness blacker than before. That last long look! I cannot describe it, but I shall remember it always. At that moment there was in Cousin Artemisia's face the suppressed longing of the imprisoned soul, the appeal for help to one that was believed to have had opportunity, the cry of the hopelessly restricted longings, the desire for companionship, suppressed for years and accumulated unbearably.

The memory of that quarter of an hour with Cousin Artemisia has driven it home to me that the young woman in the solitary farm house wants and needs the means of self-expression as much as little Helen Keller needed the means to reveal herself that would take the place of the hearing and speaking and seeing that had been denied her. What would have happened to her if she had not had gateways opened to her mind and soul so that she could give out and receive, is what happens to all of us unless we have our powers developed by contact with others and by giving and taking intellectual and spiritual goods. Dumbness is a hindrance to growth. Excessive shyness and secrecy, bashfulness, a spirit of seclusion, sensitiveness, and other faults that attack young people in the growing years, are a result of the lack of the liberalizing and purifying ministry of companionship and they are an inhibition of development.

An account by a rural school-teacher presents a picture that is gruesome, and any one that wishes may omit it from the reading; but it suggests a possibility and drives home a lesson. Circumstances required her for a time, she said, to take care of an old lady, who lived with her husband and daughter on a lonely farm. All that they had in the house were the old things the mother had kept house with forty years ago. The chairs had been scrubbed till not a particle of paint was left; and their meals were alike three times a day — pork, potatoes and bread. Not a book was there to read except a few old school books and the Bible. The young woman who tells the story stayed a week, and it was the longest week she ever spent. The farmer's daughter was about eighteen years old. She seemed a bright young girl; but two years after that, while the father was gone to the factory, she hung herself in the barn. The school-teacher did not wonder; she said that if she had had to live in such a house, life would have been a burden.

Of course that is an extreme case. The suicide rate is higher for the city than it is for the country; it is higher for men than it is for women; the proportion of suicides over sixty-five years of age is greater for rural districts in our country than it is for cities. This may not especially interest the young woman on the farm; but it concerns us to see that all the younger people should have the natural normal life that will satisfy their physical, mental and moral needs; and that they should realize early that they are to be supplied with the career that their natures demand, in order that they may not despair before they have really begun to live.

A conviction dwells in the minds of many Country Girls that the quietness and freedom from interruptions on the farm form one of the chief reasons for desiring the rural life. There certainly is truth in this. The jaded city worker flees to the calm of the country for relief from people and things. But it is also true that isolation is not a good in itself and too much of it is directly harmful.   We develop not by it but in spite of it.   No man can be a true man, no woman a true woman, who has not been molded by human companionship.   We should " live in the House by the Side of the Road " and unite our interests with those of humanity at large.   We do not know ourselves except as we know others.   Whether we are above the level of average human capacity, or below it, or simply different from others, or, what is more usually the case, different in some things and like in others, we do not know except by comparison with others.   Companionship with others brings us knowledge of our defects, our omissions, our weaknesses, sometimes of our strength and power to give and to help.

Therefore, the normal development of the daughter on the farm depends largely upon having the heavy weight of rural solitariness lifted.   She may not know this herself; but the quickness with which her spirit responds to the touch of companionship between herself and a friend of her own age, when fortunate occasion brings her this pleasure, shows what her need is.   It is now said that the young men and the young women in college give to each other almost as much education as is given to them by the teachers themselves.   In other words the social contact possible where many young people are brought together has such power to quicken energy and to incite noble rivalries that it alone becomes one of the most effective means of education.

This education and opportunity should be within reach of every Country Girl, and she may herself do a great deal to bring this about.   In endeavoring to do her share in thus developing the social resources of the country, the Country Girl must, however, work for a time against a disadvantage.   At present the young girl from the country makes the impression of being less developed than the young boy.   As a general thing he has had a great deal more outlook, more responsibility, more contact with outside influences. He goes with his father to town; the father and the brother look upon this excursion as a task, and they think this is work that can be done by them and save the women-folk all that trouble. But the fact is that this going to town is a means of getting at least some outlook into the great world beyond that the farm circle did not give, an enlargement that would be just as good for the sister as for the brother. The sons come back joyous and electrified and able to work better afterward. Meantime the daughters have stayed at home in the treadmill, unexcited and dull; and because they have lacked the stimulus of the excursion into the outer world they get the discredit of being gloomy and stupid. If they had driven to the village also, or to call upon a girl friend, they would have returned joyous and eager, full of talk and energy, and with new ideas to add to the family discussion.

The efficient Country Girl of to-day is often as equal to the management of the intractable horse as a man: she rides the disc-plough and she runs the automobile. It would only be in some backward section of the country or in some tradition-bound family, where the daughter could not drive the horses and have the use of a conveyance to go to town whenever it seemed to her to be necessary. It has been suggested by an eminent authority that the farm woman should go to town once a week and should also go to a neighbor's every week for an afternoon's visit. What then should be the excursions of the daughter during the years when she is growing up and becoming a young lady, entering upon her duties as hostess and social leader? There should not a day pass when she does not have some contact with the social world of the rural community. She should have a large letter-writing correspondence and make it yield her all the culture possible. She should take part in every commendable social organization that is accessible and with her mother's cooperation make her home a center of gracious social welcome to friends and neighbors. With the new machinery there will be much greater simplification possible in the household, and in the wake of this may enter our old-time friend, Hospitality, so long and sadly missed from our ferny lanes.

Perhaps it is not necessary to suggest that the greatest care should be taken to place under the safest conditions the social life in which the daughter bears a part. In order that this may be so there is no better safeguard than that the mother should be in closest confidence with the daughter, should be present at all the parties, should be in all the fun. This is the scheme now most approved under the best social auspices and is adopted in the country wherever they live up to the most refined models. It means that the mother must never lose the thread of her daughter's confidence; and if she has done so by the mistake of some past day, she must leave no stone unturned, by tact and love and prayer, to regain the lost ground. It means joining in all the games; it means taking an interest in all the youthful plans. It means adapting her mind to the youthful mind. It means — but why should I tell mothers what that means? They know. And the daughters must do their part too in keeping the confidence-thread between themselves and their mother always perfect and golden.

When a community is really dead, we may know the fact by the absence of sociability. The whole country problem hinges chiefly upon this social matter; and as the woman is the essential upholder of the community the world over in social affairs, it behooves the young woman in rural life to prepare for these responsibilities if she will ward off from the farm and village community a deadly and intolerable inaction.

After all Cousin Artemisia was not in such a parlous state. If those eager eyes had had no expression in them at all, if the curiosity in them had long since faded into indifference and a dull unresponsive look had taken its place, then a just observer might well have had cause for compassion for that young woman into whose soul the iron of isolation had gone so deeply that it had hardened and deadened the best part of her. If a life has been lived through with all its experiences and has been one long record of unsatisfied longing for the impossible, and if the end came without ever one break in the cloud that hid away an imagined world of fulfilment and success, and if during it all there had been never an instant's let-up from the momently waiting for the sun to break through, such a life as that has been a success. Not to attain is not failure. The only failure is to cease trying, to stop aspiring, and to let the dream and the vision fade away from the face of the unresponding clouds.

Some one may say, Why then touch her in this obliviousness of her unfilled possibilities? The same fallacy lies beneath all missionary work, all philanthropy, all striving upward. We wish every Country Girl in the remotest stronghold of conservatism to be touched with that divine discontent that will stir her to an upward struggle.

Among the six million Country Girls for whom this book is written, there are many who are tremendously and honorably efficient; there are also many who are by no means awake to their duty and opportunity; but the vision will soon touch the eyes of all, and will reveal to them the part they may play in the new Country Life era.

Not for her own sake alone does any girl strive. All she does lifts everywhere as well as in her own valley. And these beneficent influences will reach out and include other and still other circles of girls who repose under the protection of the republic. Among these one may see the puzzled eyes of Porto Ricans, and of Aleutian and of Philippine girls. And there are found two larger companies: the dark-skinned girls with the tragic remembrance of slavery in their eyes, and the aquiline faces of the Appalachian mountain girls, dignified and quietly expectant and our close

racial kin.   Among these adoptive and neglected fields there
will be hollows of stagnation and delays of progress.   For
the reclamation of these we are not by any means doing
what we might as a people; they some way escape the great
abundantly filled currents of philanthropy; and if they soon
become discontented and ominous, we shall have ourselves
to blame.   It would be better to be beforehand with nature's demands and arouse noble aspirations that may forestall wrong tendencies.

CHAPTER XXIII

THE SOLACE OF READING

THE EVENING HOUR

The day is done; the clock is striking eight;
The children now are snug and safe abed;
Still on the pillow lies each little head,
Tired out, altho' they begged to sit up late.
I cover the fire within the kitchen grate,
Mix up a light sponge for the morrow's bread,
Wind up the faithful clock; with quiet tread
Depart, and leave my kitchen to its fate.
The study calls me to my favorite nook
Beside the table, underneath the light.
Here shall I joy me with a gracious book
Until at last I bid my world good-night.
O peaceful dreams beneath the homestead roof!
Ye straighten out life's tangled warp and woof!

— *Helen Coale Crew.*

CHAPTER XXIII

THE SOLACE OF READING

THE countryside does not sufficiently appreciate the value of its asset in the changing seasons. The alternation of winter and summer gives the admirable opportunity for the harvest for support, and for the fireside evenings for culture; the two combined make the possibility of an ideal life. Even in the busy time of summer, the farmer who scientifically organizes his scheme of farm work, will be able to give one day a week at least for reading and the study of the literature of farming. Perhaps the number who compose this orderly scheme of work may at present be small, nor has any such boon of system including leisure for reading reached the farm woman. How that older woman on the farm has felt about this, is one of the great complaints lying back of the Country Life Movement. Will the Country Girl be obliged to inherit this deprivation?

From the Country Girl of to-day, the report is far more cheering than from the older women. She has many books at hand. She feels no poverty in this regard. Sometimes they say: "We have a very large library in our house — as many as a hundred books," or they say, "My father left us a large law library," and they seem to love to gaze at the brown backs of these volumes. Certainly this pride in the inheritance is noble.

If you ask Country Girls what books they have for their very own, they will in many cases give long representative lists. Encyclopedias will be included and sometimes books of reference. Their library lists give an insight into the taste in reading of the American Country Girl that is most gratifying. The first impression is that her taste is well founded in classics; the second, that she keeps up with the times. She shows on the whole great catholicity.

We cannot give room to the long lists: but we may mention some of the books that, in response to our request, some Country Girls mentioned as favorites.

In a long list of books that are her own an Iowa girl stars the following as her favorites:

Life of Ellen H. Richards	*Uncle Tom's Cabin*
Shakespeare's Works	*Kidnapped*
Whittier's poems	*Quentin Durward*
Ben-Hur	*The Woman Who Spends*

The stories she enjoys reading when she is tired; the others she takes to study.

Another mentions these:

All of Mrs. Porter's	*Shepherd of the Hills*
Several of Stewart Edward White's	*Johnson's Natural History*
Several of Ralph Connor's	*Personal Memoirs of U. S. Grant*
Three of Fox's	Life of Livingstone
Two of Churchill's	Robert E. Speer's works

She adds Dickens, Poe, Alcott, Whittier as starred favorites.

In a list of twenty books, a Colorado girl stars a large number. The list is headed by " The Library of the World's Greatest Books." Then she mentions:

Laddie	*Lady of the Lake*
Freckles	*As a Man Thinketh*
Girl of the Limberlost	*The Choir Invisible*
Barriers Burned Away	*Little Women*

Her list includes also the Life of John Bunyan, the Life of Christ, the works of George Eliot and of Burns, and many more standard and popular books. She has had a course at college and reads the U. S. Bureau of Agriculture Bulletins:

Books starred by an Idaho girl are:

At the Foot of the Rainbow	*Water Babies*
Promised Land	*The Crisis*
Friar Tuck	*The Varmint*
Treasure Island	Set of Kipling
King of the Golden River	Set of W. Irving

She includes also Riley, E. B. Browning, Wordsworth, Burns.

One writer who lives sixty miles from any kind of library is so fortunate as to have all of Dickens, Scott, Shakespeare, and a copy of Longfellow, Tennyson and Browning. " I have," she says, " a great many miscellaneous books, *The Promised Land, Laddie, A Girl of the Limberlost, The Friendly Road,* and books of that kind. The first three authors are my favorites; but the Bible and Longfellow are the most comfort and enjoyment."

On the whole there are comparatively few to complain, as one did, that the Bible and a paper now and then compose their entire means of outlook into the world of literature; or as this one said: " When I was at home my only book that was my own property was the Bible." Fortunately this young girl had thus a compendium of all literature, and she is coming out all right.

It also should be a surprise that there should be so few to include a list like this: " *Prue and I,* some books on the economic status of woman, and a few books on domestic science." But perhaps Country Girls would not think to classify their interest in such studies as these under the heading " reading."

The mothers and daughters, if requested together, would no doubt mention some of the same interferences with the pleasure of reading; but the daughters give some that the mothers would never have thought to state. Work is the great interference for both. The daughters are deterred by housework, sewing, picking blue-berries, darning stockings. Weariness, the tired-out feeling, come in. There is so much work to be done in doors and out, and the barn work lasts so late; the evenings are short and when the work is finished, it is time to retire.

It is rather pathetic to see how many Country Girls will mention the moment of getting to bed and to sleep as the happiest point in the day. But then — no one has yet said that she was too tired to sleep — and that, we are sure, has happened many and many times to the mothers of yore! And when the daughter speaks of having been kept from reading by her demonstration work duties, we certainly hear a note of the new era being struck. But what farm woman of the old days ever gave " so many other pleasures," or " too many places to go," as reasons for not reading? Piano practise, too, and " friends running in " prevent the reading. There cannot be much isolation in such a farm-stead as that!

Many Country Girls insist emphatically that in spite of difficulties they do read a good deal. Such a girl says that when she has a book the hour of night draws nigh too soon. Another always reserves a few hours each week for reading, though sometimes she can not make it every day. A determined girl declares that she lets nothing interfere with a certain amount of reading. This sort of testimony reaches a height in one who says that she reads or studies five hours every day. Yet the girl who wrote that does most of the housework for a small family and takes care of a large garden.

A few lament the scarcity of books. They have no opportunity to get books aside from the few belonging to one's friends; but these are soon read and re-read. Lack of material is the chief interference with reading with an uncomplaining but very important minority.

If there does really remain any girl in the country who does not know that she can get books from the traveling libraries that are maintained now by almost every State, the glad message should be taken to her at once. And any girl with a fair share of energy could start a small library in her village or her community, even as the peripatetic librarian did in Mr. Bouck White's book, *The Mixing,* who carried the books about to every house and pressed them upon the family at its very threshold. In that case the house was the castle of the woman as well as the man, but the little librarian battered an entrance with her winning ways. After a while everybody blessed her, and her old mare and wagon were welcomed along the roads.

Or the Country Girl might begin with a book exchange club in which each member buys a book a year and these are handed from member to member by the month or as shall be agreed upon. Meetings may be called to talk the books over and fine discussions of ethical points involved in the stories read may be held. At the end of the year the books may be lodged in some convenient place to be used by others not members of the club. In this way a nucleus is made for a regular library. The same can be done with magazines. At the end of the year a " banquet " may be held; each member may be dressed up to represent some book, speeches may be made while good things are eaten, and literary conversation may to some extent drive out less worthy and less interesting themes. Almost anything can be done if there are young people enough to get together and talk over plans. The whole tone of the community may be lifted and many a young person may be saved from the evil things that creep in where the mental spaces have not been forestalled by better ideals.

Many a Country Girl has laid the foundations for a regular public library by using the country store and the schoolhouse for book stations. In one very successful attempt of this kind, one hundred books of fiction and travel, children's books, religious books, history, and biography were chosen.   Voluntary assistance was given by friends, and records were carefully kept.   The following were the appliances necessary.   Besides the one hundred books, there were five hundred book labels, one hundred borrowers' cards, four record books for the librarian, three small memorandum books for the stations, three typewritten book lists or catalogs, and one hundred hand bills.   On the borrowers' cards were printed the directions, which were these: " Any responsible person wishing books may borrow them one at a time; no book may be kept out longer than two weeks; no charge is made for the use of books; please take care of them and return them promptly."   The librarian visited the stations at regular intervals and took up the books that were returned.

There can hardly be a more definite way in which a girl may serve her community than by starting some such scheme as this.   If her own home were conveniently situated, she could use it as book station.

It is to be feared that the Country Girl does not make the most of one great privilege: namely, to lead the family to indulge the luxury and joy of reading aloud together on winter evenings from some interesting author.   Even in a family that is fond of reading, each member of the circle will be seen when lamps are lighted to settle down to read from the book or paper that interests himself or herself alone, and all the good of unified thought, that might be theirs if they had read aloud, of vital interruption and comment, of living together in mind and growing together as the story develops, of enjoying the humor and romance together, are entirely lost.   To read great pieces of literature together in the family is to put a personal consecration about the genius-crowned work of the master spirit. Never can a great epic or drama mean so much to any one of us by closet perusal as it would if we had shared it with our next of kin.   This is another place where losing our life is gaining our life. Our treasure is doubled by giving it to others. Winter evenings and Sunday afternoons all the year round, may be made memorable by association with the greatest minds through their preserved works.

The complaint has been made that there is no literature of farm life — that our literature is now completely urbanized and industrialized. There certainly is a tendency in this direction, especially in the realm of fiction. But it is possible to find some that are giving the country its due, and the writings of Mrs. Porter, so dear to Country Girls, are a proof of the fact.*

But if the Genius of Fiction has become absorbed with the problem of the city, that of Poetry has remained true to its first love among the fields and streams. It is a joy to know that the poets will always be found among the books chosen for the happy winter evening in the country home. There, if not in fiction and tale, countryside people find a reflection of their thoughts. Perhaps this is because poetry is the one art that can conveniently penetrate to the distant homes in remote rural places. Since time immemorial country life seems to have been not only an inspiration to poets, but also to the development of our powers of expression in that highest of the arts. What is there about life in the open that gives to genius its incentive? The beauty of the surroundings ought to be a sufficient answer. But perhaps that very individuality that we blame country life for overdeveloping may be the favorable ground for the upspringing of this noble human blossom. At any rate it seems that if a soul is born with the endowment of genius, the psychical offices of country life will carry those native qualities to their highest power. Many a city child has been born with the light of genius in its

* In the Appendix to this book will be found a reference to a special bibliography made as a guide to certain works of fiction that do illustrate country and village life in various States.

eyes and has had this fire smothered out in the close air and wild rush of the metropolis. But the woods still face the window where Bryant looked out into their mysterious depths, and the brook still sings its way down from the mountains and past the farm where he spent his early years. To him the Berkshire groves were God's chosen temples, first and last.

It is because of this that the poetic writers of the present day and hour should find a sympathetic hearing in the country realm even when the turmoil and drive of the metropolis are deaf to their music. If our living poets may have the people of the countryside for their great and widespread audience they need ask no greater joy.

Mr. Vachel Lindsay, a wandering poet who has traveled almost all over this country preaching his Gospel of Beauty and Democracy, says that in almost every ranch-house " is born one flower-girl or boy, a stranger among the brothers and sisters," a " fairy changeling." The land, he says, is being " jeweled with talented children," from Maine to California. These children of to-day, though they may not be adapted to the strain of heavy labor, yet they will be infinitely patient with the violin, or chisel, or brush, or pen. Country people should be on the watch for those rare wonder children who will be the poets of the future. One of these may seem at the beginning like a simply unusual child. Afterward it may be seen that what was thought queer or different, may have been higher or supreme. We may not have been ourselves sufficiently attuned to the supreme in human accomplishment to recognize the elements in their beginning. Great genius is not " to madness near allied," but is the sanest and most normal thing in the whole realm of creation. The extension of human powers in the field of what we call " genius " is what makes the benefactor of the race in any field most successful and the reformer most influential.

Moreover, every child has the right to find forces in his

world that will make his powers, however great or however small, grow to the full measure of which he is capable.   If one has a little ability in the field of any one among the arts, he has a right to experience the joy and the benefit that as much training as he is capable of taking shall give to him. Therefore artistic training should be given to every child. And since poetry is the art that is most widely disseminated, the one most practical in its service and cheapest to get hold of in places far distant from picture galleries and concert halls, therefore there should be in all the homes in the open, a great deal of poetry, in order to satisfy the demand that is deeply imbedded in every human being for the satisfaction of the love of beauty.

Here is indeed a great service for the daughter in the family to supply.   She is the poetic individual in the home circle.   It will be readily acknowledged as fitting that she should know poetry by heart.   That she should sing poetry feelingly and speak it effectively will be forgiven by a business-hardened parent and a rough, deriding brother, more readily than if any other member of the family circle should make the attempt.   And the persevering and enthusiastic girl will be repaid by finding that the tight outer case of the father will after a time be loosened and that he will be surprised to find himself enjoying what he did not know he liked.   She will be gratified again when the heroic ballad, told to appeal to the brother who is in the chivalrous and fighting era of boyhood, fulfils its mission not only by amusing him, but by leading him up to the chivalric motives and to the conquest of selfishness by the higher ideal of honor and devoir.   If, too, she will select for her evening reading volumes of the poets who are writing today in her own country, writing out of today's life and mood and hope and pain, she will be far more likely to find a sympathetic response in her living audience, than if she chooses from the pages of any souls of poets dead and gone, however classic.

CHAPTER XXIV

THE SERVICE OF MUSIC TO THE COUNTRYSIDE

HARMONIES

The scrubbing's done; my kitchen stands arrayed
In shining tins, and order reigns supreme.
And on the table, like a fairy dream,
A row of pies and cakes, all freshly made
And full of spicy odors, stands displayed;
While from the oven, like a rising stream
Of incense, comes a fragrance, warm, supreme . . .
The bread, its final browning still delayed.
Now while I sit beside the oven door
I take up my guitar upon my knee,
And singing the old songs I knew of yore,
My happy youth comes back again to me.
Music and incense rising on the air!
Courage is mine, and all the world is fair!

                                — Helen Coale Crew.

CHAPTER XXIV

THE SERVICE OF MUSIC TO THE COUNTRYSIDE

MRS. GENE STRATTON PORTER in her book, *At the Foot of the Rainbow,* makes a certain Scotch character say that he does not care for better talking than the " tongues in the trees "; for sounder preaching than the " sermons in the stones "; finer reading than the " books in the river "; no, nor better music than the " choirs of the birds." This music he calls the music of God; he would rather have this, every time, than " notes fra book."

This philosophy of Dannie Macnoun's is excellent; but we must not forget that God made the " notes fra book " also, and gave us our power to design and to enjoy them. It is true also that there is little man has done in copying after the ideas of God that comes so near to the divine as do his attempts in the realm of music. This field nearly all, if they have ears to hear and a voice to sing, can approach in some, at least, of its aspects.

The service of music to the human soul is so excellent that it seems as if it must be one of the necessities. Why does the shepherd invariably possess a flute? The answer is this: some kind of music he *must* have in his solitary life, and the flute is the instrument that can be carried in the pocket. The ills of isolation may be measurably alleviated by this harmonious companionship and this fact seems to meet a fairly widespread appreciation along our countryside. The emphasis is however placed almost entirely upon instrumental music. The piano of course predominates; but the organ frequently takes its place, the violin, 'cello, cornet, flageolet, guitar and trombone are also found.   Then there comes in the phonograph, the graphophone, the Victrola, and the Angelus music-box; the instrument that stands for "all that ever went with evening dress" appears among country customers also, and there seems to be room for mouth-organ and jew's-harp when nothing else offers.

Now a jew's-harp is better than no harp, a mouth-organ is better than no organ; and an accordeon can happify a lowering twilight.   The banjo is an all-round-the-world delight and a guitar may be almost heaven to a music-hungry boy or girl.   A twenty-dollar organ worked by foot-pedals may be a household blessing, and a flageolet has kept many a sheep herder from insanity on a lonely mountain.   But any report on music makes on the whole a sad impression when the human voice is not mentioned; and a hundred will tell of having a musical instrument and some song book or other, where one will speak of singing in the family. Almost every conceivable collection of songs will be mentioned but the general impression gained will be that the American countryside is not filled with singing; that the people do not sing at their work, and that not one hundredth part is there of the joy due them in community music.

In the art and joy of singing together our people seem to have retrograded.   Perhaps the dominant influences at the beginning were not favorable to this art.   Whatever love we had for music was cherished, however, in the church of New England, but the advent of the soloist in the choir loft has put a quietus upon the musical expression in the pew.   Harriet Beecher Stowe tells us how those old billowy fuguing tunes used to be sung, with what gusto the men and women, bass, counter, soprano, and tenor, trained in that national institution, the singing school, would chase the melody around, racing after one another, each singing a different set of words, until at length by some inexplicable magic they would all come together again and sail smoothly out into a rolling sea of song. To her those tunes, as she remembered them from her childhood, were like the ocean aroused by stormy winds, when deep calleth to deep in tempestuous confusion, out of which at last is evolved union and harmony.

It is a pity that such musical impulse as this should be allowed to go to waste. And it is not as if the primitive musical quality were extinguished in us, but the impulse remains submerged unless something brings it out. Professor Peter Lutkin of Northwestern University, head of a school of music that constantly draws students from the Western States, says that you cannot give musical culture to an acre of the Western land without having music talent spring there.

We should follow the example of little Wales, that sturdy sister in the confederation of the British Isles. How wonderful is the singing of the Welsh when they come together in their great national Eisteddfod! There they have a national contest in which many singing societies join, and a prize is given to the victorious one. How do we account for this great interest in singing? Why, there is a Choral Society in every village of Wales. Between village and village, between city and city, there are competitive tests, and this annual event is the outcome of all the smaller ones, the crowning engagement for the highest honors. How much must this mean to the people of the villages! What a comfort to the isolated ones! For twelve miles about any village or town center the people come walking in every Sunday evening, to attend rehearsals for practise in sacred music, hymns and chorals being their mainstay. In northern England we find the same musical feeling, and in Italy. Why these special parts of the world should move in this direction, who can tell? It is enough to know that those rougher, more hilly, and more secluded regions do this service for the people. They make them feel the impulse and the necessity for song.

That the case with us is not by any means hopeless is shown by the story of Norfolk, Connecticut. Here a great musical movement has been led by the Litchfield County Choral Union, a musical society that was founded and led by an inspired man, the keynote of whose life may be found in his own words when he said: "Had I my life to live over again, with such slight knowledge as I may have gained, I would become an humble laborer in a primitive and ignorant farming community where by word and example I might perhaps help to raise its members to a higher standard of life in material and spiritual matters; and could I but implant one better thought into a single soul, life would not have been lived in vain." Such was the quiet but radiant ideal of Robbins Battell, the man that tuned all the life of the lower Berkshires to lofty music. The Choral Union as it now stands is a federation of the musical societies of the larger towns of the county, and includes seven hundred members. Each of these societies has many concerts and festivals for the expression of its own skill and joy in the compositions of the masters; and besides this there is an annual three-day meeting and concert at the great "Music Shed" in Norfolk.

In the festival of 1912 they gave the *Elijah* with a chorus of four hundred and fifteen voices, all chosen from the members of these county Unions. The year before, the same chorus gave excerpts from Gluck's *Orpheus and Eurydice* and the *Hora Novissima* of Horatio Parker; the year before that they gave *Verdi's Requiem* and *The Song of Hiawatha* by S. Coleridge-Taylor. Other concerts accompanied these in which noted soloists took part and great composers were present and conducted their own compositions as given by trained orchestras. So, in 1906 about thirty-six thousand people of the region were able to hear pieces from Wagner, Beethoven, Haydn, Vieuxtemps, Liszt, Rossini, Schumann, Strauss, and Mendelssohn — these were the names represented in the program of 1906, while selections from Goldwork, Beethoven, Tschaikowsky, Saint-Saens, Grieg, Mozart, and Wagner, in 1912 were heard by eight thousand persons.

It is quite impossible to estimate the effect of such musical opportunity or the meaning of these rehearsals from January to June to those villages. The people become consecrated to their art, like the Oberammergauers. Personal ambition is swept away in the success of the song or the oratorio. As there is no entrance to the concerts except by invitation, all mercenary and selfish desire is removed. There is one aim — to express the music perfectly and in the most lofty spirit; therefore the festival is both a vital element in the community and a welder of the people into a social unity. The chorus is also an influence for democracy. There is a weekly rehearsal. Women sometimes walk several miles to attend this and members rarely miss a meeting. One couple came twelve miles every week for eight years. There is no expense except for music and sometimes the sum does not go over sixty cents a year. The possession of a voice is the one condition for entrance, and the land does not assign tuneful voices according to man-made aristocracies; maid and mistress, bank president and store clerk, sing side by side. Into many lives, otherwise inert, the music brings a motive and an inspiration. They sing with wonderful enunciation and with a fervor that can come only from spontaneous rapture. When in *Elijah* the prophets of Baal cried out their prayer for " Fire! " outsiders ran, it is said, and notified the fire department!

To have a large part of the community thus trained, to have all the community thus interested and inspired, to have every least member of the community honored by citizenship in a village where these nobly cultural influences are found, is certainly a great thing. And when we remember that this could happen or rather, could be developed, in any town or village in the land, we can but mourn our silent roadsides, our unsinging lips, our wicked waste of the good gifts of God.

Another rare expression of musical enthusiasm comes from the Central West. The little town of Lindsborg, on the broad high prairies of Kansas, holds each spring during Holy Week a musical celebration called, naturally, the "Messiah Festival." In this case a college is the leader — Bethany College, where there are a thousand students with regular standard courses of study besides varied and excellent choruses, orchestras, societies, and classes for musical development. In the spring of 1914 there was a chorus of six hundred voices; another of children alone contained four hundred and fifty; distinguished singers gave the solos; a week was filled with concerts of classic and modern renderings; Brahms, Dvorak, MacDowell, Sibelius, were found together with Beethoven and Handel, and the whole reached a wonderfully high level of attainment.

What interests us most, however, is to see what this work does for the people of the region. Men and women come from fifteen miles away to attend the rehearsal, and this in winter; three generations of one family sang in the chorus at the last Festival; they play and sing for the pure love and enjoyment of the music. It is altogether impossible to state in words what all this must mean to the moral and spiritual development of the region, to the binding of the hearts of the people in the community, and to the forging of those ties that will hold the young people true in their loyalty to their homes.

It is not claimed that every country community can have such a concourse as this for concert work during the winters; but something like the old singing school might be installed, and home music might be made far more of a joy and comfort than it now is.

That this can be the mission of music in community service is being discerned by many. In the always forward-looking University of Wisconsin, a plan has been made for the development of musical feeling among the people. The desire is to make the people realize the immense social power of music and to give a chance for this welding and delighting influence to have its way in the home, the schools, the churches, in musical organizations of all kinds, in all places of amusement, and in entertainments of all kinds. No doubt other universities in other States will follow this admirable example.

But we do not need colleges and universities to tell us that we should do more with singing than we at present do. Here are six million girls of the countryside — what can they do to redeem the country from this dull silence and unmelodious tedium? What, in fact, might they not do? Let every one of them resolve that she will wake up every morning singing; that she will sing at her work all day long; that she will call for songs in the evenings, with the whole family around — not one, of any age, allowed to be absent from the circle; that she will require that music of some sort shall be part of the ceremony of every society and club she belongs to; that she will get the young people together to sing once at least every week; that she will suggest that the older people should sing together — it is unnecessary and absurd to let the singing days disappear along with youth into the background; and that she will persevere in this till the whole countryside shall ring with song from east to west, and until the stigma that we are a people that do not care for music shall be forever removed. We have some magnificent old folk songs; we have glorious national songs; we have some religious songs with a marching rhythm and a fervor that make them good for every day in the week, for threshing times and for all times; we have a song for every mood and every experience; why not use our songs and enjoy them?

The larger breadths of musical repertory are not so far away from the remote country places as formerly, now that the victrola and other instruments of like kind bring a knowledge of the great orchestral and operatic passages to our very sitting-room. Every village should have this help in order to understand the great music that without it might be shut off from us. There should be one in every social center for general use in the community. A good way is for some member of the music-study committee to give a description of the opera or the oratorio, with comments on the particular passage that the instrument can render; then the listeners are better able to understand what is being played and by the imagination to place the solos in their right background as they are being heard; an impression of the work as a whole will be thus gained that will to some extent approach the composite scene as it is shown on the stage. " Ah! can you imagine what the victrola means to us out here on this prairie! " wrote a friend from western Nebraska. This may be the experience of every rural circle the country over if it will only have community spirit enough to work together and acquire the music-reproducing apparatus.

Another thing that can be done is to get together all the people in the community that can play on any kind of instrument, and make them play together. Do not despise the day of small things. There must be a beginning. It will not be long before we can do more in any village, and at last we can have music of a higher order to drive the ills of isolation out of our atmosphere and introduce a healthful harmony in their place. If a boy belonged to an orchestra that met on Monday and Friday evenings for practise, to a class in voice on Tuesday evening, and had engagements with groups of young men and young women to train for concerts all the other evenings of the week and was to sing in the church choir on Sunday, is it possible that he would feel that he could be spared to go away to the city to live? The case of the Country Girl will be exactly parallel. Her voice is the leading voice in the quartette; she is necessary to the musical atmosphere of the vil-

lage; she is the hostess everywhere; she cannot be spared
from any village and country life that is full of musical
and other social engagements. And among the influences
that beneficently endow human beings, the one that is at
once most welding, most unifying, and most delighting is
music.

CHAPTER XXV

THE PLAY IN THE HOME

O little bulb, uncouth
  Rugged, and rusty brown,
Have you some dew of youth?
  Have you a crimson crown?
    Plant me ánd see
    What I shall be —
    God's fine surprise
    Before your eyes!
                — *M. D. Babcock.*

CHAPTER XXV

THE PLAY IN THE HOME

THE development of musical taste and the power to enjoy the works of the great composers is closely akin to the ability to appreciate the sister art of the drama. The art that has grown out of that imitative impulse, which is so deeply implanted in human nature and has reached such heights in the hands of genius, has modest stages of growth that may be seen in the daily programs of the home, the school, the playground, in all the walks of children and of grown people. To be able to tell a story, and show it up with a little dramatic imitation, is to add to the success of the social queen, the drummer, the one who influences and manages men or women in any field. There are people who think it well worth while to spend much time in the study of the art of expression, just to add to their powers of entertainment when they wish to use this form of culture in the home circle only. It is not at all a bad thing to do. Thus to train the voice for sweet and fine or for powerful and striking modulations, to give the face new power of showing emotion, to win also the help of gesture, is to add to one's resources and to make them a greater source of enjoyment in the daily walks of life.

It is hardly possible to think of society in any age of the world since we became human beings when the intercourse of people was not lighted up with electric bits of humor, joking and ridicule, based on the dramatic principle of imitation. But when the day came for our solemn ancestors in New England to appear on the scene, they concocted a theory of duty that was not favorable to these pleasurable forms of activity.

Yet, as we have seen, these subdued people loved music and they loved beauty in all forms. And when beauty could be had along with what they considered a pure and dignified aspect of expression, they winked at the keen pleasure that they felt and said nothing against it.

An interesting story of Catherine Beecher, daughter of the great New England theologian, Dr. Lyman Beecher, illustrates this. It is related in the autobiography of her father that she once devised a play and prepared, unknown to her parents, to give it in the kitchen of their home in Litchfield, Connecticut. The unsuspicious parents, it seems, did not notice that the neighbors were dropping in with a very unusual simultaneousness and that after supper an unwonted fire was being built in the parlor. Soon the door into the kitchen was opened with a flourish, a curtain was seen to have been strung across the room, Roman senators began to stalk across the stage — the kitchen floor — and a good rousing dip was taken by all into the fountain of antique romance. After it was over the stern father, who had been too greatly overwhelmed by the events of the evening to make any objection, whispered to that favorite daughter of his that it had all been very interesting but — better, not do that again! Catherine got off easily, considering the repute in which dramatic representations were held by our forefathers. Temptations to evil, at least, they were considered to be, if not the very path itself.

Yet Catherine Beecher made many plays, devised in large part from the plots of approved and semi-pious story-books, and these were enacted at school and at the picnics of her large circle of brothers and sisters. Moreover her sister Harriet (afterward Harriet Beecher Stowe) being at about this period of her youth filled with the aspiration to become a great tragic poet, wrote reams and reams of blank verse on a classic theme developed in dramatic form. By this time, however, the elder dominant sister Catherine must have seen the error of her ways, for finding Harriet one day in the act of composition, she took her precious play away from her, bidding her to cease this waste of time and go to work on her Butler's *Analogy of Nature and Religion*. And Harriet obeyed.

This story is told to afford one illustration of the fact that the divine endowments of human genius cannot be so easily crushed out. A theory will not accomplish it.

Catherine and Harriet Beecher were not the only possessors of glowing dramatic inspirations in the early days. We had not been fully settled here very many lustrums before the submerged river of artistic feeling came to the surface in the form of vivid oratory and elaborate dialogue; and when there began to be Sunday Schools there were Sunday School concerts with tableaux of an unworldly sort, with dialogues and with companies of young people who, in a small and innocuous way, engaged in exercises that might be called acting. This was found more or less all over New England and went with the New England migration into New York, and Ohio, and then farther west. Many thousands of angels with tinsel crowns and tissue-paper wings have filled the spaces between pulpit and organ in the little white churches that have sprung up beside every hill along what we may call the New England belt — the course of the travels westward across the continent as the generations of descendants have passed on and built and subdued the soil and planted schools and churches along the northern latitudinal lines.

The story of Catherine Beecher illustrates too the fact that the prejudice in the dwellers in country districts against the use of dramatic forms of entertainment is based after all not so much upon the dramatic representation itself as upon certain conditions and associations often found connected with theatrical displays as carried on in larger towns and cities and believed to be necessary to the existence of theatrical life.

There is a village in Illinois with a population of nine

hundred where the majority of the church-going people — and most of the inhabitants of the town belong to that class — have been of the opinion that it is a wicked thing to go to see a play if it is enacted by some company of play-actors such as might come along on their theatrical route; yet in that town for years the townspeople have been giving plays of their own, in which nearly the whole population of the place would join, old and young, rich and poor, wise and unwise. The whole family from grandmother to grand-child will sometimes appear in one play, and all the cousins and relatives of the whole " team-haul community " will come to see. They give many standard melodramas, and they have also tried their hand at Shakespearean drama, to the great enjoyment and uplift of themselves, both those that thoroughly capture the meaning of the play by training for the parts, and those that closely if charitably attend and listen. Why should not this be done in every small town? Why should not the unused building, an old barn, a store-loft, be transformed into a country theater, where the whole village may assemble twice a week or oftener, and run through a play together, getting joy and culture at once?

If once the ingrained, inherited prejudice, handed down from those misinterpreting honorable ancestors of ours, could be overcome, the plunge might be taken and the drama could become the education and inspiring agent that it has the capacity to be in our homes, our schools, and our towns and villages.

Especially to the remote village and to the lonely farm would this form of entertainment be a benefit. Do we not need this also to help lift the ban of loneliness and to supply that elasticity of spirit that means life to us? Companion-ship is our lack, the impact of various lives upon ours, the stirring of resentment against wrong or of enthusiastic approval of the good and noble that comes from the clash of motives, right and wrong, wise and unwise. If we are denied the opportunity to see and feel all this in the scenes from actual life in which we ourselves in our own persons participate, we may receive some portion at least of the education to be derived from such impact by living for a time in the imagined world of the dramatist's creation and by watching the constant intricate play of emotion in the dialogue. And this we can in no other way do so well as by taking a part in the drama and appropriating it for our own; by living in that part, adopting the imagined circumstances for our own and following out the problem in the character represented and pursuing his fate to the bitter end. To do that is to gain to some extent the effect of companionship and its enlightening, enlarging and satisfying influence. To the extent that we are able to do this shall we combat and overcome the stagnation and the pain of loneliness.

As a by-product of the same exercise, we shall gain a new knowledge of our own capacity. We shall take a long step in the direction of obeying the old dictum to " know thyself." If, for instance, we are reading the part of Hamlet, and are trying to adopt his life and problem for the time being for our own, we learn how much we could suffer, how strongly we could determine, how fiercely we could doubt and yet struggle on, how tenderly we could love and yet resign, how all these things we could feel if we were really the Hamlet of the great play of Shakespeare.

In this way we gain an enlargement of our own nature and receive inspirations to heroism on our own part. This is not wasted time, for there is no life that does not afford opportunity for heroism or that does not need inspirations to courage and fortitude.

There are people who do not enjoy reading a play. They miss the constant running description of movement and gesture, of scenery and color and background, of meaning and prophecy and scope that are found in a story or in narrative of any kind. They are not accustomed to supplying the pictures of the story from the resources of their own imagination. However valuable a discipline it may be for them to learn how to make up imaginary backgrounds instead of depending upon the writer's aid, to that form of discipline they will not give the trouble. But if such readers will take the play into the family circle, and using several copies of the text, assign parts to each of the family, and thus read the text aloud, letting the words spoken by each of the characters give the suggestion for action, and encouraging each one to give the proper expression and gesture as he reads his part, the meaning will come clear as the scene goes on, and the proper enjoyment of the play as a play will enter into each one that shares the cast. If this does not happen with the first reading, it will come with the second or third. It is a pretty poor play that will not bear several readings; while as for the greatest of dramatists, Shakespeare, his plays will stand many and many a reading. It would be a good winter's enjoyment on a far away farm, for the family to set apart one or two evenings a week to be given to reading of the plays by the greatest poet and dramatist. Several plays would do for one winter and the whole thirty-six of them would last for several years, and then one could begin again at the beginning and read them over with renewed interest and understanding. Thus the farm home could have a theater of its own in the warm sitting-room while the soft snow covered the acres all about, hushing every disturbing sound.

Perhaps that lofty master of the dramatic art should not be the first one mentioned. It is quite easy to understand that some Country Girl will think this poet to be hard reading for one who has not had the chance to go through high school. For those who are timid about taking a bold leap into the field of more advanced literature there are many plays made from our present-day lives that are easy to read and to enact, plays adapted to any number of people, plays that may include father, mother, and the children down to the smallest; and there are many kinds of tableaux and smaller plays that can be represented on the lawn of the farm-house or in the kitchen after the work is done.

Of course the greatest thing of all would be to make one's own plays out of one's own circumstances or out of the things that one is thinking about every day. In making a play one must first choose a hero or a heroine; then imagine something that this hero wishes to do. After that some great difficulty is to be planned that he must meet, some opposition he must overcome. In constructing a drama you tell the story of a struggle or endeavor of this kind, putting it all into the words the people speak and nothing at all into any account of the action, the gesture, or the dress. All those things must be seen to by the people who take the parts. And the background may be selected that will come nearest to being the right and fit one for the people and action suggested by the words of the play.

There is an infinite possibility before those who will make the attempt to let the playing of plays have part in the amusements in the farm home. All ages can be suited with plays, the simple ones for the smallest children, the more complex and finished for the older ones, the great ones for the oldest and most educated among the members of the family. As drama is one expression of the play spirit (using the word here in its meaning of " recreation "), and the satisfaction that comes with the feeding of this hunger in people of all ages, has but to be once known for us to seek earnestly for its food another and yet another time.

To show how this instinct has been made effective in one home I quote, with kind permission, a play made by one little girl of eleven years old. In reading it over the reader will see what the child has been reading and where she got the material of the thoughts she has embodied in the action and atmosphere of this naïve and delightful little play.

TRUE LOVERS

By Julia Carolyn Horne

THE CAST

King Eric .... Betsy Horne
Princess Elaine, his daughter ....Harriet Benger
Sir Constantine, knight, in love with Princess Elaine
Julia Horne
Omar, a page .... Billie Horne
Three ladies in waiting to the Princess — Jessielyn Lucas, Helen
Ecker, Helene Timmerman.

Scene I.— Court of King Eric.

King *seated on throne.* Princess Elaine *beside him, attended by her three maids of honor. A loud knocking is heard.* Omar *goes to the door and returns.*

Omar [*bowing low before throne*] — Your Majesty, a visitor has come.

King — Bring him in.

[Omar *ushers in a knight.*]

Sir Constantine [*bowing low before the throne*] — Most noble King, I beg of you your daughter's hand in marriage.

King [*stamps impatiently*] — No! Out of my royal presence at once!

Knight — Farewell! Farewell!

[*Bows low and withdraws.*]

Princess Elaine. [*rising*] — Alas! Alas! It is so sad! Father, if ever thou carest for my happiness, grant him my hand.

[*Withdraws.*]

King — Come back, daughter, be not so foolish.

Scene II.— Under the Window.

Knight [*kneeling, sings*] —"Oh, ma charmante. Dost thou love me, fair one?" etc.

Princess — Yea, Sir Knight; Cupid's arrow hath in truth pierced my heart.

Knight — And wilt thou elope with me? Fear not.

Princess — I fear lest thou should think I bear no love for my father, or that I am too easily won. But yea, I will.

KNIGHT [*bends low and kisses her hand*] — I will come even on Wednesday next. Will it be long, sweetheart?

PRINCESS [*waves hand and tosses a kiss*] — Yea, it will be long.

SCENE III.— THE ELOPEMENT.

KNIGHT — See, dearest, I am come, and we shall flit away to my castle. Step forth from thy lattice. Quick! Spring into my arms.

PRINCESS — It is even so.

SCENE IV.— KING ERIC'S COURT.

KING [*rushes in excitedly*] — Where is my daughter? My daughter! [OMAR *appears in response to bell.*] Omar, scour the kingdom for that wretched Sir Constantine. He no doubt knows something about my daughter.

[OMAR *retires, while* KING *walks up and down stage in anger until* OMAR *returns.*]

OMAR [*returns and bows low*] — Your Majesty, I have searched everywhere except in the forest.

KING — What! not found my daughter? Now methinks the forest is the very place to which she and her scoundrel Knight would take themselves. Now will I creep all through the forest, and mayhap I will find these madcapped lovers. Their ill-gained happiness will soon be brought to an end.

SCENE V.— THE FOREST.

[KNIGHT *and* LADY *enter arm in arm.*]

KNIGHT [*radiantly*] — We are now safe. Thy father would never hunt us here. We shall spend our day in the forest.

PRINCESS — It is even so.

KNIGHT [*looking around joyously*] — The birds shall sing at our wedding. Fragrant wild flowers shall be thy wedding bouquet. Oh! let us scorn not Nature, for she and Love are great friends.

PRINCESS — Yea, 'tis so.

[*The* KING'S *voice is heard without.*]

KNIGHT [*suddenly in alarm*] — Ah, woe! woe! Here comes thy father. I must not flee, but fight.

PRINCESS [*clinging to* KNIGHT] — Oh! go not forth, my Knight!

KNIGHT — That angry voice! I hoped never to hear more. I am young, I thought experienced. He is old, yet mighty.

KING [*enters*] — Fight with me, Sir Knight, and defend your lady with your body. Do your best, for I am come to test your fame.

[Duel with swords, KNIGHT *falls.]*

KNIGHT — Alas! I am weak and my courage fails. Spare me, O King.

KING — So, thou pleadest for mercy. Yea, mercy thou shalt have. But go thou away, far away. Be banished, nevermore to return.

*[*KNIGHT *departs mournfully.]*

KING *[embracing daughter tenderly]* — Weep not, daughter. I shall banish thy lover till thou shalt be more careful how thou dost elope. Have done with thy weeping. Thou shalt have no tears left for thy other lovers if they dare to come.

PRINCESS *[in tears]* — Ah, cruel father! dost thou have no pity for me?

KING — Why did'st thou not tell me before, oh, daughter! I knew not how true was thy love. Would I could call the brave Sir Constantine back. But that is against the law.

SCENE VI.— THE KNIGHT'S DEATH.

KNIGHT *[calls]* — Oh, Omar!

[Enter PAGE.]

Faithful bearer of my letters, take this to my Lady and tell her that I have died of grief.

[Sighs, falls and·expires.]

SCENE VII.— COURT OF KING ERIC.

*[*LADY ELAINE, *with* MAIDS.]

PRINCESS *[as* OMAR *enters]* — Ah! see! here comes a messenger. Now will I see what my dear Sir Knight will say to me.

*[*OMAR *gives her a letter.]*

[Reads:]

" Dear Lady — I have died of grief, and shall never see thee more.

" CONSTANTINE."

PRINCESS — Alas, Alas! My Knight, I will join thee.

[Screams, falls, dies.]

KING *[enters sorrowfully]* — Oh! 'tis but to-day that my daughter had a letter saying that her lover had died of grief. She, too, has died of sorrow, and I shall have the same fate. Woe, that I had no time to repent!

[*Falls, dies.*]

THE END

The utter childlikeness of this playlet is one of its chief charms. Any one may play it — it is not copyrighted. And if it may seem forbiddingly dark in tone, perhaps in spite of the empurpled tragedies of its ending, the pang will be turned to joy when the king and the princess arise promptly from the ground and assume their proper character as father and little daughter amid the wild plaudits of the audience, consisting probably of mother only.

Nothing can be better for the children than to engage them in the making of little plays such as this. There are now many books of plays for children and young people. Of course there are not enough. There should be one hundred where there is now but one. If all the young people would go to work devising plays we would soon have more; and plays made by themselves for themselves would be better for their use than any others could ever be.

Where the life of the sixteen-year-old daughter in the home may become most useful may perhaps consist in getting the parents and the children to join her in carrying through the great endeavor of presenting a play, some winter afternoon in the kitchen, for their own delectation and education. It is easy to imagine the whole family, including the father, whatever his age may be, taking part in a play; and if the father finds it hard work to fall down dead at the proper minute, it is good enough for him for allowing himself to grow so stiff! And if he finds it difficult to feel at home in a helmet of pasteboard trimmed with gilt paper and decorated with dust-brush plumes, he may remember that he is ridiculous in his own eyes only, not in those of the enraptured boy and girl who are fellow actors with him.

An unfailing source of good plots is always at hand in the Bible; and no better way to impress these stories upon the memory could be found than by turning the incidents into little plays and tableaux for the family to show. The Sabbath School lesson could be metamorphosed into a joy and the symbolisms of Christmas and Easter could be made a reality by the legitimate use of the dramatic instinct that is innate in all of us.

A form of art akin to the play is the moving picture. This source of amusement and of education is within the reach of every country community that has learned the secret of joining hands. The men and especially the women of the community should be invariably present and should instantly and firmly object to any film that seems to them harmful. This being provided, the young people are safe and may have the pleasure and instruction that come from seeing displayed the clean, adventurous story, the doings of other lands and of historic events long past.

CHAPTER XXVI

PAGEANTRY AS A COMMUNITY RESOUR·

Truth is eternal, but her effluence,
With endless change, is fitted to the hour;
Her mirror is turned forward, to reflect
The promise of the future, not the past.

— Lowell.

CHAPTER XXVI

PAGEANTRY AS A COMMUNITY RESOURCE

THE swiftly awakening artistic energies of the Country Girl are finding still another outlet in the new national interest in pageantry.

Now that we realize our puritanic mistake about the God-given powers for artistic enjoyment, we are taking to our heart the ravishing delight that the quick and vivid sense of beauty can yield. The pageant is one expression of this; along with Old Home week, and other celebrations of local history, it is also a blossoming of our quickening historic sense. We see that there is a great deal of education to be found in the pageant itself, and a great deal of community spirit in the making and in the representing of this form of dramatic art.

The pageant is a form of drama in which the greatest freedom is allowed as to the dimensions of the stage, the number of the actors, and all the provisions of properties and scenery. Instead of a constricted box-like compartment such as the audience faces in the usual theater, the hillside or the village green may be the stage. In the place of a few accurately balanced characters, whole congregations of worshipers, audiences of citizens, or armies of soldiers, may assemble, flocks of faeries may fly by, unreal spirits of the winds and very real spinsters or bachelors may hold conversation with each other, and throughout the whole structure of the work the fancy may have its way with the actual and disport itself freely with the romantic.

It is not many years since the pageant began to be taken up in this country as a form of artistic expression. When we began to realize how strangely romantic our course of history as an American people had been, when we viewed our past struggle to subdue the soil and overcome the difficulties of pioneering as a most tragic story, as a heart-moving tale fitted for the great epic and for the great tragic drama, then we felt the impulse to place these tales of old-time heroism in fitting artistic form before the eyes of the people.

It was not without meaning that the desire to express in dramatic form the pictures of our historic past had its earliest origins not in the metropolitan square but on the village green, with a background not of skyscrapers but of sequoia groves. Again we see rural conditions more favorable to the budding powers of human genius. There our newly awakened enthusiasm for community betterment promptly seized the pageant as a fitting means of expressmg its urgent emotion. Looking forward into the future we desired to express our hopes for enlargement as we had expressed our vision of the meaning of past struggles.

There are plain reasons why this loose and easy dramatic form is especially adapted for the use of a town or village when it wishes to portray dramatically its own historic and community experiences. In fact, American pageantry has had from the earliest attempts a distinct reference to the welfare of the community and to the development of the rich resources of fellowship to be found in concerted action. This was amply shown at Thetford, Vermont, where one of the earliest and most successful pageants was given. That was as late as 1911. The author of the text frankly stated that the pageant seemed to him the expression of a movement for the general development of the resources of the town, agricultural, educational and social. The work should become, then, a study of the rural problem, and a contribution toward the effort to make the country town fulfil its ideal as a place to live. In this effort the pageant has been a success; it has proved a molding, unifying and inspiring influence; it has quickened into life the slumbering

The swiftly awakening artistic energies of the Country Girl are finding an outlet in the new national interest in pageantry. The farm, meadow or field makes an ideal stage.

One of the many Eight Weeks' Clubs organized throughout the country by the Y. W. C. A.

energies of the people. By awakening pride in the characteristics of the town and the region, interest in the history of their past, and hopes for the better things of the future, it has created a shoulder to shoulder feeling and a vivification of energy that have brought new ideas to life and given courage to try them.

In the pageant reality may be mingled with symbolism — the latter for passages not susceptible of representation on so large a stage as the village green, or for certain elements of village life that could not be put into direct dramatic form. For instance, after some scenes from the early history of a town have been shown, the conditions of modern times may be symbolized by embodying the new life in a character to be called the Spirit of Pageantry or the Spirit of Putting Joy into Work. She will be radiant with hope and joy, and her motions will be stately and ritualistic. Prone upon the ground before her may lie a character representing the Village of Time Past, clothed in a dingy dress and expressing melancholy in her whole appearance. The Spirit of Pageantry may lift her up and give her encouraging words. Following this a figure on a white horse who represents America may enter and the pageant may close with the orchestra and chorus singing " O say can you see by the dawn's early light? " Something a little like this was done at Thetford, Vermont.

The pageant at St. Johnsbury had an advantage in that its name suggested knightliness and gave opportunity for armor, processions of knights, and chivalric poems. They had also the Fairbanks' Scales as a motive suggesting an interesting symbol for their historic treatment. In Meriden, Vermont, Education for the New Country Life was taken as a theme and the founding of their Academy was the central feature. The individuality of every town may be expressed in its pageant. No two would ever be alike.

How a pageant idea may be used to illuminate a sacred or ecclesiastical subject may be seen in a masque that was written for the dedication of a chapel. The plan is very simple. One character represents the church as a whole, and another, a younger woman, stands for the Spirit of the Chapel. This character presents a model of the chapel to the Church, who in stately measures of verse, receives the gift, and asks to know what the services of the people are to be. A series of scenes are the answer. Women and children come with their burdens of sickness and poverty and are helped. A battalion of boys show their drill and receive prizes. Various clubs offer entertainment. Strangers of different nationalities are welcomed one after another, and before the evening is over one has seen an exhibition of model devices for making a church touch every side of the life in a community. Of course a church that has no benevolent activities in working order could not hope to provide a pageant that would have dramatic interest. A dead church could only betray its poverty. And yet — perhaps it would be salutary for some churches if they could be stung into such betrayal: it might awaken them to a sense of their own losses of the joy of giving and of doing.

A story that has been passed down from generation to generation can be used in a pageant. This is delightfully illustrated in a scene from *The Mohawk Trail,* a pageant given in the summer of 1914 at North Adams, Massachusetts, in honor of the re-opening after many centuries of disuse of an old path over the Hoosac Mountain that used to be the connecting link between the Iroquois Indians of New York and the tribes of New England. Eleven hundred persons took part in this great play. There were Indians, early settlers, Quakers, Revolutionary soldiers, Spirits of the Pines and Spirits of the Waters, the Little Creatures of the Swamp, and so on. The inhabitants of several towns took part and the Muse of Cooperation (a newcomer in that select Greek group!) must have waved happy wings over the whole mountain region.

The scene referred to was based on the following story: There were many Quakers among the early settlers in that region and among them was a pretty young Quaker sister that an English officer fell in love with, thereupon asking her father to give him her hand in marriage. The old gentleman said: "If thee will give up thy fighting, thy sword and thy sinful coat of scarlet, and become a good Quaker gentleman, thee may have my daughter, sir, for she loves thee." The officer, it is said, did give up his commission, marry the pretty Quaker and adopt the Quaker garb and the Quaker principles.

In the pageant this quaint incident appears in this wise: The British officer alights on the pageant green near the meeting-house and stands waiting. The young Quakeress comes demurely along, picking flowers as she approaches. While they are conversing, the people begin to enter the church. As they pass they look with curiosity upon the two young people, who when the father and mother come near, show the very picture of woe. The British officer however steps toward the parents, leading the maiden by the hand and says: "Friend Bowerman, may I have thy daughter for my wife? I love her, sir, and will guard her with my life. Do not, I pray thee, say me nay. My happiness and hers depend upon the decision." Here the soldier and the maiden kneel before the stern parents. Says Friend Bowerman: "Rise from thy knees, Friend, kneel only to thy God. Thee may have my daughter, sir, upon one condition. Thee must give up thy fighting, thy sword, and thy sinful coat of scarlet and become a good Quaker gentleman. Think well on this, good friend, before making thy decision."

Then Friend Bowerman and the mother go toward the meeting-house, leading the daughter sorrowfully with them. The English officer now seats himself to think and decide. Immediately thereupon things begin to happen. Enter Cupid with his little bow and dances about him. Next the

Spirit of War rides across the green; the soldier sees the war-horse and runs eagerly toward it. He leads it forward as if about to mount, when presto! Cupid runs forward, and draws his bow. The officer returns to his seat, drops his face and thinks some more.

Now the people come out of the church and gather in groups shaking hands with each other. Friend Bowerman comes along with wife and daughter. Cupid hides in the bushes. The British officer rises from his meditation, steps forward and says:

"Friend Bowerman, I have made my decision. I lay my sword, my scarlet coat and my commission at the feet of thy daughter whom I ask to be my beloved wife."

Friend Bowerman says to Rachel his wife, "What sayest thou, Rachel?" and she nods acquiescence. Then he says to the officer, "Thee may have her, Friend, for she loves thee."

Then the people gather around the couple, the wedding ceremony is performed, the officer and the pretty bride mount and ride away, the Quakers disperse, and Cupid dances gleefully about the green.

There were ninety Quakers in this scene and nearly all of them were direct descendants of the true Quakers of the earlier time. This adds, of course, immensely to the interest of the scenes. To think that one is enacting a story that our great grandparents lived, making history as they lived, is a wonderful experience. But we are living too; we are making history. And perhaps the things we do shall be thought worthy of remembrance.

The pageant in this country has an opportunity that almost no other land on the globe can afford. This is illustrated in one of the scenes of the St. Johnsbury play, a town whose business of scale-making has called to the town many people of many different nationalities. In one of the Interludes of their pageant companies of people entered in the costumes of the countries from which they had come and danced the folk dances of their various nations.   So for instance the French Canadians came in and danced the old Vintage-dance to the proper folk-music accompaniment. Following them the Germans danced the German Hopping-dance; then the Scandinavians gave their Kulldansen, the Scotch the Scotch reel, the Irish the St. Patrick's jig, the Italians the tarantella.   After these separate dances were finished, all the different companies came in together across the greensward and marched in and out in interlocking wheels, until they formed themselves into one large glorious united wheel together.   The beautiful lesson is very plain.

In such scenes as these full opportunity is specially given for the young people to take part.   They can be choruses; they can be pioneers or fairies; they can be flowers and birds and butterflies; they can be spirits of waves, of breezes, of leaves and brooklets, all in appropriate costumes of tissue-paper wings or khaki Indian suits, or blue denim cloth with patterns cut out and sewed on.   This gives every one a feeling of being a part of the day's great celebration and awakens the spirit of home and community in the heart.

To represent a pageant with broad historic effects one must have many characters and a great deal of perspective. But the beauty of it is that this great piece of work is one that can engage the interest of every last man, woman or child in the whole town.   There are so many parts to the completed whole, there are so many kinds of ability that can be brought into play that every member of the community can be given a portion of the structure for his or her responsibility; and the final joy of achievement is gained, the sense of being a part of a great whole, the joy of the community working together.

There must be committees.   All the noted and leading people of the town and county may be made into a Committee of Patrons and Patronesses.   To these may be added the names of any people of note whose interest can be gained.   The honor of heading the committee will perhaps not be declined by the Governor of the State, and any literary people who may live in the vicinity will be proud to give their names. The author or authors of the text, the composer of the music and the Master of the Pageant who has main charge of the dramatic presentation, will be in a distinctive group by themselves. There should be a suitable person to see that the historical matters are correctly used, a historical censor or critic. There must be a committee to take charge of funds incoming and outgoing, one for advertising, one for costume, one for properties. Other committees will have charge of buildings and grounds, of seating and lighting, and any other matters that are likely to come up, such as care of horses or oxen; and if there are to be any eagles, ostriches, rattlesnakes or giraffes — why, safety and agreeableness would seem to require that there should be a committee for each of these! It is evident that the pageant will find use for all the tastes and abilities of the whole village, not to say the entire township. Many and many a meeting will be held and many a discussion about the olden time and what the grand-parents now have to carry on their various industries and household and town activities. And every boy and girl who takes part in those discussions will have a deepened realization of the hardships that our ancestors went through to prepare the way for the blessings that we now enjoy.

The pageant not only cultivates the historic sense; it also makes us better understand ourselves in the present; and it quickens our sense of living for the things that are to be and that are to be a growth from the things that are, as what we are now has come up from the past. The picture of the heroism of our ancestors gives us the enlargement that always comes from the view of great ideals of courage and nobility. So our culture and our spiritual height are enlarged, our sense of the dignity of the human race is heightened, and our determination to live highly is intensified.

It is a good thing to present any dramatic piece that has been created by the great minds and poets of earth. This should also be a part of our endeavor. To do this brings us into a closer touch with the mind of the great artistic creator than we can come in any other way. We have then held up before our mind the ideal of great artistic form and the influence of this model will be incalculable upon our education and development. But there is a certain spontaneity of self-expression, a certain arousing of the intellectual powers and of the artistic feeling, that comes with the making of our own play, that can hardly be otherwise gained. Both experiences are within the opportunity of any village or community. Both joyful means of self-expression can be mastered and experienced. The play and the pageant form the greatest means for the expression of the artistic energy of a community that can be devised.

The pageant may be the happy means of bringing the whole town together. It breaks over all dividing lines because every individual in the community can have at least some part in it. The pride in the success of the whole can be shared by every least child, by each most important person, by the rich and the poor, by the wise and by the unlearned; for there has been a place for each one, according to his ability. The pageant is democratic; all individuals work for the success of the whole, not for the glorification of any single one, never for the glorification of self. It develops a personality of the community itself.

Above all things it gives the person and the community a chance to gain the joy that comes from the expression of that creative sense that lies at the base of all artistic ability, that power in which the human being is most near to the God-like. Here the poets and dramatic writers of earth, the great souls of the Greek and of the Elizabethan ages have been partakers of the fervor that was with God under the symbol of " Wisdom " as that wonderful poem in the eighth chapter of the Book of Proverbs, relates, when with joy He created the earth.

Among all the good things that may come in the new up-springing of this artistic interest, the young women in the rural realm have a distinct function. In the planning of the play or pageant the young people will be brought together in social ways that are full of opportunity for high-toned acquaintanceship and culture under the best auspices. Ladies and gentlemen, young men and young ladies, will be working together for an artistic purpose; the result will be not only an enlarged community spirit among all, but a great number of personal ties that will be of enduring value. May not this be still another interest that will bind the younger members of the village life more closely to the home place so that they cannot be lured away?

There are pageants that may be enacted by young girls alone when fairies and sylphs and angels hold the stage and delight the eye with their many-hued robes and their beautiful movements. The Young Women's Christian Association has given some altogether delightful masques and pageants; the Camp Fire Girls have done the same. In their societies, whatever the kind, Country Girls may undertake some of the plays of smaller scope but quite as beautiful in their way as those in which the whole community join, and in this way find their hands filled with pleasing and recompensing labor.

CHAPTER XXVII

ORGANIZATIONS, ESPECIALLY THE YOUNG WOMEN'S CHRISTIAN ASSOCIATION

Raise the stone: thou shalt find me there;
Cleave the wood, and there am I.

—Logia of Jesus.

CHAPTER XXVII

ORGANIZATIONS, ESPECIALLY THE YOUNG WOMEN'S CHRISTIAN ASSOCIATION

IN a Memoir that belongs to the classic traditions of our country, that of David Brainerd the Missionary, we read that he besought the Lord that he might not be too much pleased and amused with dear friends and acquaintances one place and another. We have now a new and different ideal of community feeling; we pray that we may be " pleased and amused with dear friends and acquaintances," for we realize that only by having ideas together and working together may we reach the highest ideals not only for the community but for the individual.

Where isolation becomes really intolerable, the Country Girl cannot be blamed for taking the first means to relieve herself of its dangers. But where there is a possibility of making a stagnant place become healthily busy and interesting, she must be blamed for not making an attempt in that direction.

An association of the girls alone is always possible if there is even one more than one to start with. Perhaps others will soon join. The most unpromising material, if it is human material, can be brought into line and made something of. But there must be a start.

Now and then we know there is a girl found among the good people of a village who has thoroughly bad inclinations. Such a one, after the case is made clear, must be put into the hands of some person of trained experience and mature judgment. This is not to be managed by the girls themselves. Because of this possibility it is thought best that every club for girls, especially for the younger girls, should have a guardian or a secretary of older years. Whatever rules are made, say, for instance, by the Young Women's Christian Association, in the fundamental plans for societies of girls, we may be sure they have been devised by people who are good, and who desire the best for the girls, and who understand the whole situation and speak and act from this knowledge.

It may be that the girl who will entertain the bold idea of forming a club or society is not by any means the one who most needs the club. She thinks of it because some happy circumstance has developed in her a power of initiative, the courage or instinct for beginning something new. It takes courage sometimes to undertake an absolutely new work; and the girl who has been always helped, never told to go ahead and do things for herself, will not have developed that power. The ability to start things can be hypnotized out of anybody; the faculty for it, if once possessed, can be deadened or suppressed beyond the last degree of vitality. To take the first step is a matter of life or death with such a long suppressed nature; but that one step over, the crushed vitality springs strangely to life and then every step is easier. Then the beautiful experience lies before you of constantly growing life; faculties that you hardly knew you possessed spring into being. This is growth, and growth is the only life.

There will sometimes be in the village one girl who cherishes a higher ideal of conduct than she sees embodied in the life about her. Where did she get it? Perhaps from a mother who, immersed in her home cares and burdens, has taken little part in the affairs in the town. She in turn received from her mother delicate thoughts that have vanished from the village when a lower standard of manners came in with certain new and less cultivated people. In this new atmosphere the daughter has tried to live and has been mostly alone. Lack of companionship has made her unsocial and somewhat unbending. Her mind lacks swift response because she has had no chance to practise swiftness of response in conversation and repartee. Moreover, she has not the influence among the girls that she ought to have because they take her search for better forms of conduct for self-conceit; they consider her proud and stiff and priggish; those touches of ceremoniousness which she chooses because of her passion for beauty and grace, they consider affectation. There is no place like the country to put affectation in its place; but it is as possible there as elsewhere to misjudge the real sources of inspiration in matters of conduct.

In the hearts of these very girls who look askance at the solitary one as she passes along the village path and talk among themselves about her primness and her pride, there may be a great admiration for her after all, a desire to copy all her little touches of elegance, a swift noting of her graces and of everything new she adds to her repertoire of manners. If she keeps her body very straight and holds her chin correctly, they will be looking in the glass to find out whether their spinal column can be stiffened to give the same effect. They may laugh at her but they try to imitate her.

After all, you see, the fundamental standards are the same; the difference being that one girl comes almost to the point of living up to them, the other girls have tried and because of ignorance or lack of opportunity have failed, and have looked upon their failure until they have despaired of ever succeeding. Fundamentally there is the same desire at the heart of both the refined recluse girl who longs to have company among the other girls, and the less agreeable, less refined and less cultivated girls who secretly envy while they ridicule, and are waiting only for the open door to enable them to walk in and leave their coarseness and bungling outside.

The first step for such a girl to take in working out her desire to be of help to the other girls, is to show them in some way that she really cares for them and that, as far as her heart goes she is one with them. If she can only get out of her seeming stiffness for a little while and get down to the real heart beneath, the other girls will respond, and pretty soon the happy influence of the spirit of unity will assert itself and the true basis in desire for better things — whatever they may turn out to be — will be a bond between the elements. Then some kind of play or some kind of work may be proposed. It does not matter so much what is done as it matters that something shall be done and done together. *Do something together* — that is the main thing. Anything, anything at all — only that it be *together!* Then after the doing of something together has begun, the next steps are possible.

The young woman in the rural community may see things that need to be done and be unable to think of any way to accomplish the reform. Here comes in the good of an association. For instance, something may be going wrong in the village. There is a dangerous manure heap by a wall. On the other side of the wall lives a family with children. The big black flies are creeping on the heap and then they fly over and light upon the baby's lips, dropping death-dealing poison as they move along over the pure skin of the child. What is there that any one girl can do about such a thing? She may feel that she is not the one to approach the old gentleman who owns the uncared-for barnyard; he would never listen to what some chit of a girl would say to him; no, evidently that would do no good. But if the young girl has some social position and some popularity among the other girls in the village, she can organize them into a club or society; she can make out programs for meetings into which some useful modern subjects are sprinkled; she can in a little time get the whole village agog about the care of their spotless town, and at last, the thought will rise

to the surface that said neighbor must do something about
the abuse of neighborliness he has committed in leaving his
barnyard untended for so long a time. The club of girls
could take for its motto, "No fly in our village"; and no
worthier one could be found, at least for a time. Other
forms of aspiration might follow. Meantime, perhaps, the
baby has died; and this thought may bring it home to us that
the keeping of the village clean is a sort of King's Business
requiring haste.

It is always a good plan to save red tape by taking advantage of any existing associations that may be made to
answer our need. The Country Girl is happy in having several such societies that she may join. Among these may be
mentioned the Young Women's Christian Association, the
Young Women's Hebrew Association, the Educational Alliance, the Girls' Friendly Society, the King's Daughters,
the Sodality of the Children of Mary, the Girls' Athletic
League, the Girls' Protective League, the Camp Fire Girls,
the Good Templars, and the Grange, a society in which the
women have the same privileges as the men and where young
and older members meet and work together. The Interna-
tional Congress for Farm Women has a section for young
women.

Among all these the one that has the most to give to the
young women of the countryside is the Young Women's
Christian Association — an association that now includes a
glorious company of two hundred and eighty thousand
young women. The fundamental thought in their work is
"character-contagion"; first the contagion of the character
of Christ as an influence in the world; second, the contagion
of the character of a Christ-like human being among others.
This thought is expressed in their handbook in these words:
"With the contagion of Christian character as a definite
object the very first ideal of the Association is that every
person placed in a position of responsibility for any part of
the work shall embody the spirit of Christ."

Flaming with enthusiasm for this ideal, over a hundred national secretaries are carrying on the work among nine hundred local societies in this country, and over thirty are sent to Turkey, Japan, India, China, and South America, that the girls of other lands also may learn to know the good that girls can do for girls.

For this association follows the theory that " every girl needs help, and every girl can give help." The declaration strikes to the bottom of things psychological in girl-life. Girls need each other. No one can help a girl like a girl. If there is any trouble with any girl or with any pair or group of girls, get a girl — the right kind of girl — to come and redirect the group. If new thoughts, new ideals, new enthusiasms embodied in a new girl can be brought in, the old thoughts will disappear themselves. There are trees on which the old leaves hang withered and dead all winter long: the rains cannot rot them away, the winds cannot whip them off. But when in the spring the new life begins to come coursing up the trunk, runs out through the branches, and presses a new end against the root of the dead stem, it yields at last and makes way for the leaf and flower and fruit that imperatively insist upon having more room. Those who wish to redirect young human life may find a practise lesson in this example of nature. To make faulty habits or low ideals or dangerous inclinations disappear, bring in new life. And experience teaches that new life can be imparted in no way more effectively in the field of girl-life than through good noble girl associates. To associate girls under some noble banner that will assure their enthusiasm and loyalty, will therefore be one of the most direct means of lifting their standard of living.

This Association more than any other has taken to heart the problem of the Country Girl. Two of the hand bills of the Association show how they feel about the Country Girl and what she needs and what she may have if she will take the right means.

THE GIRL IN THE COUNTRY

"Where the wide earth yields
Her beauties of fruit and grain."

If the country is to continue to produce not only the food but the hardiest young men and women, and much of the idealism and best leadership of the nation,

Life MUST be made

Less Solitary	*Freer from Drudgery*
More Comfortable	*Happier and*
More Attractive	*Fuller of Opportunity*

For the 21,000,000 girls and women on the farms and in the villages!

Solving the Rural Problem
Through
The Country Young Women's Christian Association.

It brings to the girls in the country and small towns
  The opportunity of self-development and self-expression
  The chance to work and play with other girls
  Higher social standards
  Spiritual growth and Christian ideals
  Contact with a world-wide organization
  A community consciousness.
These girls give back to their community
  Trained leadership
  Joyful, rich, vivid lives
  Improved economic conditions for women
  Consecrated homes
  Christian spirit in work and play
  Cooperation.

The Young Women's Christian Association feels that it is its " privilege to reach the Country Girls in terms of their own environment, helping them to help themselves and to become active social forces in their own communities."

Pursuing this thought, the wonderful idea was hit upon of using the available energy of the Country Girl that goes away to college as she returns to her home full of inspiration for a " career." The career of being a good angel to her home community is offered to her.

Carrying out this purpose with energy and great enthusiasm, as they do everything they take up, the Y. W. C. A. instituted a special section of their work which they called the " Eight Weeks Club." Under this scheme, in the late winter or early spring, trained secretaries who are able to give time and strength to the work and who are touched with the flame of that character-contagion, are sent out to the colleges. Preparation classes are formed among these girls, schemes are marked out for the summer, and a suggested plan of study printed for them in the Association Monthly is gone over. In the summer of 1914 about nine hundred names of Country Girls in college who were willing to embark for the summer's work were received. They came from one hundred and fifty-eight different colleges. Not all of these were eventually able to lead clubs; some were prevented by sickness, by family reasons, etc., after they got home. But there were one hundred and seventy-two who reported promptly that they did actually lead Eight Weeks Clubs, and about 2800 girls were enrolled in these clubs. The clubs represented thirty-one States, Pennsylvania leading with twenty-two, Iowa having nineteen, South Dakota ten, Wisconsin twelve.*

If you think that there is not much that you, a lone, single

---

* If any Country Girl should write to Miss Elizabeth Wilson, Executive Secretary of the Y. W. C. A., 600 Lexington Avenue, New York City, full information would be given her about the Eight Weeks Clubs and also as to any other part of the work of this wonderful, dynamic and constantly growing Association.

girl without any help can do, listen to this story which one of the Christian Association secretaries tells of the experience of one college girl who went to teach in a small town. " The first Sunday I was in town," she said, " I went to Sunday School. There were eight people there and they were all old. On the next Sunday there were five and one of them was blind; and what do you think? They asked me to take the superintendency." Did she take it? The secretary says she held her breath for the answer, for on just such a turning-point as this hangs the solution of the whole country problem. " I did; and when I went away in the spring, there were ninety-three in that Sunday School and none of them was blind."

If one lone Country Girl can do so much as that, what might not be accomplished if all the girls in the community were as one heart and mind to work together for the Sunday School, for the Church, for the Christian Endeavor and the Epworth League, and for all the causes that seek higher things in the community? A young woman may never know what emergency she may be training for when she begins to teach a Sunday School class.

It is the hope of the Y. W. C. A. that the Eight Weeks Club for the summer may ultimately be developed into an all-round-the-year Y. W. C. A., to go on indefinitely. The desire of the secretaries is to organize the young women of country and village life on the basis of the county. A County Secretary, trained for the work, should be placed in charge and should seek to reach every girl within " team-haul " or street-car riding distance with the invitation to meetings, where music, books, and pictures are found, together with wholesome social guidance and direct religious inspiration, and above all the companionship that forms a channel for the effectiveness of those good and uplifting influences. " The County Secretary " says one of their leaflets, " must not only know country life but student life and city life and industrial life. She must be an expert in educational, physical, religious and civic questions and she must be able to lead and to organize so that clubs and groups may be produced which shall meet needs extending all the way from athletics and recreation through social and general community life up to distinctly religious and devotional service.   She must be able to use volunteer leaders and to mold them into a sympathetic cooperation for the bearing of one another's burdens which ultimately will lead them to share one another's successes. The County Young Women's Christian Association . . . is bound to come into its heritage of success and to transform the girlhood of the country and village life of our land."

If there is no college girl to come " back home " to take the lead in forming an Eight Weeks Club, and no other means at hand to carry out a plan for organization in the mind of any young woman in some rural region, the best thing to do is to write — and get as many other girls as you can to write also — to the Y. W. C. A., 600 Lexington Avenue, New York City, and tell them of the desire, and then see what happens.   They will be likely to send in good time a State or County Secretary to come and look over the field and give advice.   She will probably hold a conference with the leading people of the county, calling together the pastors and their wives, teachers, bankers, alumnæ, and others interested.   There will be parlor conferences, speeches and addresses, and personal interviews.   Giving of the necessary funds will surely follow all this education of the mind of the community, and a place will be chosen or built for the home of the new association.

Whatever institutions already exist in the community, either social or religious, the Y. W. C. A. will not retard them but will give them aid and new inspiration.   By the elastic articulation of its secretaries and departments, the Young Women's Christian Association cooperates with many organizations: with the church in training leaders for Bible study courses and teachers for Sunday Schools, in directing social life, and in encouraging federation and unity among denominations; with the school, by athletic leagues, field days, play festivals, contests in public speaking and choral singing; with teachers and farmers' institutes, Chautauquas, and the Grange, giving programs for girls and women; with agricultural extension courses, adapting them to the needs of girls; with State and County fairs, providing exhibits, contests, camps, rest rooms; with library commissions, making out reading lists and using traveling libraries.

There is not an organization for betterment beside which the Young Women's Christian Association will not stand, taking from it whatever it can use for the welfare of young women and girls, and putting its own spiritual meaning into the endeavor.

CHAPTER XXVIII

THE CAMP FIRE

RUTH THE TOILER

There is that quiet in her face
    That comes to all who toil.
She moves through all the sheaves with grace
    A daughter of the soil.

There is that beauty in her hands,
    That glory in her hair,
That adds a warmth to sun-brown lands
    When Autumn cools the air.

There is that gladness in her eyes,
    As one who finds the dust
A lovely path to Paradise,
    And common things august.

There is that reverence in her mood,
    That patience sweet and broad,
As one who in the solitude
    Yet walks the fields with God!

               — *Edward Wilbur Mason.*

CHAPTER XXVIII

THE CAMP FIRE

THE Young Women's Christian Association will frequently be found working in harmony with a sister organization called " The Camp Fire Girls," which is also a national association with many local groups called " Camp Fires."

The purpose of this organization, to quote from one of their booklets, " is to show that the common things of daily life are the chief means of beauty, romance and adventure; to aid in the forming of habits making for health and vigor, the out-of-door habit and the out-of-door spirit; to devise ways of measuring and creating standards of women's work; to give girls the opportunity to learn how to ' keep step,' to learn team work through doing it; to help girls and women to serve the community, the larger home, in the same ways that they have always served the individual home; to give status and social recognition to the knowledge of the mothers and thus restore the intimate relationship of mothers and daughters to each other."

The field of endeavor in this organization is seen to be a wide one. It is interesting to learn how they have worked this fine ideal out into practical form.

In planning and building up this association the picturesque field of American Indian life has been drawn upon for an elaborate and fascinating system of ceremonial, that masks some very definite psychological principles and ideals for future development in character and customs. What seemed attractive in Indian life to the founders of this society has evidently been the out-of-doors aspect that our Amerindian predecessors' way of living always suggests.

Then the primitive industries were taken into account, and perhaps the fact that the mother was among the Indians the center of the community, the chief laborer, the owner of all the property and the giver of the family name, may have had influence in the choice of their thoughts and ways of symbolism. The picture writing, the delicate craft of bead embroidery and bead weaving had a strong appeal. There was much about Indian lore and Indian craft that could beckon modern girls along a path of adventure, poetry and romance into the realms of industry, service and patriotism.

Indian symbolisms are used in the prettiest manner. There is a Camp Fire costume cut and fringed so as to look like that of an Indian maiden. There are many attractive signs filled with mystic meanings. The watchword is "Wohelo," a word that sounds like an Indian name, but really is made out of the first letters of three good American words: work, health, and love. Each member is expected to choose a name for herself; it must be something that shall express her own wish and desire. For instance, the girl whose aspiration was to sing and to grow, chose for herself the name "Songrow." Then the member is expected to weave this name into the bead band she is allowed to wear about her forehead in the supposed fashion of Indian women. Around her throat she wears a necklace, and on this sacred ornament each bead represents some achievement she has made, the color of the bead indicating the class of service that has been performed by her. All this is most fascinating to the story-book quality in the mind of every young girl.

In order to become a Camp Fire girl the applicant must repeat "The Wood Gatherer's Desire." In this she testifies to her desire to obey "The Law of the Camp Fire," which is to

> " Seek beauty
> Give service
> Pursue knowledge

        Be trustworthy
        Hold on to health
        Glorify work
        Be happy."

These seven laws of the Camp Fire she promises that she
will strive to follow. Later on she may receive a higher
title, that of Fire Maker. To do this she must learn by
heart and repeat " The Fire Maker's Desire."

> " As fuel is brought to the fire,
>   So I purpose to bring
>   My strength,
>   My ambition,
>   My heart's desire,
>   My joy,
>   And my sorrow,
>   To the fire
>   Of humankind.
>   For I will tend
>   As my fathers have tended
>   And my fathers' fathers
>   Since time began,
>   The fire that is called
>   The love of man for man,
>   The love of man for God."

But in order to win the honor of becoming a Fire Maker,
she must do much more than merely to recite a short poem.
She must also perform a service of a housewifely sort, such
as the purchase and preparation of a meal; must be able to
darn stockings, keep her own cash account, tie a square knot,
sleep with open windows, take a half hour's outing daily,
refrain from chewing gum, from candy, sundaes, sodas and
commercially manufactured beverages for at least a month,
report on a study of infant mortality, on the rudiments of
first aid, and of personal hygiene, including the right use of
baths, a nice care of the hands and of the feet, exquisite cleanliness of hair, shiny whiteness of teeth, perfect sweetness of
breath, care in regard to eyesight, sleeping, and exercise; she

must know by heart some one poem twenty-five lines long and the whole of " My Country, 'Tis of Thee," and the career of some woman who has done much for the country or State. Besides all this the candidates must present twenty elective honors; but to learn what these may be a prospective Fire Maker will have to consult the long and elaborate lists in the Camp Fire Girls' book of specifications, where she will find them covering eight pages of fine print, arranged under various heads.

Here is where the brightly colored beads come in. It is no meaningless honor — that necklace of many-colored beads! Let us briefly run over this list of possible honors.

The red beads are for honors in Health Craft; and this represents attainment in a special knowledge of First Aid to the Injured, in personal conquest over colds for a certain length of time, regularity in attendance at school, proper diet, sleeping out-doors or with windows open wide, a certain time spent in playing games, attainments in swimming, rowing, canoeing, sailing, skating, coasting, snow-shoeing, riding, mountain climbing, tramping, bicycling, automobling or folk dancing. It is plain to see that the ideal of the Camp Fire Girls in regard to health and vigor is to be sought with determination and to be gained specially through the good out-of-doors.

The flame-colored bead represents Home Craft. Here a large variety of activities are grouped under the heads of cooking, marketing, laundering, housekeeping, a term used here to include all departments of scientific house-cleaning, making beds for baby and for grown folks, care of baby and making toys for the little ones, care of waste and garbage, washing dishes, storing clothes for the winter, and care of domestic animals. To this formidable array is added the devising of some invention that shall be useful in the household. Then comes some non-professional instruction in the care of the sick; and the wide field of entertainment follows, such as song, playing some musical instrument, reciting poetry, getting up a dialogue or play, writing a story or working out a program of some sort, giving a pantomime, telling stories, or adapting them to dramatic representation, and giving these forms of entertainment at some home, hospital, or settlement where there are sick people to be helped to forget their suffering.

Next come the blue honors. The bead of this color is given for attainments in Nature Lore — knowledge of trees, flowers, ferns, grasses, mosses, birds, bees, butterflies, moths, stars. If the girl knows the planets and seven constellations and their stories, she may wear the blue bead. Also if she does a certain amount of work in a flower or vegetable garden of her own, raises a crop of something and cans, pickles or preserves her product, or if she carries on an experimental garden, planting, for instance, one plot with pedigreed and one with unpedigreed seeds and recording the results, she wins the blue bead. This is but a faint sketch, of course, of the interests in this department.

A wood-brown bead is given for Camp Craft. Here there are tent craft, wood craft, fire lore, camp cookery, weather lore, camp packing, and all kinds of knot tying. Added to this is an attractive group called Indian craft. Under this head the member may win a wood-brown bead if she knows six Indian legends or twenty-five signs of the Indian sign language, or six blazes. Is there any one who does not know what the word " blaze " means? It is the mark you cut on the tree with your hatchet by which when you are on the trail you may tell your way back home again. The applicant for this brown bead honor may know three Indian ways of testing the eyesight, or how to make a totem, an Indian bed, an Indian tepee, or a bead band eight inches long. Any one of these achievements wins the wood-brown bead.

Then come the green honors. Here the artist in the young member of the society has a chance for development. If the girl chooses she may win this bead by work in clay modeling, or in brass or silver work; in basketry, wood carving, carpentry, dyeing, leather work, stenciling, sewing, photography, hat trimming, original designs in embroidering, and many other kinds of beautiful expression through the arts.

Yellow honors are given for any sort of business positions, earning certain sums for an accomplishment worthy of the yellow bead, keeping accurate accounts, saving a definite amount, making budgets for the family. and so forth.

Then come the red-white-and-blue honors, which includes helping in the celebration of some historical day, the national birthdays, or some day connected with the history of the town in which the member lives, like a pageant or an historical tableau. Knowledge of the customs and laws of our country come under this head, and service to the community in any way, helping about keeping the town clean and about making it a better and more healthful place for all. This bead may be won by a knowledge of what the great ones of the past have done for the public good, such as religious leaders, missionaries, educators, great women, statesmen, scientists. A sketch of the life of that great woman, Harriet Beecher Stowe, or of that other wonderful woman, Frances E. Willard, would take this honor; and the ability to repeat from memory a certain number of verses from the Bible or a number of the world's greatest hymns, would be equally valued among these achievements.

It would certainly seem as if a girl who could win honor beads enough to string a necklace for herself might be forgiven for some slight tinge of vanity. But there is not much excuse for any girl in the land to fail to be worthy of acceptance in this honorable company, for the requirements cover so wide a range and the girls of America are so ingenious in taking hold of new ideas and moreover are already so filled with activities in all the realms touched by these inspiring suggestions, that the Camp Fire spirit ought to become a household interest in every State of the Union.

This photograph of a Camp Fire Girl shows the opportunity
country life affords for good sport.

A school garden where the children are taught to love and understand the growing things as well as to cultivate them.

When a member has gained the precious testimonials of her attainments in these artistic and household and community services, she procures the leather cord that is essential in the proper Indian method for stringing beads, and in some shape that her original fancy shall dictate she arranges a necklace to suit her own taste. The beads are of good size; they are colored in delicate, unstaring tints, and the hole in the bead is large enough for the leather to pass easily through.

More and more honors may be worked for and won as time goes on, and the bead string may be made more and more beautiful; the wearer may thus become more of an inspiration to her friends and associates.

There is a still higher rank than Fire Maker; it is that of Torch Bearer. The one who reaches this rank by special study and work, is an assistant to the Guardian, who is the leader of the society and is a person of maturity and of training for the work of guide to the younger ones. The Camp Fire Girls as an association is especially adapted to charm and interest the girls of from twelve years old to sixteen, while it is good also for older girls.

It is evident that the useful activities that lie back of the attainment of these varied beads in the Camp Fire Girls' necklace will influence every girl that undertakes them in the direction of the aims and purposes of the society. The camp craft and wood craft will awaken the outdoor spirit, and the health craft will help to establish habits making for health and vigor. The same red bead brings games and exercises that will teach girls how to do team work, how to work together to gain the power of quick decision, to take defeat casually, to acknowledge the rights of others, to perceive justice when its laws are thrust upon one in fair play. When the red-white-and-blue bead is gained, a service to the community has been emphasized; and throughout all the list the emerging standardization of women's work is seen. In this respect the Camp Fire Girls as an organization joins with many other movements in working toward placing home economics on a more respected and honorable platform.

Just how the system of activities is to make a closer and more intimate relation between daughter and mother is yet to be revealed. The daughter's appreciation, developed through actual experimentation, of what the mother has perhaps been doing all alone in carrying household burdens, will no doubt tend to make a more cordial relation and intimacy between the house leader that has been and the house leader that is to be in the home that goes on forever. At all events there is a crying need just to-day for a closer understanding and sympathy between mothers and daughters: and if this organization of young women and girls will help in that phase of our life, it will be performing a great national service.

A great deal of poetry has been written for and by the Camp Fire Girls and much fine music has been composed for them to sing in their ceremonies. What could be more beautiful than this, by Katherine Lee Bates:

" Burn, fire, burn!
Flicker, flicker, flame!
Whose hand above this flame is lifted
Shall be with magic touch engifted,
To warm the hearts of lonely mortals
Who stand without their open portals.
The torch shall draw them to the fire,
Higher, higher,
By desire.
Whoso shall stand by this hearthstone,
Flame-fanned,
Shall never, never stand alone;
Whose house is dark and bare and cold,
Whose house is cold,
This is his own.
Flicker, flicker, flicker, flame;
Burn, fire, burn!"

The whole ritual is so poetic that it seems to have touched the young life into creative energy.

The ceremony of receiving a girl into the various honors is altogether beautiful; but we must leave something for a surprise to the young girl who is hoping to become some day a member. It must be remembered, however, that the honors are to be earned. The friend of a member is not begged to join the Camp Fire Girls; she is allowed to join if she will enter into the spirit of the society and make herself worthy. To do that she may have to alter her point of view. If she has been in the habit of thinking of the humble duties of life as a drudgery, she certainly will have to change her mind in that respect. To throw romance and beauty and the spirit of adventure about the common things of life is the avowed object of the association. And these are the common things of life — dish washing, house cleaning, first aid to the injured, darning stockings and keeping accurate accounts. To view these as adventures, as bits of romance, is what the Camp Fires are aiming toward. And they are succeeding; for there are hundreds of groups of girls all over the country who are struggling to win the beads by study and service, that shall make these prized necklaces represent their endeavors. The mothers are welcoming this spirit that turns a disliked piece of household work into an adventure of high emprise. They find themselves rushed away from a task they were about to begin lest the daughter should fail by chance to gain a bead she was striving for, and prevented from various branches of work by the rules the daughter was following. But it is not the spirit of vanity and self aggrandizement that forms the basis of the girls' endeavor; it is the love of achievement; it is the game!

If one looks over the books of directions for Camp Fire Girls, one is delighted and fascinated by the pictures that show the many ways the girls have to carry out the intention of the society. Here are girls in the ceremonial costumes, the hair braided Indian fashion, the decorated band drawn around the forehead and fastened behind at the back of the head. In one picture the girls are sitting by the tent at camp, sewing and carving and carpentering for honors. Here they are in a big canoe with paddles lifted all together; again they are starting out for a hay-rack ride, or building a gigantic bonfire for Independence Day, setting up the logs in tepee-shape, while eight girls are bearing the next log to the pyramid. We see them wading, swimming, and making fire in antique fashion with bow and drill; they are cooking in house and in camp; they are washing, they are ironing, they are mending; here they are serving the community by teaching some little girls to sew, or by helping to fight a real forest fire; they are holding ceremonial meetings and conferring honors on those that by hard work have won them. One can only say: O happy, happy girls in this happiest of countries, that have so much done for them, that have so great opportunities, that are so diligently and joyously making the most of their chance in life!

CHAPTER XXIX

THE COUNTRY GIRL'S DUTY TO THE COUNTRY

Are you sheltered, curled up and content by the world's warm fire,
  Then I say that your soul is in danger!
The sons of the Light, they are down with God in the mire,
  God in the manger.

The old-time heroes you honor, whose banners you bear,
  The whole world no longer prohibits;
But if you peer into the past you will find them there,
  Swinging on gibbets.

So rouse from your perilous ease: to your sword and your shield!
  Your ease is the ease of the cattle!
Hark, hark, the bugles are calling! Out, out to some field —
  Out to some battle!

— Edwin Markham.

CHAPTER XXIX

THE COUNTRY GIRL'S DUTY TO THE COUNTRY

VARIOUS societies are now trying to supply one of the greatest needs of the girls in country life: namely, good times. The young life is doing the most natural thing possible when it demands recreation, and grave losses must be sustained if satisfaction is not given to this pure and normal desire.

The countryside itself seems to be painfully, culpably wanting in the first efforts for the supply of the need for normal, healthful play times. If public health is valued, if pure morals are desired, if home comfort is coveted, not to say if there is a wish that the girls and boys should remain and sustain the rural commonwealth of the future, the first thing to do to gain these ends would be to answer their unconscious outcry for more development of the play instinct. A wonderful woman of our time has written a book about the spirit of youth in the city street; some one should write one about the spirit of youth along the country road. We should awake that spirit and set it to singing on every road and lane, up hill and down dale, all over the prairies and all along the canyons.

That this is a very vital matter is shown in a letter from a Country Girl. She wrote:

"There was one thing I did want to ask you about and that was the need for social recreation, girlish recreation, wholesome, whole-hearted recreation. Judging by the girls I have taught both in country and village schools, it has seemed to me that they need to be taught to be girls, real girls, more than anything else, and to cherish that girlhood.

There exists such a false relation between the girls and the boys. They are little stagy grown-ups playing at life, when they should be natural, wholesome children. I have wondered whether, if their social entertainments' were different, and, if the true way could be shown them, they wouldn't leave the false and the sham, and be natural. Often the play ends in real disaster and young lives full of possibilities go down into the deeps. It is hard to express this in just these few words on paper but if you know country life as it still exists I am sure you will understand."

This wise young woman has here linked the need for recreation and the dire necessity for moral restraint in a way to appeal to every student of country life and to every one that desires the well-being of the boys and girls there.

When the factors in this problem are thus reduced to simple terms, it seems so easy to manage. The little things to do, the appalling disaster to be prevented! More recreation in the village — more girls saved from direst sorrow and downfall! Who would not spring to help? Is not the duty of the girls who are a little older or who have been away to school or college perfectly, translucently clear? Can you fail to see and feel it?

There was a story of lost opportunity unconsciously revealed in the letter of a college girl, who lives in a long valley between mountains where the young people come in great numbers to do the hop-picking. The plan for living included tents and an eating-table in common. There were dances at night and much drunkenness. The writer added a tragic description of what happens under these circumstances and of the terrible results that follow the orgy.

What is that Country Girl thinking of, that she should waste this opportunity? Why does she not do something for those girls?

What can she do? Organize something! Form some kind of an association. Get the girls together — but not at just the last moment before the great wave rises above their heads. We must build up beforehand; we must start in at foundations; little by little we must undermine wrong likings and insert slowly in their places better likings. We cannot force the growth of the better things; they must grow naturally. Working thus for days and months and years, we may at last cause a better feeling, a better taste; we may develop greater self-control that will be permanent because based on higher ideals and nobler desires.

The young woman who wrote that letter was educated in an Eastern college and went from there to a farm in the West, finding a home at last in this beautiful valley. Who knows but that her whole life and career was ordained in this wandering way in order that she might come to that special valley and seeing the need there, should put her shoulder to the wheel to make a moral uplift for the whole region! The young woman that will accept this high education and then neglect such opportunities for social service has not gained the chief thing — the socialized spirit, the spirit of social responsibility for the world; no, nor even for the very town for which she ought to be first to feel it. Surely she could ask for no better or larger career than to be able to make in her home town a radiant life for all the young people, full of charm, a counter-charm against which the lure of the city would have no power, and thus keep girl life safe and pure, and prevent the sorrowful fate that would befall her young townswomen if they should yield to the temptation that knocks at their door.

The seriousness of the situation for those unprotected from such dangers can scarcely be exaggerated. While the number of native-born American Country Girls that deliberately choose a low or vicious life is, in the opinion of experts, comparatively small, still it is not to be tolerated that any country or village girls should lack safeguarding.

Happily this is the story of an exceptional incident; but how may it be prevented from becoming common? By making the life about the country home interesting in the work and in the play; by building up a complex social structure in every village with music and pageantry, with clubs and societies, with vigorous religious influence and activity, with traveling library and magazine exchange. Not one of the possible means for intellectual and social interchange, however joyous, but is justified in its philanthropic aim. The farm home, the country village *must* be made a happy place for the young folks. It must never for one instant be dull.

To preach this ideal no one can be so useful as the girls themselves. Natural hostesses and social leaders, they are adapted to create wholesome good times in the community. But may we not expect even more? If among the girls of the village there is one who has been away to college and has seen anything of the outside world, ought she not to use her influence among the girls of the village to show them what the real danger is likely to be to one who goes unprepared by industrial and social training to cope with the situation in the city? Ought she not to consider herself to a great degree responsible if any girl from her village or her country community does go away unequipped into the struggle and becomes lost in the oubliette of vice? Ought not the girls with superior knowledge and better outlook not only to do all in their power to keep the home girl amused and interested in the life of the village, but to see that in each individual case the better wisdom is at hand for her as warning and as deterrent? " I should have known better " is small comfort afterward. When the wrong is done, and the girl is lost, does the college girl in her home town take it to her own heart as in part her responsibility? Should she not do so?

In case an inexperienced girl should have occasion to go to the city alone, she should learn beforehand what are the proper and fit things to do at railroad stations and in other public places, and what resources she has at hand there in case of difficulty. The Young Women's Christian Associa-

tion announce the following rules for a young girl entering
a strange city:

Do not start to a strange city or town without information
   about a safe place to stop.

Do not leave home without money for an emergency and
   sufficient for a return ticket.

Do not ask for or take information or direction except from
   officials.

Do not accept offers of work either by person or advertise-
   ment without investigation.

The Y. W. C. A. has employment bureaus and boarding-
   house directories, and cafeteria lunch-rooms.

Travelers' Aid Secretaries meet all in-coming trains.

These appointed systems of relief for girls in difficulty the
   girls should understand about, and feel free to take
   refuge in them if occasion requires.

Assuredly there are many young women in the country
who are fully as well prepared for the work of revitalizing
the life in country and village community as the college-
trained girls are.   A number of these are far more so than
some who have had the opportunity for higher education.
It is said that a man can go through college and be a fool
still.   The same is no doubt true of a woman.   But from
those to whom much has been given, much will be required;
and this requirement comes from all about us as well as
from above.

The thing to be done is to cut off this thread of inevitable
sequence at the beginning; to give the girl in the small town
the movies and the other varied amusements that will make
it impossible for her to think of going away; to give her
the knowledge of the poisonous results of vicious contacts
and companionships that will make her abhor them with her
very soul and be terrified of them; and to provide her with
the opportunity for earning that will satisfy her self-respect
as a unit in the home industrial community.   These things

cannot be done by one person alone; the parents must work at it, the better class of girls in the community must work for it, using constantly varied tactics to meet the enemy; and the minister, the teacher, the people all together must combine to prevent this bitter inroad from entering rural life.

For the Country Girls who by nature, ability, predilection and training, are endowed for special service, there are attractive fields open. The work of visiting nurse, of physician, of home economics agent and demonstrator, of social secretary, of teacher, of minister and pastor, are available fields for womanly endeavor. No Country Girl need feel called to go to the other side of the world to fulfil her mission. In her own valley she can have a life work that will be full of the rich returns for her well-directed, self-sacrificing service.

CHAPTER XXX

THE COUNTRY GIRL'S SCORE CARD

I am aware
As I go commonly sweeping the stair,
Doing my part of the everyday care —
Human and simple my lot and my share —
   I am aware of a marvelous thing: .
   Voices that murmur and ethers that ring
   In the far stellar spaces where cherubim sing.
I am aware of the passion that pours
Down the channels of fire through Infinity's doors;
   Forces terrific, with melody shod,
   Music that mates with pulses of God. ·
I am aware of the glory that runs
From the core of myself to the core of the suns.
   Bound to the stars by invisible chains,
   Blaze of eternity now in my veins,
   Seeing the rush of etherial rains,
Here in the midst of the everyday air —
   I am aware.

— Angela Morgan.

CHAPTER XXX

THE COUNTRY GIRL'S SCORE CARD

EFFICIENCY " is now the watchword in all endeavors, and every man worker and every woman worker is being put under training to secure the greatest amount of it. The factory is stretched to the strain. In every department store there is an efficiency school for the clerks, and every one has to take this discipline. All large public schools have a score card for the instructors and every teacher must stand or fall by the results of the criticisms therein set down.

In the home economics department of various colleges a section of a course of study is sometimes given to the close examination of the score card for the housekeeper. The points discussed include not only the technique of the kitchen, but the character that lies behind all efficiency and the training for making the most of native endowments.

Why, then, if the Country Girl wishes to become efficient, should she not have a " score card " of her own? At any rate it may be an incitement to her conscience, and perhaps it may give some suggestions for her life-plan.

The Country Girl's Score Card given here is not to be taken as in any way final. Let it be thought of as suggestive only.

THE COUNTRY GIRL'S SCORE CARD

Character

Notable excellencies in character, temperament, or disposition: integrity, truthfulness, trustworthiness, courage, fortitude, self-reliance, steadiness, fearlessness, generosity, magnanimity

351

Notable deficiencies in character, temperament or disposition
as shown by such actions or incidents as these:

inconsiderateness in causing unnecessary trouble to others

carelessness, causing waste or extra work

disorderliness, causing waste or worry or extra work

frequent tardiness at meals

disregarding the rules of the home, thus causing worry

forgetting (which usually means not caring)

losing things (which generally means culpable inattention)

showing a depressed will power (which means not caring enough)

tampering in the least with accurate statement, not rigorously preserving a habit of accuracy

tampering in the least with exact business relations, borrowing carelessly; borrowing money when it is not absolutely necessary; not making payment at the first possible moment

deflecting in the least from generous treatment in speech or act of companions especially of a rival or foe

Expression of herself in manners

Self-control

repose of manner, dignity, gentleness, quietness

Tact

quick perception of people's whims or foibles

avoidance of things that may give offense

ready adaptation to circumstances

Atmosphere

friendliness or cordiality; expressing enough but not too much; having a manner perfectly adapted to circumstances

cheer; a hopeful, buoyant spirit

Voice

quality, management of voice, sweetness, clearness

carrying power without harshness

Speech

use of English, good grammar, avoidance of crude language

precision in the use of the mother tongue, choice of words, use of idiom

a clear-cut enunciation

Philosophy of life

The will to live, a plucky spirit, a determination to win through, to succeed, to take the hazard and go ahead

A passion for perfection, for excellence in the result; not to give up until the end is gained and the product is as good as it can possibly be made

Artistic passion, the love of seeing things look well, of seeing harmony and proportion; love of music and pictures and all things beautiful; love for finding beauty in common things; interest in making oneself look always as beautiful as possible

Power and habit of reflection, philosophy, reasoning things out; the power to put two and two together, to see through a matter and find out why a thing is made in such a way and no other

Passion for truth for its own sake, for finding out what the underneath processes of nature are, for scientific investigation in the natural world about us

Power of growth

a teachable spirit, ability to take suggestions, and to act generously upon them; employment of means to maintain efficiency and perseverance in these efforts; ability to rise after failures and to strike in again with better knowledge

Health

Enthusiastic and persistent obedience to all the Code given in Chapter XIV, particularly as to bodily carriage, exercise, breathing, clothing, food and eating, elimination of waste, cleanliness, amount of sleep, rest, and prevention of illness. Willingness to make sacrifices in order to gain and to maintain a high state of bodily strength and efficiency

Perfect relations with the various members of the family

Attentive and affectionate relations with the father

Loving and helpful relations with the mother

Amiable and companionable relations with brothers (if nearly her own age)

Fair, responsive and tender relations with sisters (if nearly her own age)

Patient and inspirational relations with the younger children

Community spirit

Dependable and active relations with the church

Inquiring, critical, responsive relations with the school

Helpful working relations with the community societies and societies for young people

Cordial furtherance of any public work for betterment

A pure, self-sacrificing and noble influence among the village young people

Definite preparation for her home that is to be

The " hope-box " and what it should contain

A scheme for her house-plan and all its ideal details; the site, the appliances, the fittings and furniture, the decorations

Training in the business of the home

Training in the business of the farmstead

Training in the knowledge of child-life and child-psychology

Training in the laws governing the property of women

Qualities for an efficient administrator of a household:

Knowledge of the business and training for it either at home or in some school

Power to systematize work, to apportion out labor, and to keep accounts and make budgets; power to purchase and to save wisely

Ability to carry things through in a business-like way; courage to undertake things; ability to make both ends meet

Resourcefulness; ability to act promptly when things go wrong, to adapt oneself to changes, to show reserve in emergencies

Power to save time and avoid dawdling; to avoid unnecessary motions and waste of energy; to avoid unnecessary waste of materials

Passion for cleanliness in rooms, furniture, utensils, linen; passion for personal cleanliness

A real love of the work itself, a love to create good things; a love to see things done and to do them

If you, dear Country Girl, will take a score card similar to this, go away by yourself and think it all over, then conscientiously take the examination, mark yourself on all the points honestly and fairly, desiring strongly to be just with yourself and to see yourself as you really are, there will perhaps come to you an illuminated hour when you will dare to set yourself down in the group called "meritorious" or in the next group called "not-quite-meritorious-but-almost." Perhaps, however, you may feel that you ought to descend into the group named "inferior" or even into the "deficient" class. But this attempt at self-examination will spur you to greater effort, whatever your decision. For if you must say "inferior" or "deficient," there is no doubt some reason for the lacks, and the examination will help you to find these and to strive earnestly to make up for them. And if you feel that you can honestly say "meritorious," you must remember that all good qualities are but the stepping-stones to higher struggle and that life affords us many more advanced degrees to which we may aspire.

The Country Girl's Score Card may afford an appreciation of how much the young woman in rural life means to her environment. That appreciation will only make you see the more clearly the claims that country life has upon you. For you must realize that there is one link in the chain of American life that the Country Girl alone can forge. If you fail, the chain must break; but if you do your allotted part, the chain will be one of those that Milton loves to sing about, that bind the whole round earth about the throne of God.

INDEX

INDEX

A

Abbott, E., 94.
Addams, Jane, 10.
Agricultural Department. See *U. S. Agr. Dep't.*
Agricultural College of Conn., 202, 237, 238.
Amusement, recreation, 27, 30, 34, 50, 63, 64, 66, 67, 79, 291–302.

B

Barton, Clara, 10.
Bates, K. L., 338.
Beecher family, 215.
Beecher, Catherine, 292.
Benson, O. H., 189–191.
Bible, 20, 72, 269, 302; source of plots, 302.
Book exchange. See *Clubs.*
Books. See *Reading.*
Brainerd, David, 317.
Breathing, correct, 176.
Bureau of Animal Industry, 250.
Bureau of Chemistry, 250.
Bureau of Plant Industry, 55, 250.
Budget, 186 f, 192, 195–204, 223.

C

Canning in the home, 42.
Camp Fire Girls, 63, 64, 169, 321, 331–340.
Card catalog, 158.
Chase, L. G., 200.
Chemistry in household, 166.
Chicago, University of, 238.
Children in farm home, 38, 39, 56, 184, 214–216.

Christian Endeavor Society, 63, 64, 325.
Church, 3, 65.
Church Periodical Club, 56.
City: precautions, 346, 347; occupations in, 348; exodus to, 20, 66, 80, 81, 181.
Clothing. See *Dress.*
Clubs: canning, 54, 55, 189–191; book exchange, 271. See also *Organizations.*
College girls, work of, for Country Girl, 324.
Columbia University, 237.
Commission on Country Life, 3, 173.
Community spirit, 30, 43, 51, 56, 65, 67, 118, 119, 129, 216, 313, 354.
Comstock, Sarah, author "The Soddy," 94.
Congress of Farm Women, 321.
Conservation, 188.
Cooperative Agricultural Extension, Bill for, 244.
Cornell University, 187, 236, 238.
Correspondence basis of the work, 26.
Correspondence courses, 238.
Country Girl: as a class, 5; number of, in U. S., 7; wide extent, 9; in gainful occupations, 10; happiness in rural life, 9, 19, 36; experiences quoted, 33–82, 87–95, 102, 109, 112–120; as farmer, 9, 11; distinguished women, 10, 11; as homemaker of future, 25; character, 26, 30, 183; passion for independence, 29, 49; love for country, 26, 61;

needs, 66; inheritance, 85; share
in housework, 101, 102; relations with mother, 103–105; social life on farm, 118, 255 f;
magnitude of her task, 150;
wage, 181–192; opportunity, 211;
barriers to her progress, 211;
place in evolution, 207, 208; duty
to country, 216, 343–348; going
to the city, precautions, 346,
347; attitude of family toward,
353; importance of her status,
4, 17, 20, 87, 355. See also
*Earning, Finance, Spiritual as-
pects.*
Country life movement, 3, 15, 16,
224.
Country life in: New England,
61, 200; New Hampshire, 111;
New York, 34, 41, 111; South,
46 f, 189, 198, 243; South Dakota, 119; Porto Rico, 263, 264;
Philippines, 263, 264; Alaska,
263, 264; western, 65, 109, 196;
Northwest, 33, 37, 65.
Country life, favorable view, 26,
65, 70; influence on health, 28;
misunderstood by urban people,
28; nearness to nature, 29; influence on poetic genius, 274;
opportunities, 243–251; love of
animals, 27; spiritual aspects,
27, 28; influence on home life,
29; an optimistic report, 37.
Country life, unfavorable view,
49, 61, 66, 75–82, 85, 86, 99, 109,
110. See also *City, exodus to.*
Crew, H. C., 98, 136, 266, 278.

D

Dishwashing, 151, 152. See *Equip-
ment.*
Dress, 176, 196.
Dress budget, 195–204.
Drama. See *Play.*

E

Earning, 53, 64, 66, 68, 78, 182,
190–192, 195; spending, 68, 183,
187; bookkeeping, 161; parents'
right to child's earnings, 182;
wage of daughter, 181–192;
daughter's share in farm, 184.
See *Occupations, Budgets, Finances.*
Eberstadt, S., 206.
Economic position of farm
woman. See *Finances, Earning.*
Education, training, 44, 54, 64, 69,
134, 147, 164, 165, 188, 231–239,
243; instruction at farm home,
248; a four years' course, 238;
courses of study, 236–238.
Educational Alliance, 321.
Efficiency, 50, 123 f, 139–142, 147,
151–153, 157 f, 189, 192, 203, 204,
351–354. See *Equipment.*
Eight Weeks Clubs, 324. See *Y.
W. C. A.*
Epworth League, 325.
Equipment, 66, 126, 129, 131–134,
137–143.
Exercise, 176.
Experiment Stations, 55, 250.

F

Family. See *Children, Farm
home, Family life.*
Family council, 184. See also
Farm home.
Family life on farm, 33, 38, 39,
160.
Farm Bureau Agent, 249.
Farm home: wife, 79, 87, 91–95,
222; mother, 39, 103–105, 123;
children, 214 f; council, 184;
family records, 160–163; social
life in home, 42; Sunday in, 40.
See also *Efficiency, Equipment,
Children, Farm home work.*

BIBLIOGRAPHY

THE PROBLEM OF COUNTRY LIFE

ANDERSON, W. L.: The Country Town
BUTTERFIELD, K. L.: Chapters in Rural Progress
EARP, E. L.: The Rural Church Movement
FISKE, G. W.: The Challenge of the Country (*Y. W. C. Asso. Press*)
GILLETTE, J. W.: Constructive Rural Sociology
HART, J. K., editor: Educational Resources of Village and Rural Communities
ROOSEVELT, T.: Report of Commission on Country Life, Introduction by Theodore Roosevelt
STRONG, J.: Our World

THE PROBLEM OF URBAN LIFE

DEVINE, E. T.: Misery and Its Causes
LAUGHLIN, CLARA: The Work-a-Day Girl
RICHARDSON, D.: The Long Day

THE WORLD OF ALL OUTDOORS

BAILEY, L. H.: The Outlook to Nature
BREARLEY, H. C.: Animal Secrets Told
COMSTOCK, ANNA B.: Handbook of Nature Study
DIXON, ROYAL: The Human Side of Plants
GRINNELL, M.: Neighbors of Field, Wood and Stream
KNIGHT, C. R.: Animals of the World for Young People; Birds of the World for Young People
LOUNSBERRY, A.: The Wild Flower Book for Young People; The Garden Book for Young People; Frank and Bessie's Forester

DELIGHTFUL BOOKS ABOUT THE COUNTRY

ALBEE, H. R.: Mountain Playmates
BURROUGHS, J.: Wake Robin
ROBERTSON, C. D.: Down the Year
ROGERS, E. W.: Journal of a Country Woman
STEWART, ELINORE RUPERT: Letters of a Woman Homesteader
THOREAU, H. D.: Walden
WHITING, C. G.: Walks in New England

EFFICIENCY IN THE HOUSEHOLD

CHILD, G. B.: The Efficient Kitchen
CURTIS, I. G.: The Making of a Housewife
DODD, H.: The Healthful Farmhouse

FREDERICK, C.: The New Housekeeping
GOLDMARK, J.: Fatigue and Efficiency
GULICK, L. H.: The Efficient Life
LANCASTER, M.: Electric Cooking
MARCHANT, E.: Serving and Waiting
TERRELL, B. M.: Handbook of Housekeeping

WOMAN AMONG THE WORLD'S WORKERS

ABBOTT, E.: Woman in Industry
DORR, R. C.: What Eight Million Women Want
NEARING, S.: Woman and Social Progress
SPENCER, A. G.: Woman's Share in Social Culture
The Woman Citizen's Library, 12 volumes
WILBUR, M. A.: Everyday Business for Women

CRAFTS FOR GIRLS

BAILEY, C. S.: Girls' Make-at-Home Things
BEARD, P.: The Jolly Book of Boxcraft
CANDEE, H. C.: How Women May Earn a Living
KELLEY, L. E.: Three Hundred Things a Bright Girl Can Do
KLIÇKMAN, F.: The Modern Crochet Book; The Craft of the Crochet Hook; The Home Art Book of Fancy Stitchery; Home Art Crochet Book; The Cult of the Needle
LASELLE, M. A. and WILEY, K. E.: Vocations for Girls
McEWEN, D.: Stenography in Two Weeks, A Text-book for Self-use.
PARET, A. P.: Harpers' Handy Book for Girls
SANFORD, L. G.: Art Crafts for Beginners
WEAVER, E. W.: Vocations for Girls

BOYS' BOOKS THAT GIRLS CAN USE

ADAMS, M.: Boys' Own Book of Pets and Hobbies
BAILEY, C. S. and M. E.: Boys' Make-at-Home Things
BARNARD, J.: Every Man His Own Mechanic
FRASER, C. C.: Every Boy's Book of Handicraft
KELLAND, C. B.: The American Boy's Workshop

GAMES AND RECREATION

BAKER, E. M.: Indoor Games for Children and Young People
BANCROFT, J. H.: Games for the Playground, Home, School and Gymnasium
BARSE, M. E. S.: Games for all Occasions
BEARD, L. and A. B.: How to Amuse Yourself and Others
CAMPBELL, H. S.: The American Girl's Home Book of Work and Play
CANFIELD, D.: What Shall We Do Now?
CURTIS, H. S.: Play and Recreation for the Open Country

BIBLIOGRAPHY

JENKS, T.: Photography for Young People
KINNEY, T. and M. W.: Social Dancing of To-day
PARSONS, B. R.: Plays and Games for Indoors and Outdoors
STERN, R. B.: Neighborhood Entertainments

SOME PROBLEMS OF GIRLHOOD

BURKS, F. W. and J. D.: Health and the School
CABOT, R.: What Men Live By
COE, G. A.: The Spiritual Life
DANIELS, H. McD.: The Girl and Her Chance
LEARNED, E. C.: Ideals for Girls
SLACK, E. J.: A Little Essay in Friendship (*Y. W. C. Asso. Press*)
SLATTERY, M.: The Girl in her Teens

A GROUP OF BIOGRAPHIES OF COUNTRY GIRLS WHO BE-CAME GREAT AND USEFUL WOMEN

MARY LYON, by B. B. Gilchrist
ALICE FREEMAN PALMER, by G. L. Palmer
ELLEN H. RICHARDS, by Caroline L. Hunt
HARRIET BEECHER STOWE, by Martha Foote Crow
FRANCES E. WILLARD, by Anna A. Gordon

SOME OTHER INSPIRING STORIES

Jane Addams' TWENTY YEARS AT HULL HOUSE
Louise May Alcott, by Belle Moses
Helen Keller's STORY OF MY LIFE
Lucy Larcom's A NEW ENGLAND GIRLHOOD
Margaret E. Sangster's FROM MY YOUTH UP
N. Hudson Moore's DEEDS OF DARING DONE BY GIRLS

BOOKS OF POETRY COUNTRY GIRLS ENJOY

NOYES, ALFRED: Sherwood — Robin Hood and the Three Kings;
Drake, an English Epic; Tales of the Mermaid Tavern
The Golden Treasury, Series I and II
The Little Book of Modern American Verse

A GROUP OF POEMS TO KNOW AND RECITE IN THE HOME

BATES, KATHERINE LEE: America the Beautiful
BRANCH, ANNA HEMPSTEAD: Songs for My Mother
DAVIS, FANNIE STEARNS: Souls
GARRISON, THEODOSIA: The Daughter
GUINEY, LOUISE IMOGEN: The Kings
KILMER, JOYCE: Trees
LINDSAY, VACHELL: Kansas
MACKAYE, PERCY: Hymn for Equal Suffrage
MARKHAM, EDWIN: To Young America
MORGAN, ANGELA: Battle Cry of the Mothers

PEABODY, JOSEPHINE PRESTON: The House and the Road
REESE, LISETTE WOODWORTH: In Praise of Common Things
SCHAUFFLER, ROBERT HAVEN: Scum o' the Earth
THOMAS, EDITH: The Chorus of the Trees
TORRENCE, RIDGELY: Evensong
WIDDEMER, MARGARET: The Woman's Litany
WILKINSON, FLORENCE: The Cloud and the Mountain
WILKINSON, MARGUERITE O. B.: The Prayer of Summer

STORIES FOR A COUNTRY GIRL TO KNOW AND TELL IN THE HOME

Dickens' CHILD'S DREAM OF A STAR
Hale's MAN WITHOUT A COUNTRY
Hawthorne's GREAT STONE FACE
Irving's LEGEND OF SLEEPY HOLLOW
Kipling's CAPTAINS COURAGEOUS
La Motte Fouqué's UNDINE
Mark Twain's PRINCE AND PAUPER
Maupassant's NECKLACE
Poe's GOLDBUG
Van Dyke's OTHER WISE MAN
Wilde's THE HAPPY PRINCE

STORY TELLING IN THE HOME

HOUGHTON, L. S.: Telling Bible Stories
WYCHE, R. T.: Some Great Stories and How to Tell Them

BOOKS CONTAINING PLAYS

BRISCOE, M. S.: Harpers' Book of Little Plays
McLAREN, J. M. and HARVEY, E. M.: Hansel and Gretel for Little Children
MACKAY, C. D'A.: Patriotic Plays and Pageants for Young People
MERINGTON, M.: Festival Plays, and Holiday Plays
TUCKER, L. E. and RYAN, E. L.: Historical Plays of Colonial Days
WALKER, A. J.: Little Plays from American History

BOOKS ABOUT PLAYS AND PAGEANTS

BATES, E. W.: Pageants and Pageantry
HADDEN, J. C.: Favorite Operas; The Operas of Wagner
LAMB, C. and STOKES, W.: All Shakespeare's Tales
NEEDHAM, M. M.: Folk Festivals
PRENDERGAST, J.: Great Operas for Young People

A list of works of fiction representing country life and arranged by States and localities, made by Elizabeth L. Foote of New York, appeared in the Publisher's Weekly for July 31, 1915. Two additional stories may be specially mentioned:

Y. W. C. A. STORY

HENSHAW, H.: Passing of the Word

CAMP FIRE STORY

THURSTON, I. T.: The Torch Bearer

For useful bibliographies on topics interesting to country girls, send to S. J. Brandenburg, Miami University, Oxford, Ohio, for "One Hundred Good Books for Country Readers"; to the Y. W. C. A., 600 Lexington Ave., New York City, for their Eight Weeks Club leaflet; to the New York State Educational Department, Albany, N. Y., for Traveling Library Lists; to the New York City Public Library for their "Favorite Stories of the Library Reading Clubs," and "Stories of Heroism"; or to the Brooklyn Public Library for their "Books that Girls Like."

The United States Department of Agriculture publishes the following valuable papers:

Report No. 103, Social and Labor Needs of Farm Women
Report No. 104 Domestic Needs of Farm Women
Report No. 105, Educational Needs of Farm Women
Report No. 106, Economic Needs of Farm Women

Women in America

FROM COLONIAL TIMES TO THE 20TH CENTURY

An Arno Press Collection

Andrews, John B. and W. D. P. Bliss. **History of Women in Trade Unions** (*Report on Conditions of Woman and Child Wage-Earners in the United States,* Vol. X; 61st Congress, 2nd Session, Senate Document No. 645). 1911

Anthony, Susan B. **An Account of the Proceedings on the Trial of Susan B. Anthony, on the Charge of Illegal Voting at the Presidential Election in November, 1872,** and on the Trial of Beverly W. Jones, Edwin T. Marsh and William B. Hall, the Inspectors of Election by Whom her Vote was Received. 1874

The Autobiography of a Happy Woman. 1915

Ayer, Harriet Hubbard. **Harriet Hubbard Ayer's Book:** A Complete and Authentic Treatise on the Laws of Health and Beauty. 1902

Barrett, Kate Waller. **Some Practical Suggestions on the Conduct of a Rescue Home.** *Including* **Life of Dr. Kate Waller Barrett** (Reprinted from *Fifty Years' Work With Girls* by Otto Wilson). [1903]

Bates, Mrs. D. B. **Incidents on Land and Water;** Or, Four Years on the Pacific Coast. 1858

Blumenthal, Walter Hart. **Women Camp Followers of the American Revolution.** 1952

Boothe, Viva B., editor. **Women in the Modern World** (*The Annals of the American Academy of Political and Social Science,* Vol. CXLIII, May 1929). 1929

Bowne, Eliza Southgate. **A Girl's Life Eighty Years Ago:** Selections from the Letters of Eliza Southgate Bowne. 1888

Brooks, Geraldine. **Dames and Daughters of Colonial Days.** 1900

Carola Woerishoffer: Her Life and Work. 1912

Clement, J[esse], editor. **Noble Deeds of American Women;** With Biographical Sketches of Some of the More Prominent. 1851

Crow, Martha Foote. **The American Country Girl.** 1915

De Leon, T[homas] C. **Belles, Beaux and Brains of the 60's.** 1909

de Wolfe, Elsie (Lady Mendl). **After All.** 1935

Dix, Dorothy (Elizabeth Meriwether Gilmer). **How to Win and Hold a Husband.** 1939

Donovan, Frances R. **The Saleslady.** 1929

Donovan, Frances R. **The Schoolma'am.** 1938

Donovan, Frances R. **The Woman Who Waits.** 1920

Eagle, Mary Kavanaugh Oldham, editor. **The Congress of Women,** Held in the Woman's Building, World's Columbian Exposition, Chicago, U.S.A., 1893. 1894

Ellet, Elizabeth F. **The Eminent and Heroic Women of America.** 1873

Ellis, Anne. **The Life of an Ordinary Woman.** 1929

[Farrar, Eliza W. R.] **The Young Lady's Friend.** By a Lady. 1836

Filene, Catherine, editor. **Careers for Women.** 1920

Finley, Ruth E. **The Lady of Godey's:** Sarah Josepha Hale. 1931 **Fragments of Autobiography.** 1974

Frost, John. **Pioneer Mothers of the West;** Or, Daring and Heroic Deeds of American Women. 1869

[Gilman], Charlotte Perkins Stetson. **In This Our World.** 1899

Goldberg, Jacob A. and Rosamond W. Goldberg. **Girls on the City Streets:** A Study of 1400 Cases of Rape. 1935

Grace H. Dodge: Her Life and Work. 1974

Greenbie, Marjorie Barstow. **My Dear Lady:** The Story of Anna Ella Carroll, the "Great Unrecognized Member of Lincoln's Cabinet." 1940

Hourwich, Andria Taylor and Gladys L. Palmer, editors. **I Am a Woman Worker:** A Scrapbook of Autobiographies. 1936

Howe, M[ark] A. De Wolfe. **Memories of a Hostess:** A Chronicle of Friendships Drawn Chiefly from the Diaries of Mrs. James T. Fields. 1922

Irwin, Inez Haynes. **Angels and Amazons:** A Hundred Years of American Women. 1934

Laughlin, Clara E. **The Work-a-Day Girl:** A Study of Some Present-Day Conditions. 1913

Lewis, Dio. **Our Girls.** 1871

Liberating the Home. 1974

Livermore, Mary A. **The Story of My Life;** Or, The Sunshine and Shadow of Seventy Years . . . To Which is Added Six of Her Most Popular Lectures. 1899

Lives to Remember. 1974

Lobsenz, Johanna. **The Older Woman in Industry.** 1929

MacLean, Annie Marion. **Wage-Earning Women.** 1910

Meginness, John F. **Biography of Frances Slocum, the Lost Sister of Wyoming:** A Complete Narrative of her Captivity of Wanderings Among the Indians. 1891

Nathan, Maud. **Once Upon a Time and Today.** 1933

[Packard, Elizabeth Parsons Ware]. **Great Disclosure of Spiritual Wickedness!!** In High Places. With an Appeal to the Government to Protect the Inalienable Rights of Married Women. 1865

Parsons, Alice Beal. **Woman's Dilemma.** 1926

Parton, James, et al. **Eminent Women of the Age:** Being Narratives of the Lives and Deeds of the Most Prominent Women of the Present Generation. 1869

Paton, Lucy Allen. **Elizabeth Cary Agassiz:** A Biography. 1919

Rayne, M[artha] L[ouise]. **What Can a Woman Do;** Or, Her Position in the Business and Literary World. 1893

Richmond, Mary E. and Fred S. Hall. **A Study of Nine Hundred and Eighty-Five Widows Known to Certain Charity Organization Societies in 1910.** 1913

Ross, Ishbel. **Ladies of the Press:** The Story of Women in Journalism by an Insider. 1936

Sex and Equality. 1974

Snyder, Charles McCool. **Dr. Mary Walker:** The Little Lady in Pants. 1962

Stow, Mrs. J. W. **Probate Confiscation:** Unjust Laws Which Govern Woman. 1878

Sumner, Helen L. **History of Women in Industry in the United**

States (*Report on Conditions of Woman and Child Wage-Earners in the United States,* Vol. IX; 61st Congress, 2nd Session, Senate Document No. 645). 1910

[Vorse, Mary H.] **Autobiography of an Elderly Woman.** 1911

Washburn, Charles. **Come into My Parlor:** A Biography of the Aristocratic Everleigh Sisters of Chicago. 1936

Women of Lowell. 1974

Woolson, Abba Gould. **Dress-Reform:** A Series of Lectures Delivered in Boston on Dress as it Affects the Health of Women. 1874

Working Girls of Cincinnati. 1974

DATE DUE

MAY 0 1 1994	
AUG 2 6 2004	

GAYLORD   PRINTED IN U.S.A.